Colonial
Entrepreneur

DR. SILVESTER GARDINER

Colonial Entrepreneur

DR. SILVESTER GARDINER
and the
Settlement of
Maine's Kennebec Valley

OLIVIA E. COOLIDGE

With an introduction, genealogy, and bibliographical essay by Danny D. Smith

TILBURY HOUSE PUBLISHERS
& GARDINER LIBRARY ASSOCIATION
GARDINER, MAINE 1999

Tilbury House, Publishers
132 Water Street
Gardiner, ME 04345
800-582-1899

Gardiner Library Association
152 Water Street
Gardiner, ME 04345
207-582-3312

First printing: May 1999

10 9 8 7 6 5 4 3 2 1

Cataloging-in-Publication Data

Coolidge, Olivia E.
      Colonial entrepreneur : Dr. Silvester Gardiner and the settlement of Maine's Kennebec Valley / by Olivia E. Coolidge : with an introduction, genealogy, and bibliographical essay by Danny D. Smith.
      p. cm.
      Includes bibliographical references and index.
      ISBN 0-88448-205-7 (alk. paper)
      1. Gardiner, Silvester, 1708–1786. 2. Kennebec River Valley (Me.)—Biography. 3. Kennebec River Valley (Me.)—History—17th century. 4. Land settlement—Maine—Kennebec River Valley—History—17th century. 5. Boston (Mass.)—Biography. 6. Physicians—Maine—Kennebec River Valley—Biography. 7. Businesspeople—Maine—Kennebec River Valley—Biography.
      I. Smith, Danny D. II. Title.
      F27.K32C66 1999
      974'.02'092—dc21
      [b]   98-32359
                                              CIP

Design: Edith Allard, Crummett Mountain, Somerville, ME
Layout: Nina Medina, Basil Hill Graphics, Somerville, ME
Editorial and production: Danny D. Smith, Earle G. Shettleworth, Jr.,
        Jennifer Elliott. Barbara Diamond
Scans and film: Integrated Composition Systems, Spokane, WA
Jacket printing: The John P. Pow Company, South Boston, MA
Text printing and binding: Maple-Vail, Binghampton, NY

CONTENTS

MEMORIAL TABLET in the southeast corner of Christ Church, Gardiner. This tablet contains a long inscription tracing the life of Dr. Silvester Gardiner. RICHARD CHEEK, PHOTOGRAPHER.

INTRODUCTION

A S THE CITY OF GARDINER, MAINE, approaches two anniversary celebrations, this is the time to review the beginning of settlement in the Kennebec River valley in central Maine. There are few individuals who so perfectly play the rôle of colonizer as Dr. Silvester Gardiner (1708–1786). Although the settlement of much of northern New England fits into hazy theories about the depletion of land, increase in population, and social unrest, rare is the settlement which becomes an Emersonian lengthened shadow of one man. In 1999 the City of Gardiner will celebrate the sesquicentennial of the city charter, and in the year 2003 the community observes its bicentennial as a separate entity from Pittston, of which it had been part since 1779. The year 1803 was a momentous one for the sole heir of Dr. Silvester Gardiner, his grandson, Robert Hallowell Gardiner I (1782–1864), who turned twenty-one that year and claimed his inheritance

Not unlike the Biblical parable of the rejected stone which was retrieved to become the cornerstone of the building, a near miracle has preserved an important historical manuscript undertaken nearly fifty years ago. Olivia Coolidge, who will celebrate her ninety-first birthday in October 1999, retired in 1976 as a successful children's author. Several of her books are still in print, have been honored by *Horn Book* citations, and crowned by a Newbery Honor Prize in 1963. Her one book in the field of adult biography was rejected by her publisher. No fault of research or of writing style resulted in this decision. Instead an editor could not see the commercial possibilities for her biography of Dr. Silvester Gardiner. The Gardiner Library Association now has the privilege to bring this excellent study of our community's settlement to the public.

First, let us ask who is this important figure in our region's history?

Affixed to the southeast wall at Christ Church in Gardiner, Maine, is a black marble cenotaph, lettered in gold, terminating in three pointed arches, and looking down to the baptismal font. The font was given to the parish in loving memory of an infant who died in 1888, a great-great-great-grandson of the man commemorated in the marble cenotaph. Both bore the same name: Silvester Gardiner. The long Latin inscription in gold letters reads in part: "Atque hæc loca habintantibus pater-patriæ duti porfecto meruit" (translation: and by the inhabitants of these parts has richly deserved to be called father of the land). Why does Silvester Gardiner deserve to the called "father of the land," that is to say the leading light in settling the Kennebec Valley?

To understand the beginnings of settlement in the Kennebec Valley, it is necessary to return to the Pilgrims of Plymouth Colony. Their colony's enterprise was doomed to sure economic collapse within the first decade without help from England. Isaac Allerton, in seeking influence at the English court, obtained "a patente for a fitt tradeing place in the river Kennebec." This hoped-for grant was described as:

> all that Tract of land or part of New England ... Which lyeth Within or between and Extendeth itself from the Utmost Limits of Cobbiseconte, alias Comisseconte, Which Adjoineth to the River of Kennebeckike, towards the Western Ocean, and a place called the Falls, at Neguamkike ... and the Space of Fifteen English Miles on Each Side of the said River Commonly Called Kennebecke that Lies Within the Said Limits, and bounds Eastward, Westward, Northward, or Southward.

Precise terms of this grant had to be interpreted by recourse to endless litigation, but stated in broad outline, this Plymouth Patent, later called the Kennebec Purchase, consisted of one and a half million acres of land, extending from the northern limits of Bath to the northern boundary of Cornville above Skowhegan and east to west fifteen miles on each side of the Kennebec River. Dr. Silvester Gardiner owned a one-tenth interest in the patent, making his the second largest in the company.

The Pilgrims exploited the fur trade in the Plymouth Patent until the beaver population died out, at which point they no longer saw the land as an asset. Accordingly, on 27 October 1661 they sold it to four Bostonians for £400. These solid members of the rising merchant class were Antipas Boyes, Edward Tyng, Thomas Brattle, and John Winslow. To Boston investors, the Kennebec Valley boded land with rising values and immediate profits in timber, especially mast trees for the Royal Navy. However, the hopes of 1661 were soon dashed. In 1675 Indians, abetted by the French in Quebec, drove the settlers from the once advancing frontier of Maine. For nearly a century, the interior was deserted. Finally after seven major eruptions of warfare, known collectively as the Colonial Wars, the British emerged triumphant.

B Y 1759, THE FRENCH had been beaten everywhere: The British Empire had been created, an empire rich beyond all dreams. The year 1759 became the *Annus Mirabilis*, the year of miracles. Nearly every day dispatches to London brought news of another victory in the course of the Seven Years' War. Some skirmishes continued until Montreal fell on 6 September 1760. The peace treaty signed in 1763 cleared the slate. The French and Indians were no longer actors in the theater of settlement. One principal actor was needed to be the presiding genius over the Kennebec's settlement. All requisite energies and talents presented themselves in the person of Dr. Silvester Gardiner.

Silvester Gardiner, a delicate youth of scholarly inclinations, was not destined to follow his ancestors as prosperous Rhode Island farmers. Through the influence of his tutor (later his brother-in-law) the Reverend James McSparran, he was launched into an academic career in Boston. Later his father advanced him his share of the patrimony to study in London, Paris, and Edinburgh, then the only way to secure a first-class medical education. Returning to Boston, he quickly rose to the top of his profession because of two fortunate circumstances: first, he was the only surgeon in Boston with a European education; and secondly, he secured all the necessary social connections by marrying the only daughter of the leading physician of Boston who was near retirement. A bright young man with his eye on the main chance, he invested the proceeds from his professional practice into an import house for pharmaceutical supplies. Because of his aggressive nature and expertise, he made his company a virtual monopoly in New England. With a personal fortune swelling to spectacular heights, he invested with his colleagues in Boston who were trying to revive the old Plymouth Patent, soon to be renamed the Kennebec Company.

Dr. Silvester Gardiner was the one man in Boston with the acumen to meet the immense challenge of untangling the confused affairs of the company. Anyone who attempted to put the affairs aright would surely clash with rival claimants. The rare combination needed at this time, money, executive ability to organize complex details, unbridled fervor to bring Maine under Anglican hegemony, and the uncanny ability to steer a course around political intrigue raised him to an undoubted position of leadership in the Kennebec Company. Not only did the proprietors of the company elect him perpetual moderator of their meetings, but time and time again he was granted large tracts of land amounting to substantially more than his proportionate share in company stock. He acquired his colleagues' confidence (and additional land) because he personally supervised operations in the Kennebec Valley. From his own coffers, he financed mills, a post office, wharves, a Great House which served as a community center and tavern, the parish church, and roads. He paid the salary of the missionary priest Jacob Bailey, and he used his own sloop to transport supplies to the frontier.

It is hard to square Dr. Gardiner's actions and ideals with the spirit of democracy ushered in by the American Revolution. Adherence to aristocratic principles and the Church of England led Dr. Gardiner into a collision course with the patriots of the Revolution. In that collision course, he lost most of his land and fortunes in Massachusetts. Only by a peculiar quirk of the legal process was he able to return to America and reclaim his landed possessions in Maine.

Dr. Silvester Gardiner remains an enigma in the history of the Kennebec Valley. He was undoubtedly the father of civilization in central Maine. Without his genius for projecting efficient operations for the Kennebec Company, it is impossible to envision the history of interior Maine as unfolding as it has. Louis C. Zahner in a tribute booklet, *Henry Richards 1848–1949*, wrote of Dr. Gardiner: "For a vast territory he became a sort of feudal lord; a combination of supreme court justice and father confessor, a law-giving and colonizing Moses. Hewing forests, building dams and mills, making new settlements, he was the stuff of which legends are made." Legend he is. Liberal historians tend to cast him as a forerunner of the robber barons of the nineteenth century, an individual whose tactics and methods would have proven instructive to those very robber barons. Viewing Dr. Gardiner in his own regional context, the Kennebec Valley, it is impossible to envision the settlement without some presiding force. Dr. Gardiner sat for John Singleton Copley. Two descriptions of that Copley portrait tell more about different generations of historians than about the man himself. Dr. Gardiner and the facts of his career remain. How those facts may be interpreted and applied to the region's history is now our challenge. Writing in 1892, Evelyn Gilmore voiced piety:

> It is a vivid representation of a man past the median of life, and dressed in the scarlet coat of England, relieved by glittering buttons and white frills at the wrist. Between the side curls of a white wig a kindly, keen old face looks out; a face to whose humorous curve of lip and glance of eye is added the evidence of thought and practical tendencies, in the high forehead and vertical lines above the nose. The whole figure, one hand in its breast, is leaning slightly forward, the head a trifle bent, with a direct look at the beholder that gives him the suggestion of a certain watchful alertness in the intent eyes. Altogether a strong character; a man of deep feelings, firm attachments, and earnest purposes, for whose protection the struggling Church of Gardinerstown must have longed in later and more troublous day.

Eighty years later, Dr. Gordon Kershaw, an academic historian, perceived the character traces in that same portrait very differently:

> John Singleton Copley's portrait of Dr. Gardiner, probably painted in 1772, shows a vigorous, powerful man for sixty-five. The doctor confidently straddles his chair, his hand thrust inside his vest, while a warm smile plays on his lips—but not in his eyes, which defiantly engage the viewer's. He has the determined air of one who has sought life's challenges and met them squarely, willing to risk any consequences.

A generation of historians have shunted aside heroic individuals and gotten lost in amorphous social forces climaxing at various junctures. It is much more interesting to read about real people who had deep feelings, firm attachments, earnest purposes, challenges, and risks—attributes which the two above authors cite.

Events leading to the publication of this biography of Dr. Silvester Gardiner read like the "Perils of Pauline." This work of an eminent author in the field of children's biography was nearly lost but now is presented to students of New England history. Only a succession of small miracles has saved Olivia Coolidge's biography of Dr. Silvester Gardiner from oblivion nearly fifty years since its inception. But first, some account of Mrs. Coolidge is in order.

Mrs. Coolidge is one of the outstanding children's books writers of the third-quarter of the twentieth century. (Margaret) Olivia Ensor was born in London, England 16 October 1908, daughter of Sir Robert Charles Kirkwood Ensor (an historian and journalist) and of Helen (Fisher) Ensor. Her parents were close friends of George Bernard Shaw, whom Olivia met many times as a child. She studied at Somerville College, Oxford University, where he received her B.A. in 1931 and her M.A. in 1940. She taught English at Potsdam-Hermannswerden, Potsdam, Germany in 1931-32; Greek and Latin at Wimbledon High School, Wimbledon, England; English at Low Heywood School, Stamford, Conn. 1938-39; and English at Winsor School from 1939 to 1946.

These are the writings of Olivia Coolidge. All were published by Houghton Mifflin except as noted.

Greek Myths, 1949
Legends of the North, 1951
The Trojan War, 1952
Egyptian Adventures, 1954
Cromwell's Head, 1955
Roman People, 1959
Churchill and the History of Two World Wars, 1960

Caesar's Gallic War, 1961

Men of Athens (*Horn Book* honor list; ALA Notable Book), 1962

Makers of the Red Revolution, 1963

Edith Wharton, Scribner, 1964

People in Palestine, 1965

Lives of Famous Romans, 1965

The King of Men (ALA Notable Book), 1966

Women's Rights: The Suffrage Movement in America, 1848-1920, Dutton, 1966

Eugene O'Neill, Scribner, 1966

Marathon Looks on the Sea, 1967

George Bernard Shaw, 1968

The Golden Days of Greece, Crowell, 1968

Tom Paine, Revolutionary (ALA Notable Book), Scribner, 1969

The Maid of Artemis, 1969

Tales of the Crusades, 1970

Come By Here (*Horn Book* honor list; ALA Notable Book), 1970

Gandhi (*Horn Book* honor list; ALA Notable Book), 1971

The Three Lives of Joseph Conrad, 1972

The Apprenticeship of Abraham Lincoln, Scribner, 1974

The Statesmanship of Abraham Lincoln, Scribner, 1976.

From London, England to Gardiner, Maine, in the United States, looks like a very long jump, but it shrinks to a natural and obvious step, when we see why she came to write the Gardiner biography. Winsor School with its connections to the Richards, Wiggins, and Coolidge families was bound to give proper introduction to all the principals whose paths converged to propel this book into existence. Olivia Ensor married at Lakeville, Connecticut on 14 June 1946 Archibald Cary Coolidge of Boston (born 10 December 1905), son of Julian Lowell Coolidge (1873–1954), professor of mathematics at

Harvard, Master of Lowell House, author of many important works on mathematics, and a direct descendant of Thomas Jefferson. His mother was Theresa Reynolds, a direct descendant of Paul Revere. Mr. Coolidge is the namesake nephew of Archibald Cary Coolidge (1866–1928), the Harvard historian and diplomat. Mr. Coolidge's eldest sister, Jane Revere Coolidge, was the wife of Walter Muir Whitehill, the director of the Boston Athenaeum. From the time of their marriage until their retirement in the mid-1970s, they lived in Annapolis, Maryland. He was a school master at the Hotchkiss School. Now hearty nonagenarians, they reside in Essex, Connecticut, and continue their summer retreats at the Coolidge family compound on Squam Lake in Centre Sandwich, New Hampshire.

There is one other essential passage of Coolidge family genealogy to narrate before these threads can be tied together. Joseph Randolph Coolidge (1828–1925), a Boston attorney, married Julia Gardner (1841–1921), daughter of John Lowell Gardner, by his wife, Catherine, daughter of Captain Joseph Peabody of Salem. Julia's brother, John Lowell Gardner Jr., married Isabella Stewart of New York, whose Venetian palace in Boston's Fenway became the Gardner Museum. Joseph Randolph Coolidge by his wife Julia Gardner had five children, the eldest of whom was Joseph Randolph Coolidge, Jr. (1862–1928) who married Mary Hamilton Hill and the youngest, Julian Lowell Coolidge (1873–1954), noted above as the father of Archibald Cary Coolidge, husband of Olivia, the author of this biography of Dr. Silvester Gardiner. Joseph Randolph Coolidge Jr. (1862-1929) had eight children, the second of whom was Julia Coolidge (1889–1961), who married at Kings Chapel, Boston, 21 June 1910, Henry Howe Richards (1876–1968), son of Henry Richards (1848-1949), architect and director of the famous Camp Merryweather for boys, by his wife Laura Elizabeth Howe (1850–1943), author of more than ninety children's books, a daughter of Dr. Samuel Gridley

Howe, founder of the Perkins School for the Blind in Boston, and of Julia Ward Howe, author of the Battle Hymn of the Republic and one of the foremost social reformers of the nineteenth century. Henry Howe Richards served Groton School for seventy years, first as English master and later as Alumni Recorder. At the time of his death, he was still in service to the school where he had brought about one of the major literary miracles of the twentieth century. He brought the poet Edwin Arlington Robinson (1869–1935) to the attention of Theodore Roosevelt. The president then secured a sinecure income for the young fledging poet.

Olivia Coolidge by the early 1950s had conquered the challenge of presenting classical antiquities to children and aspired to write a scholarly biography for the adult market. Enter Henry Howe Richards to preside at another literary undertaking. Of course, the Groton master knew Olivia because his wife and Olivia's husband were first cousins whose paths often crossed in Boston, at Harvard, and at Squam Lake. As Olivia was to write to Richards' son, Hamilton, in 1986: "This [biography of Silvester Gardiner] came about because I wanted to write a biography and thought that I was qualified to do it well. I still think so, but my efforts were stymied by the grants available for Ph.D. dissertations at the period and by the expense and actual difficulty of travel at a time when we had very little money and were bringing up four children. Your father [Henry Howe Richards] took considerable interest in my ambition and suggested Samuel and Julia Ward Howe." Olivia Coolidge undertook a great deal of preliminary work on those subjects; but, unfortunately, others had crowded her out of the field long before she became apprised of the competition. Harold Schwartz had marked out Samuel Gridley Howe as his territory as had Louise Hall Tharp on Julia Ward Howe.

Olivia Coolidge writes of Henry Howe Richards: "Your father, bless his heart, came up with another idea to try on for size. What about the Gardiners of Gardiner, Maine? There was Silvester and Robert Hallowell. He knew the Gardiners had preserved masses of letters. This time negotiations went well. I went up to stay with two elderly ladies in residence, one widow and mother of the Gardiner owner, one her sister-in-law who, born a Gardiner, had married an English Gardiner, and being now widowed, was ending her life in the house in which she had been brought up. Silvester was really an interesting but not very pleasant person. The Massachusetts Medical Association had a diary kept by one of his apprentices over a period of years while living in the house. Poor fellow died, as did Silvester's own son Jamey, from picking up some epidemic which was going around. One had to be tough to survive as a doctor in Boston. I worked pretty hard on the Gardiners, and when I had got all the facts together, I wrote a life of Silvester, which was to be the first half of the book, and sent it to Houghton Mifflin, from whom I had not asked an advance since the material was fairly accessible to me. With considerable embarrassment, they refused to publish it. They said, as a sop to my vanity no doubt, that it was beautifully written, but that Silvester was not an important enough person to become the subject of a biography which would sell."

However that may be, Mrs. Coolidge was a proven author in the children's market. A "bottom-liner" editor would have wanted Mrs. Coolidge to continue in a field where she was a commercial and critical success. If that were the controlling philosophy at the time, hunches were right because Mrs. Coolidge produced dozens of successful publications for Houghton Mifflin for twenty more years.

By 1980 Olivia Coolidge had ended her career and concluded in her letter to Hamilton Richards: "So much for the history of the manuscript which I have. I am clearing out all my stuff and it occurs to me that it is just possible that the Richards family would like one or as many more as they care to duplicate. If you don't want one, the time has come when I am going to throw it away." Hamilton Richards preserved the manuscript for some time and then gave it to his brother Tudor Richards, who is the most genealogically minded member of the family.

Since June 1988 when the death of the youngest daughter of Henry and Laura E. Richards forced the clearance of Yellow House in Gardiner, Maine, for the first time in 112 years, I have represented the Gardiner Library Association which acquired the Richards-Gardiner-Ward-Howe family papers, known as the Yellow House Papers. I spent two years arranging the papers for deposit at the Special Collections department at Colby College, Waterville, Maine, and then another year in preparing for publication *The Yellow House Papers Inventory: The Laura E. Richards Collection* (Gardiner, Maine: Gardiner Library Association, 1991). Since the initial deposit of eighty-five cartons of manuscripts, other descendants of Henry and Laura Richards have had the foresight to sort through their collections to amplify the main collection with their own valued family books and papers. For eight years, I have been the liaison between them and the Gardiner Library Association and Colby College Library. Access to the papers at Colby is gained by using my work to describe the items and to identify the sections of record groups for their placement into the main collection. Tudor Richards and his wife Barbara have been the principal donors of the additional items to the Yellow House Papers. In March, 1998, when I had a discussion with Tudor Richards about the remaining items in his possession as potential gifts to the Gardiner Library Association and Colby College, I first learned of the existence of the Olivia Coolidge manuscript.

While I have been working on the Yellow House Papers, I have had to become an authority on the genealogies of all the families who owned the papers for over a period of two and a half centuries. I have drafted detailed genealogies of these families, and have an account on the Gardiner family nearly ready for publication. Having spent more than ten years in mastering the sources bearing upon the Gardiner family, imagine my astonishment when I was informed that a large-scale biography of Dr. Silvester Gardiner existed. In my work on bibliography, it may have been the one time I was speechless. With alacrity, I read the biography, and acted as devil's advocate, trying my best to trip up Olivia Coolidge on some detail. Bringing ten years' worth of hard-won expertise on Dr. Gardiner and his family to challenge Olivia Coolidge, I confess that she won the day. Two other Maine historians have read the manuscript and have come to the same conclusion that Mrs. Coolidge did her homework and then wrote a beautiful text. I believe that a broad range of readers from those who want an introduction to the community's beginnings to those who have a unquenchable thirst for New England history will be delighted.

Toward the end of her career, Olivia Coolidge wrote an article for the *Wilson Library Quarterly*, in October 1974, about the calling of a biographer, and this excerpt explains her approach to Dr. Silvester Gardiner: "Actually, a biographer has a different task from a man who is writing his memoirs. These last contain invaluable material, but a good biography is also concerned with the effect its hero has on other people, with environment and background, with the nature of the great man's achievements and their value. I find that I examine facts in all these and many other spheres before I form judgments and that it needs great care to do what sounds quite easy, namely to distinguish a fact from a judgment. For instance, a contemporary's opinion of my subject is a fact. Its reliability and importance are estimated by my judgment, which is shown by my decision to quote or not to quote it, and even by the tone in which I refer to it or the context in which I introduce it."

The publication of this work about our community's history is part of the mission of the Gardiner Library Association, and the Special Collections Committee which I chair. All revenues from the sales of this publication will be given to the building restoration fund for the Gardiner Public Library. Our building, erected in 1881, is in dire need of repairs for its continued use. It is to be hoped that this publication will inspire others in the community to raise the money needed to replace the roof within the next two or three years.

Many people have made this project possible, and upon the behalf of the Gardiner Library Association, I give hearty thanks to the following. Most importantly, the author, Olivia Coolidge has granted permission to the Gardiner Library Association to publish this work and has relinquished her royalities in favor of the building restoration fund. Her husband, Archibald Cary Coolidge, was also of assistance. Earle G. Shettleworth, Jr., Director of the Maine Historic Preservation Commission, is a major contributor to the publication in many ways. He has found private monies, traced needed illustrations, and worked with the technicians in the production of this book. Dr. Robert L. Bradley, historic archaeologist of the Maine Historic Preservation Commission, has read the text and offered useful suggestions. Tudor and Barbara Richards of Hopkinton, New Hampshire, originally suggested to me that this manuscript should be published and made original contact for me with the author. Nicholas and Claire (Gardiner) Burke, of Washington, D.C., have made a major financial contribution to the publication of this book and have provided advice on many matters. The following proof-readers helped: Marjory Whitehurst, Dr. John Ruffing, William A. Perry Jr., Lise Kearney, Ginny Nichols, and Jan Ayer. Marjory Whitehurst also read the entire manuscript, and I gratefully acknowledge her penetrating comments which have enabled me to mold this work in good fashion. Anne E. Davis, Director of the Gardiner Public Library, and her staff have made many resources available. John Dyer Shaw, Jr., President of the Gardiner Library Association, with the officers, and members of the Executive

Committee, have ratified the necessary arrangements to bring this project to fruition. Rosalind C. Wiggins, of Providence, Rhode Island, a descendant of the Gardiner and Richards families, has, as in many other instances, provided information to be found no where else. Jennifer Elliott of Tilbury House, Publishers has brought her expertise to bear in the production and distribution of this book. Dr. Myles Martel of Villanova, Pennsylvania, presented an original letter by Dr. Gardiner to the Library Association in 1996. It is reproduced in this book. Benjamin Keating of the Maine State Library answered reference requests. Glenna Nowell, City Manager of Gardiner, has advised the Gardiner Library Association about the formalities of this project, and will supervise the the work done to the building, partially supported by sales of this book. Dolly Ziegler, of Baltimore, Maryland, has advised me on copy editing matters, in the genealogy. The Friends of Gardiner (Kathi W. Susi, president) also made a major financial contribution to the production of this book.

Danny D. Smith
Chair, Special Collections
Gardiner Library Association
Gardiner, Maine

16 October 1998

Colonial
Entrepreneur

ROWLAND ROBINSON HOUSE, built before 1716, in South Kingstown, Rhode Island, inherited by Dr. Gardiner's sister, Abigail, and her husband, Governor William Robinson. SOCIETY FOR THE PRESERVATION OF NEW ENGLAND ANTIQUITIES.

$\mathcal{T}$HE BOY WHO BET ON HIMSELF

IN EIGHTEENTH-CENTURY Narragansett, to be unhappy was to seem unreasonable. Nothing makes for contentment in society so surely as the feeling that hard-working men are more prosperous than their fathers and may look forward to handing on improvements to their sons. William Gardiner of Boston Neck, who had been born in 1671, belonged to such a generation of fortunate people. From his own dining room where the table gleamed with a silver tankard, saltcellar, spoons, and a porringer or two, he could look back with satisfaction to the day when there had been no table forks in his father's house, and when rough wooden bowls and platters had not entirely given place to pewter ware. On holidays his mother had put her best ribbon bows on her homespun dress and had ridden on a pillion behind his father to parties or on visits to a neighbor. William's own wife had a dress of bought material, solid perhaps, but of a fine rich color and set off by a gold locket and ring as well as ribbons. Gentlemen like himself might wear leather breeches and homespun shirts for rough work on the farm, but on public occasions they appeared in scarlet coats of imported cloth worn over waistcoats trimmed with the gaudi-

VIEW OF VILLAGE at South Kingstown, Rhode Island,
birthplace of Dr. Gardiner. SOCIETY FOR THE PRESERVATION OF
NEW ENGLAND ANTIQUITIES.

est yellow lace obtainable. William's house had twice the solid
comfort that his father's had known in feather beds, extra
linen, carpets, and furniture. Three women helped his wife and
daughters with the monthly wash, the spring soap making, or
the slow churns and creaking cheese presses in the dairy. Nine
slaves did the heaviest farm work and carried on the shoemak-
ing business that William was not too proud to call his trade. In
his youth, not a man in the province had owned so many slaves.

As William had risen in the world, so had his neighbors.
They worked hard, to be sure, but an increasing amount of their
effort was spent on entertaining. Fox hunts and horse races
made gatherings for the men. Harvest festivals, Christmas parties, and weddings packed the farms to overflowing. The new-
est houses were being built with handsome parlors for such
parties, with wide doorways and large, square entrance halls,

into which oak staircases descended, edged with ornamental balustrades. Food and drink were always abundant, for this was farming country where the efforts of the hostess could be supplemented by the loan of her neighbors' cooks or by special delicacies sent over for the occasion. The huge fire dogs in the kitchen held several spits at once on which a haunch of venison or a quarter of lamb could sizzle before the open flame, in company with turkey, duck, or chicken. The punch bowl steamed invitingly, while musicians kept up lively dances, such as "I'll Be Married in My Old Clothes," until the early hours of the morning. There were as yet no roads or carriages, but people on horseback could bring a slave to open the gates, take care of the horses, and guide them home with a lantern if there was no moon.

NARRAGANSETT SOCIETY was highly interrelated. George Gardiner, who had emigrated from England in 1637, left thirteen children in the province. William, his grandson, was one of a family of five. Besides the descendants of the other twelve children of George Gardiner, there were those of his two brothers to be reckoned with, not to mention the even vaster clan of Hazard, the Robinsons and others, to whom the Gardiners were allied. This in itself made for frequent visiting, but an extra sense of solidarity was fostered by the political position in which the area found itself. The southern side of Narragansett Bay had long been the object of a boundary dispute between Connecticut and Rhode Island, and it had been finally erected into a separate dependency under the name of The King's Province. This arrangement, which lasted until 1726, had done much to cultivate a sense of difference from the more sober Puritan settlements to north and south. Narragansett land was extremely fertile, and Rhode Island ships, early active in the slave trade, had supplied cheap labor. The result was that Narragansett society was beginning to follow the gayer, more aristocratic ways of the Virginia plantations. Large estates had become miniature settlements, almost self-supporting, while their owners were freed from the hardest drudgeries and found time to relieve their work by plenty of enjoyments.

A moderate farm in Narragansett might be three hundred acres. William Gardiner owned fifteen hundred, well stocked with cattle, sheep, and pigs. Robert Hazard, wealthiest of Narragansett farmers in the eighteenth century, possessed about two thousand acres and kept a hundred and fifty cows. Twelve dairywomen, each with a girl to assist her, produced between one and two dozen cheeses daily from vats whose "second size" held nearly a bushel. Besides this, Hazard owned four thousand sheep, and all the wool and linen cloth for his household was spun and woven on his estate. In his later years he found it necessary to retrench and recorded with satisfaction that he had cut down his household to "only seventy in parlor and kitchen." Such an establishment contained smokehouses, a tannery, and a mill for grinding hominy or flour. As many as two hundred loads of hay might be cut in a season, while cheese, butter, calves, and fatted bullocks were the principal exports. William Gardiner, for all his fifteen hundred acres, had not a third of Hazard's wealth; yet he stood much closer to Hazard than to a modest farmer with forty acres and a couple of servants, who might leave his wife fifteen pounds, the use of the best milch cow, and the room with the feather bed.

FORTUNATE FOR all these reasons, William Gardiner was also blessed by an unusually amiable wife. His three daughters were industrious housewives and lively companions, while Hannah at least was a regular beauty. His elder sons were competent, energetic farmers. The problem of the family was Silvester, the youngest, who was unfortunately delicate and did not seem to fit well into the pattern of life on a Narragansett farm. In fact, Silvester was unhappy at home, and he met with little understanding from those around him, who regarded misfits not with sympathy, but with a certain rooted distrust.

Silvester Gardiner was born in 1708 and was brought up in a period when life for a delicate boy was usually rough. Work was physically hard, and the children were expected to join in it almost from the time that they could get about alone. Water froze overnight in the bedrooms during the winter, while in the daytime it was insufferably hot near the open fire and icy cold across the room by the window. Salt meat and fish were the main fare during this season, with heavy suet puddings to follow and often no vegetables at all. If this unhealthy diet resulted in sickness, doctors prescribed starvation and bleeding, while homemade remedies varied from mildly beneficial herb teas to unpleasant concoctions which had nothing but superstition to recommend them. Families were large and deaths during childhood very frequent, so much so that parents were aware of the folly of resting too many hopes on the future of a delicate boy. It was better to become resigned by degrees and to turn to the healthier ones when rosy plans were to be made.

Actually there was nothing seriously wrong with young Silvester's health, as in later life it became exceedingly good. However, his build was slight, though trim, and his head was large enough to be disproportionate until it was balanced in middle life by a slight increase of portliness. As a child, his physical strength was small, and his troubles mainly arose because his nature was furiously energetic. As the youngest of seven children, he must have perpetually taxed himself to keep up with the rest, especially since the family temperament was difficult. William Gardiner had earned himself the nickname of "Wicked William," probably by the violence of his temper and the boldness of his religious opinions. John, the eldest son, was known for his rages. Even her husband, who loved her, speaks of the beautiful Hannah as "my poor passionate dear." Silvester's temper was equally fiery, and it is natural enough

THE REVEREND JAMES MACSPARRAN (1693–1757), rector
of St. Paul's Church, Narragansett, Rhode Island, and
brother-in-law of Dr. Gardiner, portrait by John Smibert
in 1735. BOWDOIN COLLEGE MUSEUM OF ART, BRUNSWICK, MAINE.
BEQUEST OF CHARLES EDWARD ALLEN.

that he should have been at odds with his brothers and sisters,
to whom he was inferior in age and strength.

This conflict between Silvester's ambitious temperament
and his powers of endurance was heightened by the fact that
his real abilities were not appreciated. The lively squires of Narragansett were not particularly intellectual, and they preferred

to spend most of their lives out of doors. It seems to have been the exception rather than the rule to own more than half a dozen books in all. Poor college graduates who needed money would set up schools for the boys and stay a year or two, during which time work was interrupted by bad weather, harvest, and various festivals. In any case, a boy who could write and spell reasonably well, keep some accounts, and read his Bible had all the learning that was ever likely to be of practical use. From time to time one of the local clergymen who was anxious to eke out his stipend would take pupils for higher study. This gave opportunity for a chosen few, but many regarded such effort as a waste of time. In such an affectionate, social, gossipy society, pretensions of any sort were out of place.

It is hard to tell what might have become of Silvester, so unhappy and so ill-suited to the cheerful life of a Narragansett farm, had he not found someone to appreciate his real intellectual powers. By a rare stroke of luck it happened that in 1721 the Society for the Propagation of the Gospel, a London missionary organization, sent out an Episcopal clergyman to Narragansett at a salary of seventy pounds a year. The Rev. James MacSparran, born in Ireland of Scottish parents, had been educated in Glasgow, and he happily combined the warm heart and ready eloquence of one nation with the industry and sound learning of the other. In Narragansett he found himself master of a fine, tall church with spacious pews, lofty pulpit, wide galleries, and quite inadequate congregation. Though not yet out of his twenties, MacSparran had already held a parish in Bristol, Rhode Island, and had left his youthful mistakes behind him once and for all. His impulsiveness was modified by the dignity of his office, his pugnacity found expression in upholding the rights of his church, and his sociable nature endeared him alike to rich and poor. From the first the steady increase of his congregation was proof that Narragansett people found in him qualities which aroused their affection and respect.

It chanced that Mrs. Gardiner's mother had been Episcopalian, while William Gardiner was but loosely attached to the doctrines of his own church. Interest was expressed in MacSparran by the Gardiner household, and it was not long before he was a frequent visitor. In less than a year after his arrival he was engaged to Hannah Gardiner, a young beauty of seventeen with flashing eyes, fine dark locks, and a high, imperious spirit. Few men could have managed her successfully or understood the energy which was not consumed by housekeeping or entertaining, but must issue from time to time in outbursts of temper or hysterics. MacSparran did so triumphantly, and this very fact made him a fit person to appreciate young Silvester, equally handicapped by temperament, and more frustrated. His success is shown by the fact that on the twelfth of

EXTERIOR VIEW of Old St. Paul's Church, Narragansett, Rhode Island, the Gardiner family church. This building was later moved to its present site in Wickford, Rhode Island. SOCIETY FOR THE PRESERVATION OF NEW ENGLAND ANTIQUITIES.

May 1722, ten days before his marriage with Hannah, he baptized his young future brother-in-law as a member of the Episcopal church. Silvester's life-long devotion to the Episcopal cause is a measure both of his gratitude to his first friend, and of the extraordinary maturity of his mind at thirteen. Presented at this early age with the opportunity of choosing a new faith and a new career, he seems to have known precisely what he wanted, to have grasped it, and never to have altered his opinion in the slightest degree. It is hard to say which gift of MacSparran's was the more valuable to Silvester, the religion which alone imposed order on his chaotic emotions, or the education which made possible his future career.

William Gardiner, though not especially ambitious for his children, was disposed to give them all the advantages that were available to them. His daughters played the harpsichord, and his sons received as much education as was compatible

INTERIOR VIEW of Old St. Paul's Church, Narragansett, Rhode Island, the Gardiner family church. SOCIETY FOR THE PRESERVATION OF NEW ENGLAND ANTIQUITIES.

HANNAH (GARDINER) MACSPARRAN (1704–1755), sister of Dr. Gardiner, portrait by John Smibert in 1732. MUSEUM OF FINE ARTS, BOSTON. GIFT OF MRS. MARGARET ALLEN ELTON.

with the conditions under which they lived. When a sound scholar with a gift for teaching settled in the neighborhood, it was natural that young Silvester should go to him as pupil for a year or two. This attitude had by no means prepared MacSparran for Silvester's real abilities, and he was astonished at them. When, however, he mentioned them to William Gardiner, he did not find the father particularly impressed. Since Silvester did not seem likely to become much of a farmer, it might admittedly be wise to educate him for something else, though William seemed uncertain how to go about it. He gloomily confided to MacSparran that he did not think it likely such an unpromising child would ever be much good.

MacSparran, for his part, having given his opinion, might easily have left the matter there. His relationship with Hannah would hardly make it necessary for him to adopt a rather tiresome protégé of thirteen. Fortunately MacSparran was a born teacher and had felt the thrill of making a discovery. Besides, he was never a man to leave well enough alone or to count the trouble that interference might cost him. He now confidently assured William Gardiner that Silvester, if properly educated, would amount to more than any of the rest of his family. He had talked things over with Silvester, who had a decided preference for the study of medicine. If MacSparran might supervise the boy's education, he would send him to school in Boston for a while and let him learn a little of the business by lodging him with a respectable apothecary of good Episcopal background. Later on, he might be apprenticed to a doctor in regular fashion.

WILLIAM GARDINER, though relieved to entrust the burden of managing Silvester to such evidently competent hands, was far from understanding his young son's decision and seems to have supposed that after a year or two the boy would change his mind. He was therefore considerably disquieted to find that a Boston education only served as a stimulus to a new series of ambitious plans. After a year or so, Silvester was already saying that medicine in Boston was out of date, and that there were no proper facilities for study, since the town contained no public hospital nor medical school. Religious prejudices were such that severe enactments had been passed against interfering with the bodies of the dead, with the result that it was impossible to procure any objects for dissection. Meanwhile, in the large hospitals of Europe a student might see as many as two or three operations in a day. Young Dr. Thomas Bulfinch, who had lately returned from several years of study in London and Paris, was a scientifically educated practitioner beside whom Boston doctors were like children groping in the dark. Silvester had evidently been talking to Thomas Bulfinch, since London and Paris were precisely the centers that he himself had in mind.

William Gardiner's confidence in his fourteen-year-old son can hardly have been increased by these trenchant criticisms of established ways. Doctors had been satisfied to learn by apprenticeship in the past, and this new idea of foreign study actually amounted to a very cool demand for money. Though well-to-do as things went in Narrangansett, William had never been especially rich in cash. To spend several years abroad, pay apprenticeship fees to fashionable foreign doctors, live in expensive towns like London and Paris, and buy instruments or necessary books was going at the very least to cost some hundreds of pounds. To find such a sum would be embarrassing, and unless things went well it might make a considerable difference to the total value of William's estate. Silvester was but one of seven children, and so far he had done nothing to justify such a large investment in his future. MacSparran was confident, it is true, but the year in Boston had not been productive of any startling results beyond convincing Silvester that he knew better than those with many years of experience behind them. William was very much disposed to refuse the money.

At no time in his life did Silvester lack courage, and in this first adventure he showed the sureness of purpose which was to be characteristic of him always. He had been able to keep his eyes open in Boston and to come to the decision that for such advantages as Thomas Bulfinch possessed, it was worthwhile gambling heavily. He now proposed that if his father would pay the cost of a European education, the sum should be deducted from any inheritance that might otherwise have been his. On this basis William yielded, and so sure of himself was Silvester when he went abroad at fifteen that he took his time in Europe and did not return until the better part of a thousand pounds, all that he ever could have expected from his father, had been spent. He was the best qualified doctor in Boston when he set up practice in 1731. William Gardiner, no doubt, chiefly noticed that he had been remitting him money steadily for eight years.

SILVESTER GARDINER arrived in Europe at the time when the foundations of modern medical practice were actually being laid. In 1723, England had enjoyed eight years of peaceable rule since the Jacobite rebellion and nearly ten of freedom from Continental wars. This settled state of affairs gave people a chance to turn their attention to public welfare, with the result that an increasing number of attempts were being made to deal with such problems as crime, pauperism, and disease. Silvester saw several private hospitals or dispensaries in London, while the Westminster Hospital was a recent creation, and Guy's was certainly founded while he was there. Meanwhile the two older hospitals, St. Thomas's and St. Bartholomew's, had been for some time taking the lead in a revolution which was shortly to make London one of the most important surgical centers in the world.

Seventeenth-century surgery had been almost entirely military, concerning itself with amputations and the care of wounds. Civilian operations of the simpler sort, such as those for cataract, wryneck, or kidney stone, were either not performed at all, or were entrusted to quacks who had often no qualifications for the undertaking but effrontery. How far such people could sometimes advance in their profession may be gathered from the characters of two oculists appointed to attend Queen Anne. William Read had taken to the road as an itinerant doctor after failing to earn his living as a tailor. Though he never was able to read or write himself, he made a fortune by issuing blatant advertisements. Eyes were his specialty, but he also undertook to cure cancers, wens, harelip, wryneck, and deafness. In

1705 he had the bright idea of offering free treatment to soldiers and sailors, which brought him the gratitude of the Queen in the form of a knighthood and an appointment as her oculist-in-ordinary. Read's colleague, Roger Grant, though a tinker by trade, had learned his letters and put them to good use in getting testimonials. His practice was to pay some poor, preferably half-witted person half a crown to be treated with medicines for about six weeks. At the end of this time, the patient was offered a sum of money if he would sign a document that he had been born stone blind, and that all sorts of doctors had previously tried in vain to cure him. Grant then pressed the local clergyman for his signature. If he could not bribe or flatter the parson into giving it, he forged it himself.

These examples give an idea of the low esteem into which honest doctors had been brought by such competition, but the position of surgeons had been brought by such competition,

ST. THOMAS'S HOSPITAL, London, where Dr. Gardiner studied medicine under Dr. William Cheseldon in the late 1720s.

but the position of surgeons had been still further debased by an affiliation with the barbers. The Barber-Surgeons' Corporation, which was founded in 1540, had served a useful purpose in its day and established valuable rules. Four times a year it had the right to the body of a condemned criminal for dissection at Barber-Surgeons' Hall in the presence of the licensed surgeons of the capital and their apprentices. Apprenticeship lasted seven years, and apprentices must be neither misshapen or diseased and must present what was then considered a tidy personal appearance. That is to say, the Barber-Surgeons laid it down that they might not appear with a beard of more than fifteen days' growth. Unfortunately this union with the barbers had depressed the standing of the surgeons and left them vulnerable to attacks from the physicians, who had always been jealous of the rival profession. Thus at the beginning of the eighteenth century, regulations forbade a surgeon to perform any important operation except in the presence of a physician, or to prescribe medicaments for any patient in hospital without the written authorization of one. All this was bad enough; it was intolerable to find in the recent twenty-five years of intermittent war with France that a captured surgeon, instead of being treated like an officer and a gentleman, was apt to be imprisoned with the common herd as a mere barber.

THE FIRST STEP toward reform was taken when some of the younger surgeons accepted positions in the hospitals of St. Thomas and St. Bartholomew, the two medieval foundations of the city of London. Here they were intended to deal with amputations of infected limbs, or with wounds sustained in brawls. Inevitably, however, among such numbers of patients, a proportion of other surgical cases were to be found. The surgeons began to attempt new operations with complete success. Presently it began to be known that in the rough-and-ready operating rooms of St. Thomas's there was more to be seen in a single day than the Barber-Surgeons could offer through public dissections in the course of a whole year. The busy surgeons, in need of assistants, were glad to take pupils. The Barber-Surgeons objected, of course, complaining that St. Thomas's was turning out practitioners in little more than six months and for less than a quarter of the fee demanded for apprenticeship. Fortunately the governors of St. Thomas's had a good case and were prepared to be reasonable. They agreed that no surgeon should take more than three pupils at a time, and that the training should be not less than twelve months. This battle was won in 1702, and the fruits of it in the next twenty years were such that at the time of Silvester's arrival, London was already beginning to take its place alongside Paris, Leyden, and Padua.

Silvester found his way to St. Thomas's to hear the course of thirty-five lectures on anatomy given there by William Cheseldon, the greatest surgeon of the English world. He must have been pupil to some surgeon there for a twelvemonth, probably to Cheseldon himself. At any rate, Silvester became master of the new way of operating for kidney stone, which he later demonstrated numerous times to the assembled medical authorities of Boston. His skill in this operation was almost certainly learned from Cheseldon, who was its greatest practitioner and eventually brought his time for it down to fifty-four seconds. At one time Cheseldon calculated that he had performed two hundred and ten such operations, and that only twenty people had died. This is a remarkable record in the days before asepsis, especially as several patients actually died of smallpox, presumably contracted in hospital, while some others were extremely old and ill when they submitted to the operation.

As a pupil to a London surgeon, Silvester would hold the patient, or have ready the special instruments which Cheseldon was the first man in London to design. He would clean up the room and change the dressings after the operation. He would be allowed to bleed patients, lance boils, stitch up wounds, and in time to perform simple operations such as the amputation of a finger. Meanwhile there were books to be read, and he must lay the foundation of the excellent medical library he later possessed. From Cheseldon's lectures he would learn the importance of forming a collection of anatomical specimens—no easy matter in an age which furnished four bodies for dissection in a year. On the whole this period in London must have been sufficiently busy, though it only covered one-half of Silvester's future profession. In the Colonies it was insufficient to learn to become a surgeon without becoming a physician as well.

IF THE SEVENTEENTH CENTURY surgeon had been often less than a gentleman, the physician may generally said to have gone to the other extreme. The doctors satirized by Moliere and Fielding use pretentious language to impress that patient and to cover up mistakes. "The *contusion* on his Head has *perforated* the *internal Membrane* of the *Occiput*," says the doctor in *Joseph Andrews*, puzzled by a simple bruise. However, a good physician was often a highly educated man, a classicist, and a gentleman. The three most prominent in the London of Silvester's day were John Arbuthnot, a writer and wit; John Radcliffe, the benefactor of the Bodleian Library at Oxford; and John Freind, a member of Parliament and a prominent Jacobite. Such men wore satin breeches, well-curled wigs, and silk stockings. They carried gold-headed sticks and paid their calls in coaches with footmen behind to carry their satchels and gloves. Fielding in some exasperation defines a physician as a man who has "acquired a right of applying his skill in the art of physic to his own private advantage."

In fact medicine in London, though beset by quacks and showmen, had progressed further from the naive assumptions of the middle ages than in almost any other place in Europe. This advance was due to the work done in the last quarter of the seventeenth century by Thomas Sydenham, who was the first to classify sickness by diseases, instead of by symptoms. His studies of scarlet fever, measles, and smallpox showed them to run entirely different courses and to need different types of treatment. Moreover his work opened the way for an enormous number of similar treatises on common diseases which, making better sense than earlier writings, speedily became fashionable. The physicians who made such a parade of their success were men whose reputation had been established by such publications. Along with the pompous phraseology, the obscure Latin, and the scarlet coats went a scientific approach to disease and a real background of medical learning.

The most interesting single contribution to medicine at this time was the introduction of inoculation for smallpox, which had been witnessed by Lady Mary Wortley Montague in Turkey when her husband was ambassador there. Silvester was an enthusiastic convert and later spent a great deal of energy struggling for what was really the most difficult part of the procedure, the establishment of a permanent inoculating hospital. Hard though it was to persuade people to give themselves smallpox deliberately, the idea gained ground by degrees and might be hoped to prevail in time. During an epidemic, inoculation soared, and people did not object to it, particularly when smallpox was in any case all over the town. On the other hand whenever it was proposed to make this highly infectious disease a permanent part of town life, all the inhabitants made violent protests. In Boston, where such matters were decided in Town Meeting, Silvester fought a long, drawn-out battle, but a losing one. It is a pity that he never seems to have heard of the great discovery of vaccination, which Jenner made during Silvester's lifetime, but did not introduce to the public until some years after his death.

How far Silvester progressed with his medical training in London is not certain. Though he did visit Edinburgh for some time and spent a great while in France, his education, wherever traceable, appears to be entirely English. This is probably the case because his sympathies were totally alienated by the state of society elsewhere. William Cheseldon advertised his anatomical lectures in the *Daily Courant* as follows: "N.B. This course being chiefly intended for gentlemen, such things only will be omitted as are neither instructive nor entertaining, and care will be taken to have nothing offensive." This general attitude was not characteristic of either Edinburgh or Paris. Edinburgh was in fact serious enough, and was staffed by an unusually able body of doctors educated at Leyden. However, the lectures of Alexander Munro on anatomy were enlivened by unseemly riots between the students and the relatives of the criminals whose bodies were granted for dissection. On one of these occasions while the fight was in full swing, the body stirred and showed signs of life. She was revived and became for years a well-known Edinburgh character under the title of "Half-hangit Maggie Dickson." If Silvester was present on this famous occasion, as he well may have been, his pugnacious character undoubtedly led him into the thick of the battle. However, he conceived a profound distaste for the Presbyterians of Edinburgh, whose attitude reminded him of the restrictions imposed on medical research by the Puritans of Boston.

In Paris there *was* certainly a great deal to be learned. The French had been pioneers in the designing of surgical instruments and had produced some notable surgeons. Jean Louis Petit, now at the height of his fame, was the inventor of the screw tourniquet and the first man to perform a successful operation for mastoiditis. Paris was the greatest European school for midwifery, which was in most places hardly considered a fit subject for a doctor at all. Valuable, however, as was the instruction in Paris, Silvester was so greatly antagonized by the ideas current there that in later years he would not let his daughters study French, lest they learn to read what was written in it.

SCIENCE HAD BECOME fashionable in the days of Louis XIV as a bored aristocracy sought relief from the trivial round of life at court. This had supplied the patronage that medicine needed and had made dissections and public lectures possible. Now, after eight years of the corrupt Orleans regency, interest had lapsed into a desire to be shocked or to hear dirty jokes. There was no question of taking care "to have nothing offensive," rather the contrary. Silvester had no such unhealthy tendencies, but was earnest, humorless, and thoroughly down-right. He was shocked by the public attitude and reacted, as he always did, vehemently. He was also horrified to find that the violent anti-clericalism of the past thirty years had by now given way to open skepticism. Hardly anybody in polite society made any pretense of believing in Christianity at all. The consequence was that Silvester simply dismissed Rousseau and other liberalizing thinkers who preceded the French Revolution as atheists guilty of the greatest sin of all. In spite of his abilities, Silvester was a man who could not argue, for he always found his own opinions quite self-evident, and the slightest hint of personal opposition sent him into a rage. He was a practical, not a speculative thinker, since in the latter field his ideas ran on well-worn, conservative lines.

If Silvester left France with nothing but some added technical advantages, he had gained in England not only an education, but a faith. Long residence abroad and experience of other sects had hardened his conviction that the Church of England was the proper choice for an intelligent man. The Society for the Propagation of the Gospel in Foreign Parts, to which Silvester had been introduced by James MacSparran, had originally been intended to counteract that influence of French Catholicism in Canada by proselytizing the Indians.

This being difficult, and in time of war almost impossible, the Society had gradually directed its efforts to upholding the cause of the Church of England in the Nonconformists parts of the Colonies. This partisan attitude suited Silvester, who was also attracted by a characteristic of the English church for which it has not always been given credit, namely its reasonableness. The eighteenth-century divines were busily reducing the fervor of Christianity to a set of simple moral rules guided by common sense. Silvester was conscious of the liberal education and broad point of view behind such efforts and could appreciate them much more readily than the speculations of French thinkers. His own violent nature led him to struggle constantly for control, and he blamed both the stricter sects whose authority was emotional, and the radicals who rejected authority altogether.

All in all, one may say that Silvester's opinions were formed by his residence in England, and only hardened by experience elsewhere. In later life he had trading relations with England for over thirty years. He corresponded at various times with the Society for the Propagation of the Gospel. When his little grandson was sent to him from the West Indies in the sixties for a Boston education, Silvester high-handedly shipped him to England, which he declared was the only place where he would be given a good grounding. On this occasion it is notable that he had enough connections in England to be able to place the little boy. In France, on the other hand, it is impossible to discover that he ever made a single friend. He completed his training there, packed his books and specimens, and took ship for Boston, apparently without a desire to revisit France or have anything to do with it again.

TWO

BOSTON DOCTOR

IN 1731, BOSTON WAS a seaport town where even in gentlemen's gardens the smell of stables fought a losing battle with fishy odors wafted in from the busy wharves or tidal flats. Nearly five hundred ships reached Boston yearly, and in its famous taverns sea captains mingled daily with Puritan merchants and English aristocrats, exchanging news. In the narrow, cobbled lanes down by the docks, the incoming crews jostled their way past artisans, peddlers, foreign soldiers, raw immigrants, Indians, or black slaves. Diphtheria, dysentery, scarlet fever, and smallpox came in at frequent intervals with the seamen and flourished bravely in the crowded peninsula, where wells and cesspools were scattered quite haphazardly, and where rum was the safest and most universal drink. Boston was a busy town for a doctor, and it possessed about twenty, most of whom were apothecaries whose training had taught them little beyond the practical business of a druggist. In general they were intelligent men and quick to experiment with new treatments reported from Europe, where the actual discoveries were made. Smallpox inoculation, for instance, was introduced in 1721, only two years after it had arrived in England, and was supported by a vociferous party, for Boston's need was great. The chief deficiency of these doctors lay in the field of surgery, as dissection was still forbidden in Boston, and there was no public hospital. The result was that doctors had neither the knowledge of anatomy nor the actual practice of which they stood in need. Dr. Bulfinch and Dr. Douglass, who had studied abroad were quite insufficient to cope with the needs of a seaport town of eighteen thousand people where rough work meant many accidents.

Young Dr. Gardiner, unknown in Boston and recommended only by his person and qualifications, presented to the public a small, but confident and by no means unimpressive figure. To the neat hands, quick movements, and steady nerves of a surgeon, he added a naturally loud voice and a tendency to

SECOND MAP of Boston by William Burgis in 1728,
engraved in 1730 by Thomas Johnston.

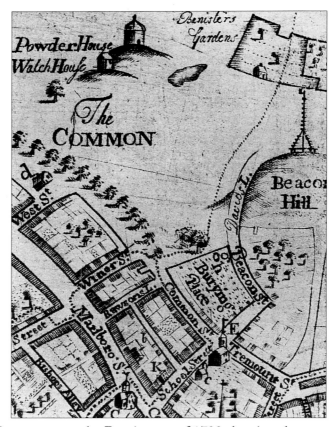

DETAIL FROM the Burgis map of 1728 showing the corner of Marlboro (now Washington) and Winter Streets where Dr. Gardiner lived and maintained his medical practice.

bully nervous people which were invaluable in a profession where it was necessary to be cruel in order to be kind. Too impulsive for dignity, he yet inspired confidence by being both rapid and efficient. Taking a short-cut to success, he did not now open his career by investing in the stuffy little apothecary shop and the slave attendant which were the usual equipment of a doctor in those days. Plenty of taverns had large upper rooms where meeting of all sorts were held and where anatomical lectures might easily be given. Silvester had brought a collection of specimens back with him from Europe and was in a position to offer Boston medicine something of which it stood in urgent need. Though tedious in argument, he was an excellent teacher on matters of his own choosing, being a persuasive and interesting talker with a capacity for throwing the whole force of his vigorous personality into his subject. No doubt a few older doctors were unwilling to learn their business anew from a self-assured young fellow of twenty-three. However, Dr. Douglass, who was firmly established in Boston, had also been trained in Europe; and there is some evidence that a progressive party among doctors had appeared under his patronage. At all events, a medical society, the first in America, was formed about 1735 and was associated with the names of Douglass and Silvester Gardiner. Its chief aims were to publish scientific articles and to draw up a qualifying examination which should exclude quacks from the medical profession. Actually, it did neither, but faded quietly into oblivion after having existed for about six years. It is evident that the new type of doctor and the old could not coalesce, though they went on existing side by side, since there was room for all.

L ONG BEFORE THE failure of the medical society, Silvester was firmly established in Boston as a result of a piece of shrewd calculation or good luck. Not much more than a year after arriving in town, he married Anne, daughter of Dr. John Gibbins, the wealthy apothecary with whom he had lodged eight years before when he had first arrived in Boston. Silvester's future was assured, for Dr. Gibbins had no son and but one other daughter, who did not marry. As the son-in-law and presumable heir of an old-school doctor, Silvester now had a foot in both camps, while a timely legacy gave him a chance to set up on his own. In 1732, William Gardiner died, and Silvester may have been surprised to discover that a promising young doctor in Boston was on a very different footing with his father from a discontented boy in school. William did leave the home farm to his eldest son, but Silvester received eighty acres and a legacy of fourteen hundred pounds, a very considerable amount in those days. He found himself able to buy a handsome, two-story brick house in the fashionable section of town on Marlborough Street, but a few hundred yards from Dr. Gibbins. Here if her husband's activities kept him from home, Anne could have her mother and Lucy to dinner or to sing duets and practice the spinet.

SILVESTER'S ELDEST SON, William, was not born till 1736, but John followed in the next year, and six more children came after that at intervals of two years each. Silvester made a fair living, but he had to work hard for it, since fees were low. One shilling and sixpence was the usual charge for a visit, and for quite serious operations about a pound. It was true that as an exceptionally skillful surgeon he could ask higher fees, but even these were not very considerable. For instance, he demanded fifty pounds for operating on Amos Turner for stone in Scituate, but this included traveling out there and staying a week to look after the patient. Moreover, Turner died, and his relatives as was often the case refused to pay for an unsuccessful operation. All in all, a man would need to work hard if he had to support a family of eight children, though it is fair to say that in some respects Silvester's household expenses were low. Meat of all kinds was cheap and good, while fine fresh fish were daily hawked on the streets for a mere trifle. Butter and cheese were plentiful, and fruits in season were a glut on the market, so much so that all but the best were frequently fed to hogs. Fuel, however, was expensive, and clothes exceedingly so, since there was a great gulf between the imported velvet and broadcloth of the well-to-do and the homespun jackets and leather breeches of the poor. A doctor must dress well, wear a handsome wig, ride a good horse, and have a servant. To be sure, he could take apprentices, who paid him and also earned him money, since he received the fees from any patients of whom they did not have exclusive charge. He could sell drugs if he could get them; in fact some sort of druggist's shop was a natural part of every doctor's stock in trade. The trouble was, it was hard to order what one needed from England in tiny amounts, while the big merchants preferred to carry goods for which there was a quicker sale. Yet if a man studied the market, a demand was certainly there, since ships carried medicine boxes and wanted to refill in port, while small-town doctors were looking for a middleman from whom they could replenish their stocks. With a little capital to start with, a very considerable profit might be made. In 1744, a modest advertisement in the *Boston Gazette* makes known that "Mr. Sylvester Gardiner, at the sign of the Unicorn and Mortar in Marlborough Street" is prepared to sell the best and freshest of all kinds of drugs, and to put up doctors' and surgeons' boxes for ships, carefully furnished with printed directions.

From this establishment, which was later moved to his father-in-law's house on the corner of Winter Street, Silvester continued to retail drugs in Boston for upwards of thirty years. In fact, an invoice of goods shipped to him in 1773 suggests that he has slightly widened his range, since in addition to such drugs as "India Rubarb ... Gum Ammoniac Lump," and "best opium," he has ordered ten barrels of "very fine Turkey figs" and two of prunes, together with a case of cinnamon and another of mixed spices, not to mention two pipes of olive oil, six half chests of Florence oil, two barrels of linseed oil, and a box of white candy.

It is difficult to realize how a doctor in active practice could find time to make a fortune in the drug business, especially if one understands the complications caused in trade by a universal want of cash. If Silvester nursed a candlemaker's son through smallpox, he was paid by a credit for so many shillingsworth of candles at the father's store. These Anne Gardiner might collect, or if Silvester preferred, he could simply hand over the credit to his tailor in part payment of a bill. The tailor in his turn might pass it on to someone else, until by rare good luck it eventually came into the hands of a man who owed the candlemaker money and was cancelled out without any transfer of candles taking place at all. Apart from the complicated bookkeeping caused by the fact that the tailor's bill was never quite the same as the candlemaker's credit, this situation was fairly simple. When, on the other hand, an upstate doctor wrote to Silvester for his annual consignment of drugs, he would generally pay in actual samples of what his creditors could give him, namely pork, leather, salt fish, or boards. This immediately forced Silvester to own a warehouse, since goods of this kind were a glut on the Boston market and could not be disposed of at once. Eventually they might be sold to someone collecting a shipload for the West Indies who would probably wish to pay in molasses on his return. In the course of time, Silvester found himself trading up the coast as far as Newfoundland, partly at least in an effort to straighten out his business to the point where he could find goods acceptable to the English market.

T HE OBJECT OF ALL this trading was to get possession of cash or credit with English merchants which could be used to pay an agent in London for purchasing and shipping drugs. One London agent might serve many people, which was an economy. On the other hand, a single merchant like Silvester, nominally dealing in a single line of goods, must have additional agents in Maine, Hartford, Newport, Newfoundland, and other places, who were engaged in handling a completely miscellaneous range of supplies. One aspect of this situation is the number of letters that had to be written, especially in time of war when it was safer to send as many as half a dozen copies by different ships. In any case, one copy must be kept by the merchant, and every one must be written out separately by hand. Large-scale traders, such as Apthorp or Thomas Hancock, kept a counting house full of clerks to do this writing, but Silvester, who was primarily a doctor, had no regular assistant for such work at all. Young William was intended to be his father's right-hand man, and he undoubtedly learned the business as a clerk when he was old enough. Sometimes Silvester used the apprentices to write for him, but they had other duties. Very often he seems to have managed the correspondence by himself.

Not only were the mechanics of trading complex, but it needed special qualities of character to make such a business profitable at all. Movements of letters of goods were immensely slow, with the consequence that long-term credits were generally expected. A doctor would write in from Machias in Maine to say that he needed such and such drugs, and that though he was precisely in a position to pay for the consignment of six months earlier, he was doing a little trading on his own account and hoped to settle presently, provided that Silvester would take payment in boards. Next year he would write again regretting that boards were not available and would offer Silvester a mortgage on a tract of unimproved land to which he said he had title, while enclosing another order. Such evasions were complicated by the universal practice of employing agents. A certain Dr. Toppan, who had previously owed Silvester money, thought it prudent to get a storekeeper named Rushton to procure him a further supply of drugs instead of asking for it himself. Eventually Silvester sued Rushton, who had not been paid for the drugs and defended himself by making out a bill in which gloves and ribbons were brought from him by Mrs. Gardiner were confused with a large number of articles which had actually been ordered by her maid. On another occasion

Silvester sold a load of boards to Robert Pierpoint and expected to be paid in cash. This being inconvenient, Pierpoint claimed that he owed Dr. Gardiner nothing, since he had bought the boards from MacFadden, the captain of the coaster in which Silvester had shipped them up from Maine.

A less pugnacious, less extraordinarily efficient man than Silvester could not have found time for all the writs of seizure and the petty lawsuits entailed by such a business, and would shortly have been overwhelmed by a vast accumulation of bad debts. Silvester not only prosecuted on every occasion, but usually took his case to the higher courts if it was not successful at first. In thirty-five years he carried more than thirty cases as high as the Supreme Court of the Province, where he almost always got a verdict in his favor, awarding him costs and some perfectly trifling sum. There is no doubt that many debtors paid him solely because he was known to be a hard man to cheat. His unremitting energies where such that he made a handsome fortune and rose to be the largest drug importer in New England. After seven years, he even found time to undertake a third profession which he carried on in conjunction with the others, besides being busy on committees which took up a good deal of his attention. Only once did he show the slightest sign of fatigue when at the age of fifty-odd he dashed off a postscript to a letter to England. "Buy for me," he wrote, "a pair of the best head spectacles for a person about 45 years." In view of his activities, the surprising thing is that he even felt as old as forty-five.

When a man turned in by the sign of the Unicorn and Mortar and rang the tinkling bell on the shop door in Marlborough Street, he seldom found Doctor Gardiner himself at home. One of the apprentices would come out to serve him from the little room behind the shop where he had been filing orders or entering bills. Usually Silvester had three apprentices, and one was always in the shop, since in addition to learning their trade, they were expected to make themselves useful where they could. Young men of eighteen are sometimes casual, and Silvester supervised their behavior with the utmost care. One boy got into trouble for writing an order to Mr. Apthorp on the best paper and was told that this enormous extravagance would practically cause the year's account to show a loss. There were reproofs for not charging "shavings of hartshorn" to Mr. Gunter, for charging Dr. Prescott's medicine without showing the bill to the master, and for giving Margett the wrong pills. This last offense might have been serious, and Dr. Gardiner was at no loss for words to impress a culprit when such a need arose. Doctor Gardiner, as the apprentice says on one occasion, "called me an Impudent, Lying, Conceited fellow & scolded at me much for putting up Galban Cnid. for Dr. Rogers, for Galb. Colat. I never was so badly treated in my life."

FAMOUS AS WAS Doctor Gardiner's temper, it does not seem badly misplaced on this occasion, and in some ways the young man had little to complain of. George Hewes, the shoemaker's apprentice, had a master who kept a leather strap conveniently handy and used it when the boy came in after nine o'clock at night. Doctor Gardiner was more restrained towards his apprentices, but he was not invariably so towards the servants. To be sure, when Betty neglected his shirts, he only shouted at her and called her a "Jayd," and though her feelings were evidently hurt, she may very well have deserved it. At any rate, the man-servant on one occasion brought his sheets into the kitchen to show the company in proof that Betty never bothered to change them. On the other hand, Silvester actually boxed his man's ears in the course of one argument and drove him out of the house with blows and kicks. Very likely the one who got most cuffs was the slave, Hasard, who carried the doctor's implements, looked after his horse, and went on errands.

Every doctor in town seemed to have a slave, and the slaves all knew each other. Dr. Gibbins's just up the street was named Carr. In 1755, Carr was approached by a fellow slave named Mark, who served a certain hot-tempered Captain Codman in Charlestown. Mark needed some arsenic "to kill a pig," he said, and Carr as a doctor's servant could easily lay his hand on a supply. Carr prudently refused all help, and Mark eventually got what he needed from Dr. Clarke's slave, Robin. Later, when Mark was arrested for poisoning Captain Codman, both Carr and Robin were naturally questioned. It is possible that Hasard, who knew Carr and Robin well, and who had a quick tempered master of his own, picked up ideas. At any rate, family tradition has it that he put poison in Silvester's breakfast chocolate, but gave himself away by warning Mrs. Gardiner not to drink. Silvester, who was by no means deliberately cruel, was at a loss how to punish such a crime, and ended by forgiving him. It appears that Mark, before taking to poison, had set fire to Captain Codman's property in the hopes of ruining him and forcing him to sell his slaves. Presumably with this idea in mind, Hasard now set fire to the Doctor's stables. At this the neighbors declared with some bitterness that the Doctor might let himself be poisoned, if such was his pleasure, but that he had no right to permit his slave to endanger them all. Silvester finally sent Hasard to Maine and settled him on his property there, providing him with tools and stock to work a farm.

SINCE THIS STORY RESTS on the slender foundations of a family tradition, a recorded fire in the Doctor's outbuildings, and the fact that Silvester really did set Hasard up on a farm in Maine, it is hard to put very much faith in it. Mark's crime was one of the most sensational in the century, and his public execution in Cambridge was witnessed by thousands. It certainly seems probable that the legend is a distorted version of Mark's story, which has by chance attached itself to Silvester's slave. Still, it may be true, and Silvester's part in it is quite characteristic, especially his unwillingness to accept defeat and get rid of Hasard. It is hard to say which is the more remarkable, the temper which would drive a servant to such lengths, or the goodness of heart which would treat a helpless dependent so magnanimously.

Over this enormous household of apprentices, men and maid-servants, slaves, and children, the authority of Anne Gibbins Gardiner was supreme. It was she who ordered the vast dinners of several meat courses and heavy pudding which were served to the servants and apprentices in the kitchen and to the family upstairs. She reproved some of the young men for eating their meals sitting on the table, an action which they resented somewhat, as manners in the kitchen were informal. It was her rule that the apprentices must be in by ten o'clock, and she threatened to lock them out on more than one occasion. Though her regime was on the whole less strict than that of Puritan households, she firmly repressed the boys when they brought in a fiddle downstairs and started dancing. She herself had married a student of her father's, but for her children she was obviously more ambitious. Young Jamey might play at checkers or shuttlecock with the apprentices, provided that he did not get into a scrape by asking them to write him an excuse note for being late to school. Billy might go out with them in the evening, as long as he did not come back smelling of punch. On the other hand, Anne, who was growing up to be a beauty, was constantly kept out of the shop. Little Hannah, aged about eight, was sent down on errands instead of her sister, until she too became a young lady and was succeeded by Abigail. Meanwhile, when John, the apprentice, showed symptoms of becoming too fond of Betty, the maid, Mrs. Gardiner found ways to prevent the two from getting off on the same afternoon.

In the shop Anne Gardiner was almost as much at home

56

Pickles.

a. To pickle mushrooms, black.

Take any Quantity of the button Mushrooms, and wipe them very clean, but, if they are very dirty wash them & dry them very well; put them into a Stewpan or Sauce pan, with an handfull of Salt; some whole Pepper a little allspice and Cloves & a blade or two of mace. Keep them over a slow Fire for an hour or more, till all the Liquor is dried, observing to shake & toss them now and then, while they are doing, to prevent their burning. When they are done, take them off and lay them by with the Spices they were done with. — Take five Quarts of Catchup to two Quarts of these Mushrooms. Give your Catchup a Boil, and when it is cold put into it half a Pint of Vinegar, after which put in your mushrooms and Spice, and bottle them off for use.

b. Mushrooms to pickle.

Gather the smallest mushrooms you can, and put them into Spring water; then rub them with a piece of new Flannel dipped in Salt, and as you rub them, throw them into Spring water, in order that they may keep their colour; then put them into a well tinned Saucepan, and throw an handfull of Salt over them; Cover them close and set them over the fire for four or five minutes, or until you see they are thoroughly hot and the Liquor is drawn out of them; then lay them between two clean Cloths and there set them remain until they are cold; when you must put them into Glass Bottles, filling them up with Vinegar, and putting into each Bottle a blade or two of mace. Stop the Bottle close. See fol. 65.

c. Mushrooms to pickle, brown.

Wash a Quart of large mushroom Buttons, with a Flannel, in alegar; chop three Anchovies small; add a few blades of mace, a little Pepper and Ginger, a Spoonfull of Salt, and three Cloves of Shallots. Put them into a Saucepan with as much alegar or Vinegar as will cover them, and let them stew untill they shrink pretty much. When they are cold put them into Bottles, with the alegar or Vinegar they were stewed in, pouring it upon them hot; cork and tie them down close with Leather.
    NB. This Pickle will be a great addition to any brown Sauce.

MANUSCRIPT PAGE from *Mrs. Gardiner's Receipts from 1763*, wherein Dr. Gardiner's first wife gives directions for pickling mushrooms.

as her husband, since she looked in frequently to see what the young men were doing, and was not above making change when the need arose. In fact, she was a thoroughly efficient wife and, like her husband, indefatigable. Silvester's temper was aroused by contradiction or inefficiency, neither of which he met with from his wife. The result was, their marriage was harmonious, and though Silvester did not always listen to Anne's tales about the young men, he upheld her authority by all means in his power. Unfortunately Anne was suspicious by nature and would nag or scold persistently when anything was on her mind. John Hartshorn, the apprentice, hated her and made a daily record of her behavior towards him which certainly suggests that she never learned when to leave a boy alone. "M.G. eadem," he would say, or "Mrs. Gardiner just the same." At times he complained of scolding, or went so far as to say M.G. was "pessima," as bad as she could possibly be. The feud between these two really dated from the occasion when John Hartshorn lost the keys of the drawer in the shop, which he had thought were in his pocket. He foolishly confided to Betty his opinion that the mistress had ordered a servant to steal them from him in the night so as to get him into trouble. When the keys turned up in the skirts of John's coat, where they had worked themselves down through a hole in the pocket, he did apologize for this outrageous remark. Anne, who was evidently not clever enough to distinguish between such childishness and real dishonesty, could never afterwards be persuaded that John was not helping himself to the drugs or stealing from the till. Her feelings were strong, and she was much too fond of discussing domestic problems with her mother and sister, or of broadcasting them to the neighborhood in general. Thus everybody knew whom her favorites were, which in so large a household was bound to make for ill-feeling.

Doctor Gardiner had his favorites too, but as far as their medical training was concerned, he did his best for all the young men and earned their gratitude. His cousin, Joseph Gardiner, and his nephew Robert Hazard, whom he educated, were both intimate with him in later life, and the later named one of his sons after Silvester. When William Jepson finished his apprenticeship and hoped to obtain a position as army surgeon, Silvester invited a colonel to dine and promoted Jepson to his first meal with the family to meet him. Jepson did not get his appointment, but two years later when he wished to open a store in Connecticut, Silvester was willing to supply capital and to go into partnership. In general it may be said that the Doctor was hard on youthful mistakes, unpunctuality, or ebulitions of high spirits and was always impatient with an apprentice for the first year or two. However, even at the worst of times when John Hartshorn complained that Mrs. Gardiner, Jepson, the Doctor, and finally even Betty were against him, it was clear that the difficulties he encountered did not interfere in the least with his medical education. Later on, as he progressed in medical skill and learned to be more reliable, Silvester took an increasing interest in him. The Doctor was a man who liked to encourage young people, even if he sometimes made the mistake of expecting them to be wiser than their years.

The duties of an apprentice were extremely varied, and they involved a great deal of practical experience. On his first recorded day as an apprentice, John Hartshorn bled a man and dressed a sore leg. Three days later he saw a broken leg set and began to study surgery. After five months he was called out in an emergency to deal with a stabbing. He found the victim with intestines protruding two feet out of the wound and almost cut asunder, and he apparently knew what to do, though he was not successful, as the man died in twenty-four hours. In general, an apprentice acted as Silvester's assistant at difficult operations and watched how they were done. He frequently took on post-operative care, and he was given regular charge of the simpler sorts of ailments, subject to some supervision. For instance, he dressed an infected leg, but when it proved impossible to save it, Silvester performed the amputation. Some of the poorer patients were handed over to the apprentice, though it is fair to say that Silvester made a habit of visiting a number of these himself. John's diary during his last year becomes full of medical detail, as he spent more of his time in actual practice and less in going through Silvester's excellent library and in making himself useful to his master in various ways.

S OME OF THESE OTHER tasks were going "a-dunning," which seemed to occupy the first weeks of the year, writing letters for the Doctor on business, carrying messages, and packing stores. One whole day was spent in sorting out supplies for the sloop going up to the Kennebec settlements in Maine, which Silvester was now active in developing. Careless again, John sent aboard the wrong barrel of pork and once more got into trouble. Another time everyone stayed at home for two days to "stow the medicines for the Governor's regiment." These tasks, though fairly frequent, were accepted as part of an apprentice's life and caused no resentment, since there was plenty of time in five years for what the young man had to learn. The quality of Silvester's instruction may be judged from its most successful product, Joseph Gardiner, who was a prominent Boston doctor both before and after the Revolution. In an age when doctors were studying in Europe increasingly, Joseph was on the defensive about having learned his medicine in the old fashion, and he liked to declare that the only way to understand illness was to go straight to the beside of a patient. Yet though he posed as a plain man without much book learning, he was in fact well educated, surprisingly so to those who did not remember the excellence of his master's medical library. Silvester's collection of over five hundred books was a formidable one for his times and was destined for Harvard. It contained many of the best medical treatises of the day and was completely at the disposal of his apprentices. Joseph became perhaps the most popular physician of Boston in his time, and he was also highly appreciated as a surgeon. Though he had not the glory of a foreign degree, people found little to criticize in the education Silvester had given him.

Silvester himself was most remarkable as a surgeon and performed a number of notable operations, particularly for kidney stone. People would often travel considerable distances to submit themselves to his skill. As a physician he had a large following, but not so great as that of some other doctors of his day. This may well be due not so much to inferior skill as to his highly unusual beside manner. George Hewes, whom he inoculated for smallpox, tells the following story which gives a colorful picture of Silvester's arbitrary treatment of an unruly patient. It seems that young Hews found the worst part of the whole disease the starvation, since current rules prescribed a vegetarian diet, and not too much of that. Hewes was an impatient, daredevil young fellow of twenty-one with a fine natural appetite, and he eventually got to the point where he could not stand the gnawing pains in his stomach an instant longer. One night he found his way down to the larder, got hold of a joint of veal, dipped it in a jar of melted butter, and ate it all, generously refusing a single bite to his fellow apprentice on the grounds that it was suicide. Sure enough, Hewes was presently seized with griping pains, and Dr. Gardiner was sent for in considerable haste. Naturally he had strong suspicions about what had caused this strange attack, and he taxed Hewes with his crime. Furious when the young man obstinately denied it, Dr. Gardiner turned to the other apprentice and tried to bully the truth out of him. He, however, though frightened of the masterful doctor, was completely terrified by Hewes and dared not give him away.

"Well, then!" exploded Silvester finally, turning back to Hewes in a rage, "you will be cold coffee, Hewes, in twelve hours from this, and remember 'tis no fault of mine."

With these memorable words of encouragement, he left. Hewes, who quite believed him, characteristically saw no reason why he should not at least die happy and ordered a mug of rum flip, "sweet, hot, and good." Sure enough, he had a terrible night, tossing and turning, and waking from fearful dreams to wonder if he were not almost gone. Towards morning, however, he sank into a sound sleep and awakened feeling much better.

"Why, Hewes!" exclaimed Silvester next morning, evidently by no means liking to be proved an untrue prophet, "Not dead, you dog? Not dead yet?"

"No, sir," retorted he defiantly, "and no thanks to you."

It certainly does not seem probable that scenes of this kind would tend to establish Silvester as the family physician, however useful they may have been during surgical operations without anesthetics. One may at least assume that young George Hewes did not trouble Dr. Gardiner with his custom any longer.

S ILVESTER MAY HAVE been masterful, but he was extremely efficient, and the town and province authorities found him a doctor very much to their mind. Between 1745 and 1760 there were two wars, so that hostilities with French or Indians were almost continuous during that period. Not only did Silvester supply large consignments of drugs for the regiments sent on various expeditions, he was also the doctor to whom the Province authorities turned when they needed help in Boston. When, for instance, a rumor got about that French bullets were poisoned, the Committee of War asked Silvester to try one on a dog by cutting a flap of skin and inserting the bullet. Needless to say, the dog lived, and the rumor eventually died. More complicated were the arrangements for taking care of sick or wounded soldiers in a town which had no hospital. A certain small sum was deducted from the men's pay for the care and medicines, but all further expenses were paid by the Province, whose practice it was to offer a shilling a day and ten shillings a cure to various doctors. The authorities then washed their hands of the business, leaving the doctors to make all further arrangements. It was necessary for Silvester to rent, and later to build a house which he fitted up as a hospital. He had to find nurses and to make a list of poor women who would be willing to earn a little by receiving sick men in their houses in case the hospital should be full to overflowing. Naturally any expedition meant the sudden arrival of wounded men, and men crippled with rheumatism or disabled by dysentery caused by rotten provisions. Very early in the war Silvester was surprised by a large contingent of sick and wounded French prisoners, for whose unexpected capture nobody had made any arrangements. For weeks at a time on such occasions he must have been almost too busy for meals, the more so since diseases brought into the town by soldiers soon spread to their nurses and presently to the civilian population in general.

IN SUCH CIRCUMSTANCES, all help was welcome. Silvester's apprentice, John Hartshorn, actually worked himself to death in 1756, having seventy soldiers in various lodgings, thirty-five town patients, and a number of sick nurses to care for daily. Silvester, who could fly into a passion about trivial matters, was a real source of strength on serious occasions. Over and over again as John Hartshorn grew more tired, he found time to record that Doctor Gardiner had been very good, had urged him to pay all his calls on horseback, and had helped him where it was possible. How Silvester managed to keep his own health is a mystery, but he evidently did, though before the close of the war he was to lose yet another apprentice. At the end of 1759, Silvester fell ill and his business was conducted by his son James, who must have been almost qualified as a doctor. Ten days later, Silvester was at least partially recovered, but James was dead.

One of the most difficult things about having no hospital in Boston was that in times of epidemics it was necessary for the selectmen to hire special houses for necessary quarantine. Silvester, who had on several occasions managed these for the authorities, was well aware how cumbersome such an arrangement could be. Quite early in the war, when he had fitted up a hospital of his own, he petitioned the town to take it over after hostilities as a permanent isolation hospital for infectious diseases. The project was defeated by a protest from the inhabitants of the south end of the town, where the hospital was located, and Silvester relinquished his plan until the wars were over. In 1761 he made a determined effort to induce Boston to accept an inoculation hospital for smallpox. He offered to receive poor patients sent him by the selectmen for the sum of four dollars per cure, plus necessary expenses for food and nursing. If the town wished, it might reserve the right to buy the whole plant at any time for the cost of land, building, and equipment. Smallpox, Silvester's petition pointed out, was particularly common in a great shipping center like Boston, and of patients infected in the ordinary way, one died in eight. In England, where an inoculating hospital had been established since 1746, only one in eighty-two was found to have died from inoculation.

Unfortunately there were drawbacks to Silvester's plan, and the committee investigating reported against it. His hospital was considered much too close to the town to be used for smallpox, even though Dr. Gardiner was proposing to erect another building enclosed by a high fence for the actual patients, and to use the present one only for inoculation and final quarantine. The fact was that an inoculation hospital would mean the permanent presence of smallpox in the community, and this the town was determined to avoid. Three years later when there was a serious epidemic, they were ready to adopt inoculation as a temporary expedient. Several doctors, Silvester among them, hired houses on Point Shirley for this purpose and inoculated both rich and poor, besides attending others like George Hewes in their houses, where patients often preferred to stay if the rest of the family had already had the disease.

These determined efforts to establish a hospital in Boston deserved success and might have been Silvester's greatest contribution to the town. As it was, his medical reputation rested largely on his work as a surgeon and a druggist, though he had as many patients as he could manage, and the majority of them certainly were not surgical. Since he was not a native of Boston, his pupils often came from outside the town, and they tended to set themselves up in practice elsewhere. Silvester, however, had a good deal to offer them, and the varied training which he supplied was in itself no small contribution to the general level of New England medicine. Silvester's fame does not rest on his success in his profession, but if it did, he must have been admitted to be a fair sample of an enlightened doctor of his day. The surprising thing is that he could have been all this, and at the same time have done so much more.

THREE

Boston Citizen

AT TEN O'CLOCK on Sunday mornings to the sound of jangling bells, the whole population of Boston would soberly make its way along the streets to church. Under the sign of the Unicorn and Mortar, a carriage was waiting, a modest, two-wheeled chaise in the early days, but later a coach with glass windows, a handsome lining, and a coachman on the box. Even this splendid affair, which was kept under a cover in the stables and rubbed until it shone, was not designed to carry a family of eight children. Most of these had already been sent ahead on foot to church, which was only two blocks up Marlborough Street and one along School. However, the Province House was nearer, yet this did not prevent the governor from ordering out his six-horse carriage and upholding the dignity of his master, the King, by rolling round the corner in state. Better-class families arrived in carriages, some with two horses, and others even with four. King's Chapel had its quota of poorer artisans and servants like other places, but these were tucked away in the gallery. In the center aisles, the scarlet coats of English officers mingled with ladies' gay silk gowns and the rich browns and olive-gree velvets of those few but wealthy citizens who were supporters of the Anglican religion.

THE FIRST King's Chapel in Boston, 1689–1749.

King's Chapel, though not the only Episcopal church in Boston, was the first and most important. The governor worshipped there and brought his aides, both military and civil, which made it fashionable for army officers and younger sons of aristocrats whose interests were in England. As Silvester first saw the church, it was a rickety wooden building with leaking roof and piercing drafts in winter which gave great scandal to godly ministers because of the Popish splendor of its decorations. These chiefly consisted of red curtains to the governor's pew, a scarlet covering for the altar, which was bare, and a row of escutcheons hanging on the pillars in commemoration of important people who had used the Chapel in the past. A decent Boston minister could only say that such pagan fittings were to be expected from people abandoned enough to celebrate Christmas or to refer to *Saint* Luke and *Saint* John instead of using the simple names which were given to them in Scripture. King's Chapel existed on sufferance, and there were those who still regretted that it was no longer practicable to close the house of the ungodly altogether.

This grudging attitude on the part of the community found a chance for expression when the congregation of King's Chapel determined that it must be rebuilt and enlarged. Henry Caner, who became minister in 1747, found that a small subscription had been raised for this purpose a few years before, but that nothing else had been done. Meanwhile, the chapel was in such poor condition that it seemed doubtful whether it could be patched together much longer, even at considerable expense. Henry Caner, who was shortly to prove himself one of the outstanding Episcopal clergymen in New England, lost no time in laying the matter before his wardens, of whom Silvester Gardiner was one. A committee was formed which was to meet at the Royal Exchange Tavern on Tuesday evenings; and as Luke Vardy, its famous London cook, was a member of the congregation, it is to be hoped that the members could combine their business with good food. In spite of his other activities, Silvester was indefatigable on this committee, and his name is signed to most of the letters that went out from time to time appealing to friends in England, and even on one occasion in Jamaica.

REBUILDING THE CHAPEL would in itself have been no problem, except inasfar as the congregation was unable to meet the expense. The difficulty lay in the fact, that when rebuilt, it needed to be enlarged. King's Chapel owned not a foot of ground, stood on the corner of two streets, and was jammed right up against the South Grammar, or Boston Latin School. After two petitions to the town, the vestrymen received permission to buy a plot of land across the road and move the school. There was a great deal to be said for this proposal, since the Grammar School itself was quite dilapidated, and King's Chapel was offering the town a new building at its own expense. Unfortunately, the town committee was disposed to make all the difficulties it could, while Lovell, the schoolmaster, was understandably anxious that the new school building should be better than the old. Lovell was particularly difficult to manage because he had been for years at loggerheads with the vestrymen, since his scholars would sometimes take it into their heads to break the windows as a sign of their animosity towards the chapel. The consequence of all this ill-feeling was that the town committee insisted on a brick building, thirty-four by thirty-six feet, with a gambrel roof, and with wood house and offices attached. As this was one-sixth larger than the present school, besides being built of much more expensive materials, a great many conferences followed. In vain the Chapel authorities tried to persuade the town to abate its demands or to build the school with the aid of a contribution of two thousand pounds. After many delays, the work was entrusted to a committee consisting of Dr. Gardiner, his father-in-law Dr. Gibbins, and one other gentleman. It was speedily completed to the unwilling satisfaction of the selectmen, who through proper to compliment Dr. Gardiner by inviting him to be one of a town committee which joined the selectmen in a yearly visitation of public schools. Mr. Lovell and his assistant in the little brick building had a hundred and twenty pupils, which may excuse him for the difficulties which he had made. In the four other public schools of the town were six hundred and forty-five pupils, and all were pronounced "in very good order." This inspection was repeated in the following year; and for several years after that, Silvester was one of the representatives of the tenth ward in a "general visitation of the town" which took place yearly.

SINCE THE AFFAIRS of the South Grammar School had been expensive to settle, Silvester and others of the building committee now redoubled their efforts to solicit subscriptions. Silvester's own contributions were liberal, and were given in sterling, which did not depreciate as the currency of the Province was rapidly doing. His time was even more valuable, for it must be remembered that in addition to his two established professions, he was at this moment engaged on the development of a large, unsettled area in Maine. The success of the committee's efforts in general may be measured by the fact that the chapel they built, which is still standing, was one of only four stone buildings in the Boston of its day. True, the fluted columns inside with their Corinthian capitals had to be of wood, and the floor and paneling were wooden; but this was only a matter of regret to those of the congregation who were obsessed by the stone churches of their native, and slightly warmer land. An altar painting of the Last Supper, which was paid for by a subscription from Mrs. Gardiner and other ladies, was duly received; but after consideration of its effect on Boston generally, the minister and vestry dared not hang it. An organ, said to have been chosen by Handel, was procured from England, and in the course of some years the church felt rich enough to afford a large, new bell. The outside was plain, but the interior made a splendid example of the rich, yet dignified effect which could be achieved by the eighteenth-century classical style. This was enhanced by the roomy, box-like pews which were sold to members of the congregation in order to raise money for the church. Silvester's two pews stretched from aisle to aisle across the center of the right-hand block, for though little Thomas was dead, three sons and four daughters

EXTERIOR VIEW of the second and present King's Chapel in Boston from a circa 1860 photograph. SOCIETY FOR THE PRESERVATION OF NEW ENGLAND ANTIQUITIES.

made a tolerable showing. Two years after the church was finished, Silvester was senior warden, and he occupied that position for seventeen of the ensuing twenty years.

These devoted services to King's Chapel undoubtedly had a tendency to set Silvester apart from his fellow citizens and cause him to form friendships with those who were like himself, or with men sent out from England for a few years only. Through his large practice evidently included men of every sect, it is remarkable that his most distinguished patients were among the Shirleys, Franklands, and Johonnots, who were all Episcopalian families. Likewise, though he dealt with the Hancocks, Bowdoins, and other merchants, and was well acquainted with Paul Revere, it was with Charles Apthorp, the fabulously wealthy Episcopalian, that Silvester shared a warehouse. His dinner guests were usually out-of-town doctors, ship captains with whom he had dealings, and business acquaintances of various sorts. Dr. and Mrs. Gibbins, the Apthorps, and Henry Caner, the Rector of the Chapel, were the only people he asked frequently and apparently for pleasure. In fact, the little Church-of-England communities had never been popular among the colonists, many of whose forefathers had been driven across the seas by persecution. Recently the Society for the Propagation of the Gospel had been so successful in subsidizing missionaries wherever little groups of Episcopalians might get together and ask for them that antagonism had been growing, not declining as the century advanced. Two important issues had by now inflamed this feeling to such a degree that they may be considered among the indirect causes of the Revolution.

INTERIOR VIEW of the second and present King's Chapel in Boston from a circa 1860 photograph. SOCIETY FOR THE PRESERVATION OF NEW ENGLAND ANTIQUITIES.

When the Rev. James MacSparran first came to St. Paul's church in Narragansett in 1721, he had found that the proprietors of the Pettiquamscut Purchase, which comprised a great part of this area, had set aside three hundred acres for the support of an "orthodox" minister. On the advice of his congregation, he commenced a suit to obtain this for his church. It would not be worth while to go into all the arguments introduced into this protracted case. The question which aroused the most intense feeling throughout New England was that of the definition of the word "orthodox." MacSparran's supporters contended that the Church of England, as the state church, was the only orthodox church in any British possession. This naturally aroused the fury not only of Rhode Island, which had no established church, but of states like Massachusetts, which had religious constitutions of their own. This, they declared, was what they had always suspected. Not only were the royal appointees men who despised the religion of the Colonies, but the very church which had driven out their forefathers by her tyrannical ways was now using the royal courts to re-assert her dominion over them. The case, it is true, was finally decided by adjudging the three hundred acres to the Congregationalists or Presbyterians, on the grounds that the original donors had belonged to these two sects. This was not done, however, until it had been carried by appeal to the highest courts, and before the bitterest feelings had been aroused. Meanwhile, when in 1735 a committee was appointed by King's Chapel to raise funds from the congregation for supporting MacSparran, it very naturally included Silvester, who was MacSparran's brother-in-law and under the strongest obligations to him.

The second difficulty of the church at this period concerned the installation of bishops. There being at this time no American bishop, it was necessary for every Episcopal clergyman to be ordained in England and to report to superiors there during the whole of his ministry. This arrangement pleased

"An Attempt to Land a Bishop in America," an eighteenth-century political cartoon portraying the fear of New England citizens that a resident bishop in America would extend the authority of the British crown.

nobody. The Episcopalians resented the expense and inconvenience of going to England to obtain orders, and the best of them felt that a divided allegiance was not to the interest of their church. The Colonists hated the special connection with England and above all disliked and feared the influence of the Society for the Propagation of the Gospel. Unfortunately, to talk of installing an American bishop, which would actually have resolved these grievances, was like waving a red flag in front of the Colonial bull. The colonists were no more reasonable on the subject of bishops than the English on the subject of the Pope. It might in fact have been better for the leading Episcopalians if they had never brought the matter up. Since, however, they were conscious that the appointment of a bishop was really the best answer to all problems, they could not refrain from pressing it. James MacSparran took some part in this controversy and at one time had hopes of becoming the American bishop himself. Though he saw eventually that this was impossible, left his estate for the support of an American bishop on his death in 1752. All in all, one feels that Silvester might have been more fortunate in some respects if he had not been drawn into these quarrels by having James MacSparran as a brother-in-law.

Meanwhile Silvester's active benevolence, not satisfied with his work for the church or his plans for a hospital, led him to interest himself in a society which was established to improve the condition of the indigent poor. The efforts of the merchants who formed this group were directed towards founding an enterprise which would at the same time teach the poor a trade and give state encouragement to the production of linen. Much flax was grown in the Province, but primarily for seed, though the arrival of Irish immigrants had lately aroused interest in the use of the fiber. In 1753, the charitable society petitioned the Province to grant fifteen hundred pounds for the erection of a suitable building, in which the promoters undertook to give free instruction to at least one person over eight years old from every town which chose to send one. This promising scheme persuaded the Province to grant a tax on coaches, carriages, and chairs for the next five years. Thomas Gunter advanced money for erecting this Manufactory House immediately, while the town agreed to advance a loan for the purchase of equipment. In the meantime, the society arranged an exhibit on the common, where three hundred women sat at their spinning wheels, while a band escorted a moving platform supported on men's shoulders, on which weavers clothed in their own cloth were working at a loom.

IT IS AN INTERESTING commentary on the times to find that the carriage tax only raised half what was expected, with the result that the Province was embarrassingly indebted to Thomas Gunter and was forced to let out parts of the Manufactory House in order to raise some cash. In any case, however, the linen manufacturing company was a failure from the beginning. All that the town finally received when its assets were liquidated was eighty-nine pounds, five shillings and six pence halfpenny in cash, together with two looms, a caldron, and two pairs of worsted combs. Part of the difficulty was that though flax was grown throughout the Province, it was too much trouble to collect in small quantities, while flax from abroad was not readily available. In general, however, the dismal fate of the enterprise was very like that of numerous efforts to teach the poor a trade in England, and probably was due to similar causes. Linen manufacturing was done on the same simple machines and with the same techniques in the factory and in the home, with the result that it might fairly well be considered a good trade to teach the poor. However, this also meant that it was still a skilled occupation, needing much practice. The factory also suffered from competition with people who spun in their spare time at home and grew their own food.

Thus prices for finished work were low, and were simply not adequate to cover the expenses of lodging and feeding the workers. It may be added that the members of the charitable society were acting as trustees, not managers of the business, and their meetings were held about three or four times in the year. Individuals, among them Silvester, were personally active in matters connected with finance; but not one of the promoters thought it necessary to let the business have first call on his time.

In these circumstances, the linen manufacturing company was a failure from the start. Presently the equipment was rented out to a linen weaver called Brown, who lived in the Manufactory House and employed some children, possibly members of his family. The charitable society, however, continued to meet and to hold annual dinners at the Bunch of Grapes or the Royal Exchange Tavern. In 1768, the Manufactory House burst into the news as Brown, the weaver, was besieged in it by the sheriff, who wished to turn him out in order to make room for the troops which had been quartered upon Boston. In the following year, when ladies throughout the Province were holding spinning parties in order to clothe themselves in homespun, the town once more approached the charitable society, which made a second attempt to revive the large-scale manufacture of linen. Silvester was once more active in this effort, which failed almost as soon as it started. Eventually he was instrumental in winding up the affairs of the company and handing over all its assets to the town.

To keep so many balls in the air at once undoubtedly called for great efficiency and an unusually good physique. Silvester was hardly ever ill, and unlike many contemporaries he seems to have kept his teeth until late in life. His activities were ceaseless. In addition to his own affairs, he found himself called upon to transact business or execute wills for people as far away as Newfoundland in cases where he had commercial obligations. His legal business took up a very great deal of time, and he must have been at committee meetings two or three times a week. True, such gatherings took place in taverns or in private homes, where there would be a large punch bowl and excellent madeira, while those who wished could relax over a long-stemmed pipe. As a doctor, Silvester even paid calls on Sundays, though nobody of any other profession was allowed to appear on the street for any purpose except going to church. How busy he was may be seen by the fact that on purely social occasions, though other gentlemen were present, Mrs. Gardiner and her daughters very frequently appeared alone. Occasionally he would drive out into the country with his wife to join in a barbeque or pay a visit, and sometimes no doubt would combine the trip with business of some sort. Once he even found time to go out fishing and had a good time, though he apparently never repeated the experiment. Quite frequently he was bearer at a funeral, dressed in black gloves and scarf and heavy mourning ring presented as a compliment by the relatives of the deceased. At home he entertained often, though his guests were mainly business connections. Now and then he would give parties on a very large scale. In general, however, Silvester was a man to whom business and relaxation were one and the same, namely a meeting with congenial friends where a little wine and much discussion enabled his superior abilities to make themselves felt. No group that he ever joined refrained from electing him as an officer.

ONE OF THE MORE active of Silvester's partners in the linen manufacturing scheme was that very Andrew Oliver who was appointed Distributor of Stamps in 1765, and who had his house entered, his windows broken, and his wine drunk by the Boston mob. Since the company directly associated itself with resistance to British imports during the occupation of Boston by troops, it may be seen that people's political positions were by no means so clear cut as the partisan journals of the time would have us suppose. In later years, Silvester liked to maintain that he had never taken part in Boston politics. Unfortunately for him, times were coming in which men would be judged by their language and by the company they had kept. Silvester's personal friendship with Governor Shirley, his official connection with the army as a doctor during two wars, and his education in England made it natural that he should move in Loyalist circles. He was not Boston born, and the harmless gaieties of Narragansett had not prepared him for the peculiar strictness of Boston views, especially as these were reinforced by the tenets of a sect to which he did not belong. There was dancing in his house occasionally, and his sons played cards with the apprentices. No doubt the freedoms of English society seemed less provincial than the restrictions imposed throughout the town.

Mrs. Gardiner, though a native of Boston, was ready to share her husband's views, since she was socially ambitious for her children. John, the second son, who was studying in England, came home for a brief visit in 1755, and a great number of the officers in town were invited to meet him. There were large parties for him, and for Nancy or William, at which Mrs. Gardiner clad in voluminous silks sailed through the minuet. The young people began to complain that their father ought to make a new entrance on the other side of the house, as they were ashamed to bring young gentlemen of good English families in through the shop. Silvester had the sound sense to insist that as long as he made his money in a shop, people who wanted to know him or his family must not be too proud to recognize that fact. Eventually Sir William Pepperell, Governor Hutchinson, Admiral Graves, General Gage, and many other notables made their way through the drug store to pay their respects. Even the second son of an earl was not above passing through the shop when he was courting Nancy.

ANNE (GARDINER) BROWNE (1741–1807), daughter of
Dr. Gardiner and wife of Colonel the Honourable
Arthur Browne, portrait in 1756 by John Singleton
Copley. PRIVATE COLLECTION.

Copley's portrait of Anne Gardiner, or Nancy as her
brothers and sisters called her, shows her as a fine looking
young woman with her mother's full, determined chin, her
father's strong mouth, a slightly aquiline nose, dark eyes and

REBECCA (GARDINER) DUMARESQ (1745–before
1820), daughter of Dr. Gardiner.

hair. Captain Arthur Browne, the Earl of Altamont's son, was
a pleasant young man of no great force of character on duty
with the Twenty-Eighth Regiment during the French and Indian War. He seems to have got into some financial trouble by
issuing bills on his agent in London which he had no resources
to pay, and it is doubtful whether the splendor of the connection really compensated in Silvester's eyes for such imprudence. Anne probably loved him, but she was also well aware
that his elder brother was sickly and that she might easily live
to have a coronet painted on her coach. Unfortunately, Arthur's
brother recovered his health and, adding insult to injury, his
nephew became a marquess. Anne was left a widow with four
children at a comparatively early age, and was forced to make
as much use as she could of her aristocratic relations, and to
make up by arrogance for her straightened means and her early
connection with a shop.

Philip Dumaresq (1739–1800), son-in-law of
Dr. Gardiner.

Rebecca and Hannah, who were the next two daughters, married Bostonians, but in rather different circumstances. Rebecca somewhat offended her father by choosing Philip Dumaresq, who had pleasing manners, but no property on which to support a wife. He appeared to rely more on his hopes of patronage than his own exertions, and when Silvester tried to help him by introducing him to some business connections, he contracted debts to them which he was not able to pay. Hannah, on the other hand, made just such a match as her father might have selected for her, had he picked out her husband himself.

Robert Hallowell, who married Hannah Gardiner, in 1772, was an exceptionally amiable and pleasing young man whose father, Benjamin Hallowell, was a wealthy Boston merchant and one of Silvester's colleagues in his Maine enterprises. Robert's eldest brother, also named Benjamin, was an

ROBERT HALLOWELL (1739–1818), son-in-law of Dr. Gardiner, portrait by Gilbert Stuart. PRIVATE COLLECTION.

extremely able man who had risen to command a British privateer as early as 1746. He was now Collector of the Customs at Boston, in which capacity he had already drawn upon himself the fury of the Boston mob. In August, 1765, they had broken into his house, destroyed his furniture and papers, stolen his money, and drunk the contents of his cellar. Two years later he had gone down to superintend the seizure of John Hancock's sloop, the *Liberty*, for infringing customs regulations. He had been too proud to make for safety on the appearance of the mob, and had been set on in in such a fashion that his life was at first despaired of. With such patronage, Robert's career was simple. He had already been appointed Collector of Customs at Portsmouth, and it was understood that when Benjamin was promoted to Comptroller of Customs, he would move his brother up to take his place in Boston. In the meantime, Robert came down frequently from Portsmouth, being not especially energetic in business, and having friends among the British frigate captains, who were always happy to take such a pleasant fellow along.

HANNAH, WHO WAS a gentle, sweet-tempered girl, was a great loss to the family circle, especially as Abigail, the youngest and the only daughter left at home, was the plainest and had the most difficult temper. Abigail, the youngest and the only daughter left at home, was the plainest and had the most difficult temper. Her brothers and sisters, with some of whom Abigail was not a favorite, implied that it was not easy to find anyone to marry her. Silvester certainly missed his other daughters and was glad to see Hannah and Rebecca in the house. He was an affectionate father, though his overbearing ways cannot have made life easy at home and may explain why all four of his daughters married men of charming manners, but not very effective character. One of his most difficult traits was his unusual ability to concentrate on one thing at a time and to forget personalities in dealing with business. In the long series of business letters he later wrote to Oliver Whipple, who had married Abigail, he mentioned "Nabby" once or twice, but generally filled up the letter without leaving room to send her his love. When he had time to think of Nabby personally, he preferred to write to her directly and send her a book. On the other hand, Oliver Whipple, who was very well aware that the old man had a considerable fortune to leave, never let a chance go by of sending messages from Abigail, or from little Silvester, who could not possibly remember his grandfather, but who was supposed to be longing to see him. Oliver Whipple was in some ways an unattractive person, but he would have been an easier father for a large family of children.

Of Silvester's three sons, all older than their sisters, James, who was to have been a doctor, died suddenly at the age of twenty, in 1759. This must have been a great loss to his father, neither of whose remaining sons entirely suited him. John was far too like himself to get on with him, while William was deficient in ability and force of character.

JOHN GARDINER, Silvester's second son, was sent to England for his education, became a lawyer, married an Englishwoman, and apparently settled down with the intention of staying in England for the rest of his life. Perhaps this was fortunate for his own sanity and that of his father, since John had inherited not only the small, trim figure inclining to stoutness, but the quick, loud, commanding voice, the energy, and the vehement temper. Moreover, he combined these qualities with an eccentricity of behavior from which Silvester was entirely free. His nephew Robert, who remembered him well, declares that in winter John slept in a chest with a small air hole in the lid, because it was warmer. What is more, he liked to go to bed early, and he let his guests sit up and play cards on top of his chest, only calling out occasionally that he could not sleep if

JOHN GARDINER (1737–1793), son of Dr. Gardiner,
portrait by John Singleton Copley.
COLLECTION OF WESTMORELAND MUSEUM OF AMERICAN ART,
GREENSBURG, PENNSYLVANIA. ANONYMOUS GIFT BY EXCHANGE.

they struck it too hard with their knuckles. This last may be an unlikely embellishment, but it is undoubtedly a tribute to the way in which John's behavior struck his relations. This sort of thing is hard for a dominating father to put up with. The gentle Hannah may have consented to be swept out of her drawing room to go and talk with her brother in the cellar, where it

THE REVEREND John Silvester John Gardiner
(1765–1830), rector of Trinity Church, Boston,
grandson of Dr. Gardiner, portrait by Gilbert Stuart.
PRIVATE COLLECTION.

was cooler, but Silvester would have raised a storm if any such nonsense were proposed to him.

John's abilities were considerable, and his success at the bar seemed for a while assured by his gaining the favor of Lord Mansfield, the greatest English jurist of the time. Unfortunately,

GARDINER FAMILY coat of arms as used by John
Gardiner, son of Dr. Gardiner. The inscription beneath
the shield describes him as a member of the Inner
Temple, a professional society of lawyers in London.
PRIVATE COLLECTION.

his opinions, though equally definite, were entirely opposite to
those of his father, since he became intimate with some of the
extreme Whigs who were leading the attack on the Court
party, through which George III was attempting to govern. At
the closing of Parliament in April, 1763, the King's speech,
which was as usual on such occasions the product of his ministers, referred to the peace lately signed at Paris as having been
concluded "upon conditions so honourable to my Crown, and
so beneficial to my people." This was too much for John Wilkes,
editor of the *North Briton*, who had been lately setting new
records in the freedom with which he attacked the Court party,
Lord Bute, the late Prime Minister, and the terms of the Peace
of Paris. He immediately pronounced the King's speech "the
most abandoned instance of ministerial effrontery ever attempted to be imposed upon mankind." This attack, which was

strictly on the ministry, George III took to be personal, with the result that he insisted that the government take action. Accordingly the Secretary of State issued a general warrant, without specifying names, for the arrest of authors, printers, and publishers of the offending number of the *North Briton.* Forty-nine people were arrested under this warrant, including Wilkes, though he was a member of Parliament, and as such should have been immune.

THIS HIGH-HANDED ACTION raised a terrible storm in which the whole legality of special warrants which did not mention names was brought into question. John Gardiner was one of the lawyers for the defense, and helped to inflict a resounding defeat on the Court party. His victory cost him the favor of Lord Mansfield, the approval of his father, and his future in Great Britain. Shortly afterwards he was glad to accept honorable banishment in the form of the attorney generalship of St. Kitts. He retired there, taking with him a silver plate presented by Breadmore, the printer of the *North Briton,* and inscribed as follows:

> *Pro libertate semper strenuus*
> To John Gardiner, Esq.
> This Waiter
> Is presented by Arthur Beardmore
> As a small token of gratitude
> For pleading his cause and that of his clerk, David Meredith
> Against the Earl of Halifax, then Secretary of State
> For false Imprisonment under his Warrant,
> That Canker of
> English Liberty
> MDCCLXVI

SILVER TRAY presented to John Gardiner in
commemoration of his successful defense of John
Wilkes in 1766. ALLEN'S *HISTORY OF DRESDEN*.

It would not be fair to dismiss Wilkes' opponents as being
none but the Court party and its hangers-on. The character of
Wilkes was such that many high Tories to whom moral conduct was a important as a political issue were honestly outraged
to find he had any defenders. He was an open profligate and
was proved to be privately printing obscene literature to dis-
tribute among his personal friends. Worst of all, he was a member of the Hell-Fire Club, notorious for its Black Masses at
Medmenham Abbey, where it parodied the most sacred rite of
Christianity. Silvester, who had rejected liberal ideas in France
because of the open atheism of their supporters, was not the
man to understand why his son made common cause with such
a fellow. He was not a slavish supporter of the government, witness his dislike of the Stamp Act at this very time, and his joy
when it was repealed. On the other hand, just as he did not
approve of the Boston mobs which plundered the houses of his
friends, Oliver and Lieutenant Governor Hutchinson, so he
would be the last man to sanction defense of the even greater
lawlessness involved in mockeries of the Christian religion.

Most of the thunderous letters which passed between John and his father from this time onward are now lost. One of Silvester's great-granddaughters came upon some of them, and burned them in horror at the sort of language they contained.

William Gardiner, the eldest son, was educated in the earlier building of the Boston Latin School, right up against the side of the King's Chapel. He and his brother James both graduated from the school, on which occasions their father gave a dinner for the masters and the whole of the graduating class. William was a pleasant young man, but totally unable to stand up to his father or mother. At an age when Silvester had already been for some years in Europe, William was called out of a party by one of the apprentices, got a scolding for drinking a little punch, and dared not walk out with a girl unless he could avoid his mother's eye. When he incautiously tried to make peace between his mother and John Hartshorn, the only result was that he ran into trouble himself. He learned the business under his father's supervision, and when he reached the age of twenty-one, Silvester sent him over to England with two or three thousand pounds to invest in goods. The idea was that he should make a quick profit, for it was wartime, and prices in America were unusually high. No doubt William set out on this adventure crammed with good advice, but the moment that he was out of sight, Silvester could not refrain from sending a letter after him and repeating it all. "This is the critical time of your life," he warned him solemnly, "a wrong step may now ruin you forever, therefore I would not have you think this is a Voyage of Pleasure; but business, thought, and reflection." William was to send his goods in a ship of force, not to waste time, and to be back by fall, lest peace break out and ruin him by spring.

Poor William was quite unequal to these demands upon his abilities or prudence. He did not get into any serious trouble, and if he did not get back by fall, at least he was there before the following spring. However, he did not make his fortune, and it was shortly evident to his father that he showed no business judgment at all. One more attempt to set him up failed, after which he was demoted to the position of general handyman and errand boy. Silvester, who used capitals for emphasis, calls him "billy" in most of his later letters, and not without justice. William was lazy and not very clever, with the result that when he undertook to help his father, very little seemed to get done. Such inefficiency drove Silvester almost into a frenzy, and yet he never quarreled as violently with William as he did with John.

T HE LAST YEAR OF Mrs. Gardiner's life, 1771, may be fairly said to have marked the highest point of her husband's fortunes. Silvester had not only made himself wealthy and respected in Boston, he had also by this time built up an immense estate in Maine for his successors. Nancy's noble connections would have had no reason to be ashamed of her family if William had taken his place among the landed aristocracy, as his father designed. William might be a poor business man, but he was certainly a gentleman, and his father had come to consider this estate as primarily for him. Meantime the rising tension between the Colonies and England only so far concerned Silvester that he was ready to express his opinions to all and sundry about what ought to be done. John Adams, who dined in company with him in this very year, had heard him often, "I shall hear," said he before he went, "philosophy and politics in perfection from Hallowell; high flying, high church, high state from Dr. Gardiner; sedate, cool moderation from Bowdoin; and warm, honest, frank Whiggism from Pitts."

Like many other wealthy Boston merchants of this time, Silvester regarded the political situation with mixed feelings. He did not approve of the Stamp Act or of prohibitive customs duties, but at the same time he had an intense dislike for mob

violence, accentuated in his case by scorn for the more demo-
cratic and in some ways more emotional sects to which the
common people belonged. He seems to have welcomed the introduction of troops into Boston to restore order, but to have
been honestly outraged at the situation caused by their coming.
Rum was cheap, and an honest Tory coming home through the
unlighted streets with a lantern was no more safe from a drunk-
en soldier than an insolent tradesman might be, or a woman.
When the men-of-war in the harbor found their crews depleted
by sickness or desertion and began impressing seamen, they
seized a man from Silvester's coastal sloop with just as much
readiness as if the ship had belonged to a smuggler like John
Hancock. Marlborough Street, being central, was well placed
for observing riots; and indeed it was from in front of Silvester's
shop that a man was attracted by a commotion and went over
to find a group of soldiers rescuing a comrade by force from the
hands of the civil authorities. The climax of all such unrest was
the Boston Massacre of 1770; and though Silvester felt it was
actually provoked by the mob, he was bound to approve of its
result in the withdrawal of troops to the harbor.

In the brief interval that followed this explosion, the merchants in general were glad to accept an uneasy truce. The small
tax remaining upon tea was not burdensome, and well-to-do
men did not trouble themselves too much about the principle
involved, just as long as smuggling was possible and there was
a rising volume of legitimate trade. They thought that grievances would lessen as prosperity increased, which indeed might
have happened if the government had not seen fit to grant the
East India Company a monopoly on tea. As for the dangerous
cleavage between the English interests and the ordinary townspeople of Boston, which was accentuated by religious difference, people were used to it and did not measure its growing
significance. Revolution was not even talked of yet, and as long
as high Tories like Silvester had plenty of criticisms to offer the

government, it was not at all clear that they did not stand on the Colonial side. The King's special claim on loyalty as the head of the English church did not prevent Silvester from supporting the cause of the Colonies as he saw it and considering himself one of a misunderstood and mishandled group. In 1771, he no more expected his "high flying" to offend people seriously than he had anticipated the Boston earthquake in 1755. Indeed, Silvester's whole attitude towards political discussion is best expressed in a letter he wrote to Paul Revere as late as 1785. "altho we should not as you Say agree in Politicks; that ought not to make any difference between Gentlemen of liberal Sentiments any more than if they did not look like each other."

At this last moment of prosperity, when Anne Gardiner was still well, and Silvester was unconscious of the vast reversal of fortune coming upon him, it was so very appropriate that Copley should have painted both their portraits. Each is a remarkable study and sums up in itself the nature and the background of its subject, giving a vivid impression of the achievements of their busy married life.

ANNE GIBBINS GARDINER is portrayed as the very image of satisfied social ambition. The painter has made much of her voluminous, golden brown silk, and has rounded her arms and tapered her fingers fashionably. She has the large, impressive figure of a dowager, together with the full double chin and the watchful, rather hard expression. However, the dark, smoothed hair, tight mouth and long determined face are not those of the born hostess, but of someone a little lower in the social scale, and more interesting. She actually does look like a woman whose husband has made a fortune out of a shop he has been running in her front parlor for the last twenty-five years. The seven children, the servants, the apprentices, the petty cash, and the door closed at ten o'clock are far more typical of Mrs. Gardiner than her laced front and stain bow, or the

ANNE (GIBBINS) GARDINER (1712–1771), first wife of
Dr. Gardiner, portrait formerly attributed to Copley but
reassigned to Joseph Blackburn. PRIVATE COLLECTION.

fine ruffles on her short, full sleeves. These details only serve to
remind us what she has won from life, and her whole expression shows her pleasure in it.

Silvester's portrait by contrast is much more informal. To
be sure, he has on his best dark-red suit and has taken up a

DR. SILVESTER GARDINER (1708–1786), aged sixty-five,
portrait by John Singleton Copley. PRIVATE COLLECTION.

conventional attitude, one arm flung over the back of his chair
and the other tucked inside the front of his vest. By a striking
effect of light, which falls on his head and shoulders and ob-
scures the rest, he gives a vivid impression of being about to
lean forward out of his frame. The effect is to present him as a

man who never sat still for an instant. His head is a powerful and intelligent one, with a fine forehead, heavy eyebrows, and strongly marked features. The mouth is particularly firm, and there are deep lines at the corners, which give it a decided, but by no means ill-tempered expression. The eyes are very bright and are aware of his audience, as though he meant to take part in whatever was going on. His might stand for a picture of the founder of a family, and it is undoubtedly in this light that he would wish to be regarded. He made his own without troubling himself much about George Gardiner, Benoni his son, or Wicked William; but he intended his own descendants to look back to him. So, indeed, they do. In spite of the Revolution, the exile, and the inadequacy of William, Silvester is the ancestor, while Robert, who came after him to carry out his work, is but the descendant.

⚬⚬⚬

$\mathcal{T}$HE PLYMOUTH
PATENT

B Y SIX O'CLOCK ON A December evening, Boston streets had fallen quiet. Country people who had come in to set up market stalls at dawn had long ago trudged off down Marlborough Street with their packhorses and rattling carts. Oystermen, sweeps, and peddlers had silenced their bells and disappeared. Fashionable ladies paying calls in chaises had tired of taking the air when it grew dusk. In the Town House on King Street, the pillared stock exchange was quite deserted, while the little windows of the bookshops on the square around it were shuttered tight. Unwary citizens groping their way home without a lantern must feel their way by the stout row of posts set up to protect pedestrians from the roaring horse traffic in the middle of the road. In the universal blackness the warm, steamy windows of popular tavern sent welcome beams of light across the cobbles, while the noise of cheerful voices steamed out across the square whenever a door was opened to let some newcomer in.

Business had gone inside for light, warmth, and well-earned refreshment. In the Bunch of Grapes on the square, merchants, sea-captains, soldiers, shopkeepers, and travelers of all sorts were forgathering to warm themselves with a glass of punch in the taproom, where one might glance at the *Boston Gazette*, or idly read the notices of slaves for sale, a bison to be seen for three pence down by the wharves, or a public execution four days hence at Roxbury Neck. In the public dining room twenty or thirty merry souls were settling in for an evening of punch and singing, which might end with a round of visits or an impromptu dance from which the latest revelers would stagger home at five in the morning. Upstairs in the private room where a group was gathering for some more serious purpose, lemon squeezer, sugar, tumblers, a china punchbowl,

BUNCH OF GRAPES TAVERN, also known as the Royal Exchange, at the corner of Kilby and State Streets, Boston, where the Kennebec Purchase Proprietors reorganized their company in 1749 and regularly conducted business.
SOCIETY FOR THE PRESERVATION OF NEW ENGLAND ANTIQUITIES.

and long tobacco pipes were evidence that the time of day had come when business could be combined with well-earned relaxation. Such meetings were of almost nightly occurrence at the Bunch of Grapes, whose central position had made it one of the favorite taverns for the Boston well-to-do. If in December 1751, a member of the casual group downstairs had asked the landlord the purpose of the meeting overhead, he might well have been puzzled by the answer "Plymouth Company," especially if he had not noticed the recent revival of this organization, which had existed in a more or less moribund form for ninety years.

THAT SOME COMMERCIAL speculation was intended by the Plymouth Company might well have been deduced from the characters of the gentlemen who were passing up the stairs. Differing in age, in politics, in religious background, and in training, the majority of them were united in having money to invest. Tall, middle-aged Benjamin Hallowell was a wealthy shipwright and merchant, trading extensively in provisions with Newfoundland and already conspicuous in Boston politics by the activity with which his family upheld the government cause. The half brothers, William and James Bowdoin, with James Pitts, their brother-in-law, formed a solid family group with great wealth and extensive commercial interests. Nathaniel Thwing, the well-to-do baker, Silvester Gardiner, the high-Tory doctor, Edward Winslow, Jacob Wendell, and Thomas Valentine were all prominent Bostonians, but of very different kinds. Yet another type were red-faced Samuel Goodwin and John Bonner, out-of-doors men and captains in the Provincial army who brought enterprise and energy to the cause instead of capital. Most solid figure of all was Thomas Hancock, whose showy costume, swollen, gouty legs, twinkling black eyes, and jovial, beefy countenance concealed one of the sharpest minds in New England when it came to bargaining.

JAMES BOWDOIN II (1726–1790), the only other propri-
etor of the Kennebec Purchase Company who owned as
much land as Dr. Gardiner. He was governor of
Massachusetts and namesake of Bowdoin College.
PORTRAIT BY ROBERT FEKE AT BOWDOIN COLLEGE MUSEUM OF ART,
BRUNSWICK, MAINE. BEQUEST OF MRS. SARAH BOWDOIN DEARBORN.

BENJAMIN HALLOWELL (1724–1799), another major
proprietor of the Kennebec Purchase Company and
brother of Dr. Gardiner's son-in-law, Robert Hallowell.
Portrait by John Singleton Copley. COLBY COLLEGE
MUSEUM OF ART, GIFT OF THE VAUGHAN FAMILY OF MAINE, BY
DEED OF GIFT WHICH IS SHARED BY THE BOWDOIN COLLEGE
MUSEUM OF ART.

THOMAS HANCOCK (1703–1764), Boston merchant and
uncle of John Hancock. He owned Great Lots 11 and
20 in present-day Richmond and Farmingdale.
NATIONAL PORTRAIT GALLERY.

Starting as a modest little printer at the sign of the Bible and
Three Crowns, he had risen by shrewd judgment, and some
said by smuggling to be one of the richest men in Boston, and
he was increasing his business every year.

In contrast to the vast resources of Thomas Hancock, or
even of Hallowell and the Bowdoins as things then were, the

modest fortunes of Thwing, the baker, or of Silvester Gardiner might well seem petty. The fact was, however, that the assets of the Plymouth Company, a million and a half acres of undeveloped land in Maine, offered a form of investment as new to the merchant as it was to the doctor, the baker, or the army officer with comparatively modest resources. In 1751, the Plymouth Company was occupied in founding a new township, and the problems of transport, surveying, and supply of settlers were dealt with by those who cared to be most active, irrespective of their financial position. Such men were not Hallowell and Hancock whose mercantile interests were capable of almost indefinite expansion. These had invested for the future when they bought a share of undeveloped timber land. For the present they were content to hold it and to assist, though not too actively, the schemes of others. The driving forces behind the Plymouth Company were Samuel Goodwin, the Bowdoins, and Silvester Gardiner.

Unlike Thomas Hancock's business, Silvester's was limited by nature, since he was primarily a dealer in spices and drugs. His operations in barrels of fish and loads of boards were undertaken solely when it was necessary to receive consignments of this sort instead of cash. In consequence, this highly specialized trade was yearly producing more money than Silvester could spend. In his personal life, as he himself remarks, he had got to the stage where he never knew a want he could not gratify. He lived over the shop because he wished to, and made a fair rather than an extravagant showing because this suited his taste. He was one of those men who actually prefer a measure of economy because it hurts them not to feel that they are getting their money's worth. This being the case, he was unable to fritter away his surplus gains, while he could not put them back into the drug business because it was incapable of absorbing them. Short of letting his money lie idle in the form of credits with merchants of various sorts, Silvester had reached the point where he was bound to branch out in some way. He was consequently ready to regard this new investment as an extension of his active business and to devote to it the energy which Hancock or Hallowell might have put into the acquisition of new ships. Perhaps his upbringing in Narragansett, where the aristocracy all owned land, and his constant association with English people in King's Chapel had taught him to despise a tradesman to some extent. For all his own sturdy insistence on his position, it was evident that he intended his son William to hold his head high in any society at all. Thus it was that Silvester really worked hard for the Plymouth Company and enjoyed an importance in it which was entirely disproportionate to his wealth. In the twenty-five years before the Revolution, Silvester alone did more for Maine than the entire company of Plymouth proprietors had achieved since their purchase of the territory in 1661. In doing so, he influenced history far more profoundly than by all the bewildering series of his activities in Boston, which perished in the upheaval of Revolutionary times.

THE KENNEBEC RIVER, like most of the chief rivers in Maine, runs southward, reaching the sea amid a tangle of islands, some of which are too small to be resting places for anything but seals. In 1625 a little shallop built by the house carpenter of New Plymouth had beaten slowly up the long, narrow channel past Arrowsic Island, and run through the rocky gorge where Bath lies now, and where strong tide races called for accurate timing. She came late in the season, and the deck over her midships which protected her cargo gave no shelter whatsoever to her crew. It must have been a relief to emerge into a still, blue, landlocked bay three miles across, whose flat shore, bordered by a wide green band of marsh grass, was alive with the quacking of ducks at dusk and dawn. In this bay, which is called Merrymeeting, six rivers join, the largest of which is the Kennebec entering on the east. The other considerable stream, the Androscoggin, flows southward parallel to the Kennebec for about twenty miles before curving inward sharply near the coast to join Merrymeeting Bay on its western side. There was good anchorage in the bay, and the New Plymouth men already understood from hearsay that the Kennebec Indians were friendly. The chief stronghold of this tribe lay at that time in the river, which divides into two channels almost immediately above its mouth in Merrymeeting Bay. Swan Island, which it surrounds, is four miles long. Here the westward banks are high, though not so steep that the forest could not come clear down to the water's edge, where a thin band of marsh grass marked the level of high tide. With the Indians on Swan Island the little shallop did good trade, returning to New Plymouth with seven hundred pounds of beaver and other fur in exchange for their home-grown corn.

In a year or two New Plymouth merchants had erected a permanent trading house somewhere north of Merrymeeting Bay, which they stocked not only with corn, but with shirts and blankets, biscuit, peas, and even prunes. The English fishermen wintering on the coast soon learned that it was worth their while to sell the traders a few extra supplies, and blue beads bought from the Narragansett Indians proved to be in much demand, since wampum here was only made with black and white shells. Beaver skins became a sort of currency on the river, passing for six or eight shillings' worth of goods among the Englishmen themselves. Very soon the New Plymouth men had ventured above Swan Island, where the whole river may for the first time be clearly seen, three hundred and fifty yards across and flowing strongly through a narrow plain broken up by headlands and never more than a few hundred yards in width. Beyond it, low hills rise sharply, receding into gentle slopes or plateaus on their other side.

Maine is a land of streams, but of the many tributaries of the lower Kennebec, only two appeared considerable. Opposite Swan Island, the Eastern River made a wide, flat estuary almost at the Kennebec's mouth. Fifteen miles higher, another river had worn a chasm through the hills and came foaming down to the Kennebec from the westward in a series of rocky falls. This stream the Indian guides called Cobbosseecontee, the place where sturgeon are caught, and in the flat land above the falls they traced its windings past a series of small ponds into a chain of lakes.

By 1636 there were already a hundred white men on the Kennebec, trappers and traders who passed up and down with Indian guides in canoes. How far above the Cobbossee they went is quite uncertain, but those who penetrated the Indian territory of the interior found the river way become harder as they ascended it. Five miles beyond the Cobbossee there was a portage around the falls at Cushnoc. Above came Ticonic Falls, the Five-Mile Ripples, and more falls at Skowhegan and Norridgewock. Higher up still, explorers would meet a tangle of falls and dead water which finally became one continuous rapid between high walls of rock. From its source in Moosehead Lake, the Kennebec descends eleven hundred feet to meet the sea, and most of this during the first thirty miles of its length. Before this last stretch, however, the Indian trail had left the river for a tributary and a chain of ponds leading westward to the watershed which runs up from the White Mountains and along the frontiers of Canada. Here lay the source of the Chaudière, the route to the St. Lawrence. By its mouth near Quebec, Frenchmen listened year by year with jealous alarm as tales passed down the river of English trappers, trading houses, forts, or settlements pushing up the Kennebec on the Indian road to Canada.

The coast of Maine had early attracted attention on account of its valuable fish and furs, so that King James the

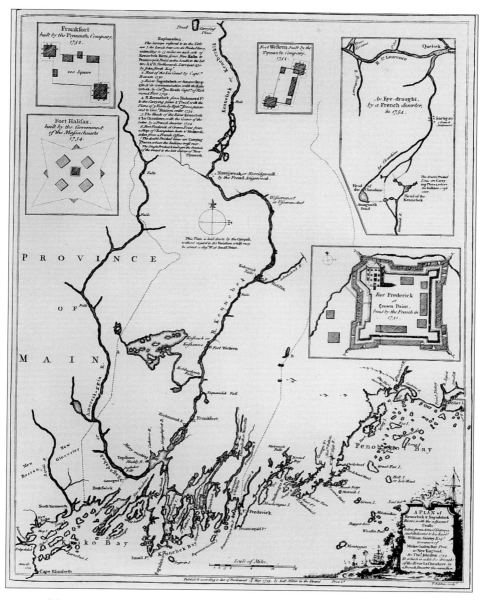

THOMAS JOHNSTON Map of 1775 delineating the claims of the
Kennebec Proprietors fifteen miles on both sides of the Kennebec
River from the ocean to the headwaters of the river to the
exclusion of rival land companies. MAINE HISTORICAL SOCIETY.

First had granted a huge, ill-defined tract of land to the Plymouth merchants as early as 1606. Various charters followed as the area became more accurately known, and presently the task of exploiting this portion of the coast was handed over to the New Plymouth Colony. In 1629 the Plymouth Council granted to William Bradford a patent which was later transferred to the New Plymouth Colony as a whole. The tract of land given away in this document, on whose authority later claims were chiefly based, was roughly defined as fifteen miles on either bank of the Kennebec River from the limits of the Cobbosseecontee to the sea. In fact, however, Indian deeds and conflicting claims of other people later forced a great readjustment of the southern boundaries of the patent. This eventually started below Swan Island, where the river enters Merrymeeting Bay, and ran north fifteen miles from either bank to the Wesserunsett River just below Skowhegan, including a territory of very nearly a million acres and a half. In 1629, the Plymouth Colony had not thought of pushing its claims so far inland, but was attempting to assert a right to the outer islands, the narrow entrance gorge, and the landlocked Merrymeeting Bay itself.

The efforts of New Plymouth to keep the Kennebec as its own preserve raised numerous difficulties, even though the colony stationed a number of agents on the river, headed by two magistrates who were empowered to try all cases except capital ones. Part of the trouble was that it was comparatively easy to obtain conflicting charters, either from authorities in England or from Indian chiefs. All Englishmen were alike to the Indians, who looked upon land as hunting ground and saw no confusion in granting the same area to several people at once. One chief actually sold the land from the lower end of the Cobbossee to the upper Wesserunsett, over a million acres, for two skins of liquor and a loaf of bread. Meanwhile in 1634 Lord Say and Sele and Lord Brook commissioned a certain Captain Hocking to trade in the Kennebec area. John Alden, one of the

New Plymouth magistrates, after remonstrating in vain with Hoskins, went with three men to cut his cables and turn him adrift. They parted one, and Hocking, leveling his musket, threatened death to any man who touched the other. A man laid hold of the cable, and Hocking shot him, and was in return immediately shot and killed. Alden was tried and convicted of homicide, but the jury pronounced it justifiable and acquitted him. Feeling ran high in Boston, while the two lords wrote angrily to the governor of New Plymouth, "we could for the death of Hocking have dispatched a man-of-war and beat down your houses at Kennebeck about your ears." In fact, however, the affair did much to establish the right of the Plymouth Colony, which took twenty hogsheads of beaver in trade that very year. Their outposts had already pushed twenty miles upstream to Cushnoc, where a Indian village now formed the most important center of the Kennebec.

I N VIEW OF THIS success against the Puritan lords it comes as a surprise to find that in fifteen years trade on the Kennebec had so greatly declined that it had become more trouble than it was worth to New Plymouth, which leased the patent in 1649 to five individuals for the inconsiderable sum of fifty pounds a year. Moreover, the lease was later renewed at lower figures, and by 1660 rent had sunk to the miserable total of ten pounds. The causes of this decline were various. In the first place, the area controlled by the Plymouth patent was ill-defined and was overlapped by all sorts of conflicting claims. The Kennebec runs south between two rivers, the Androscoggin twenty miles to the west, and the Sheepscot seven or eight miles to the east. Of these the Androscoggin, which was manifestly not included in the patent, enters Merrymeeting Bay, whose exit to the sea the Colony was trying to control. On the other hand, the Sheepscot, though less than fifteen miles from the Kennebec, has a separate mouth through which other persons might reasonably enter to trade or settle. This confusing topography, added to the fact that the areas granted away in England were imperfectly mapped and had never been surveyed, produced a conflict of claims which were not settled until the middle of the eighteenth century when Silvester Gardiner and his partners were in control of Kennebec affairs.

Maine woods were vast, and the Abenakis, to which group the Kennebec Indians belonged, were widely scattered. However, it soon appeared that their resources in beaver were not endless, and after twenty-five years of intensive trapping, the number of pelts obtainable was considerably reduced. Nor were the Indians so easy to trade with now that experience had taught them the value that the white man put on furs. The Abenakis as a whole were growing unfriendly as they saw the first settlers push up the banks of the river and experienced sharp practices or downright brutality at the hands of the invading strangers. For all these reasons trade reports from the Kennebec were quite discouraging, while settlement lagged because of the remoteness of the area, its climate, the uncertainty of title, and the absence of any local government there. By 1661 New Plymouth was ready to sell its patent, which was bought for four hundred pounds by Antipas Boies, Edward Tyng, Thomas Brattle, and John Winslow. The heirs and assigns of these men were later known as the Plymouth, or sometimes the Kennebec Company, while the tract was hereafter called the Kennebec Purchase.

THERE WAS SMALL reason to suppose that Boies, Tyng, Brattle, and Winslow would be able to make good where the Plymouth Colony had failed, and to maintain their claim against adventurers who were pushing inland from the coast. In fact, they did little or nothing, and asserted no control over the thirty families on Arrowsic and Parker's Islands, or the twenty north of Merrymeeting Bay, who were scattered from the mouth of the river to about ten miles upstream. The trading houses on Arrowsic and the mainland, together with their outposts at Ticonic thirty-five miles up the river, belonged to Richard Hammond and the partners, Clarke and Lake. Consequently, though the patent owners did nothing, they also lost nothing in the mid-coast area when the devastating series of frontier wars broke out in 1676. Hammond, whom the Indians hated because he made them drunk in order to cheat them out of furs, was killed with twenty others by his trading house, where sixteen prisoners were captured. Lake was also killed at Arrowsic, and no less than thirty-five were carried away from there. On the Sheepscot only one family was captured, as the rest of the settlement was warned in time to take refuge in their garrison house. Being strictly besieged and having no means of flight, they began to work frantically on a boat, the women sitting down to their weaving in order to have sails ready by the time the carpenters needed them. Only the masts remained to be stepped when the Indians succeeded in firing the vessel. Fortunately, however, a single scout had made his way out through the woods to get rescue, and in the nick of time a ship with fresh provisions and some troops on board was sent up from Boston. The unfortunate settlers, seeing their houses burned and their cattle driven off, and finding the soldiers who had saved them were preparing to return home, lost heart and abandoned the place, which rapidly reverted to the wilderness. By 1690 there were only four settlements left in Maine, while on the Kennebec a few overgrown cellars and the remains of orchards were the only evidence that white men had ever lived there.

These disasters, which made it impossible for settlements to exist on the river without the powerful protection of a fort, were very largely the work of the French. Their representatives, the Jesuit missionaries, had been far more persistent in pushing up the Chaudière than the English in spreading along the

Kennebec towards them. By the middle of the century a Jesuit was actually on the Kennebec, and had established centers of influence as far down the river as Cushnoc. By 1691 the Indian stronghold had receded to Norridgewock, five days' journey from Quebec, but only two from the river's mouth, where persistent English traders were beginning to reappear. To Norridgewock the Jesuits now sent Father Sebastian Râle, who proved to be far the most influential white man who had so far established himself along the Kennebec. Simple in his personal tastes, he yet understood the need of his charges for a religion of pageantry and color to replace the conjurations of the medicine man. His mission church was decorated with an altar painting of the Virgin and a gold image of the Son, while pictures in bright, colors such as the Indians loved ran all around its walls. The Kennebecs kept his altar ablaze with candles of bayberry wax, and forty Indian boys in homemade cassocks and surplices swung the censers, or walked in procession carrying gilded banners on the holy days. One of the two chapels by the banks of the Kennebec was sacred to the Virgin, but the other was dedicated to the guardian spirit of the Abenakis, a being in which the old religion and the new were skillfully combined.

Presently the colonists began to realize that besides the Latin mass in the morning, the vespers in Abenaki, the lesson in Christian doctrine, and the Abenaki dictionary of Father Râle, a political alliance of the whole Abenaki tribe with France was being cemented. A crusade was actually being preached against the reviving settlements of the heretic unbelievers in the South. At the outbreak of Queen Anne's War in 1702, it was the influence of Father Râle which kept the Abenakis to the French alliance. Two hundred settlers were killed and five hundred captured by the Indians in this war. In 1710 the government actually offered a thousand pounds for Father Râle, but in vain. Eleven years later, he went down to Arrowsic Island in person with a few French and two hundred Indians to threaten that the cattle would be killed and the settlements burned if it were not immediately evacuated.

Nothing could be done on the Kennebec until Father Râle's power was broken. In 1722 the Colonial Government in Boston sent an expedition against Norridgewock which surprised the Indian village and actually got possession of Father Râle's private papers. He himself had broken both legs in a fall some time before and could only with difficulty hobble into the woods a short way ahead of his enemies. It seemed as though he must be captured, but he stepped behind a tree, and in his own words, "as if they had been repelled by an invisible hand, they turned away and retired." Though Râle's guilt was proved to the colonists by the examination of his private letters, his own conscience justified him in all that he had done. With the courage of his convictions, he refused to leave for Quebec. Next year he sent the Indians down again to Arrowsic, where they burned the houses, killed three hundred cattle, and carried off a child, the rest of the settlers escaping into their fort. Finally in 1724 a band of two hundred and eight experienced woodsmen went up the river to Norridgewock and surrounded it before the alarm could be given. Father Râle fired on one of the rangers from the doorway of the little bark hut in which he lived, but before he could reload, he was himself shot down. Eighty of the Norridgewocks, including most of their chieftains, were killed. The scattered remnant retired to the François mission on the Chaudière.

The power of the Kennebec Indians was broken, though not yet destroyed, and a better Indian policy, which was initiated at this time had its effect. Fort Richmond had been built in 1719 on the west bank of the river just north of Swan Island. It was now strengthened and enlarged by the government, which built a new and larger complex on a nearby site in 1740. In addition a truck house was opened there for Indian trade, for which goods were purchased wholesale and sold for only

ADVERTISEMENT.

THE Proprietors of the *Kennebeck* Purchase from the late Colony of *New-Plymouth*, hereby inform the Publick, That besides the twelve Townships mention'd in their Advertisement of the 16th of *February* last, they have agreed to appropriate a Tract of Land on each side of *Kennebeck* River for the Accommodation of such Families as may be inclined to settle there. The Land refer'd to, is situated a little above *Cobbiseconte* River, where the Navigation of *Kennebeck* River is good for Vessels of 100 Tons Burthen, and continues so several Miles higher as far as *Fort-Western*.

THEY propose to grant to each settling Family 250 Acres, *viz.* 100 Acres front upon *Kennebeck* River, 50 Rods, and run one Mile back ; and 150 Acres at two Miles from said River : On Condition that each Family build an House not less than eighteen Feet square, and seven Feet stud ; clear and make fit for Tillage five Acres within three Years ; and dwell upon the Premisses personally, or by their Substitutes for the Term of seven Years more. As this Land is exceeding good, and is attended with many natural Advantages, the Families that apply for Settlements there must be well recommended for their Sobriety, Honesty and Industry ; and such of that Character, who apply first, will have the first Choice of the Lots to be granted.

FOR further Particulars enquire of *James Bowdoin, James Pitts, Silvester Gardiner* and *Benjamin Hallowell*, Esqrs of *Boston*, and Mr. *William Bowdoin* at *Needham*, Committee to the *Kennebeck* Proprietors.

PERSONS at the Eastward inclining to settle on the Lands aforesaid, may apply to Major *Samuel Goodwin* at *Pownalborough*, and *James Howard*, Esq; at *Fort-Western*, who will communicate their Minds to the Committe aforesaid.

David Jeffries, Proprietor's Clerk.

Boston, 20th *February* 1761.

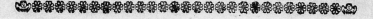

BROADSIDE published by the Kennebec Proprietors in 1761 to promote settlement in Central Maine.
MAINE STATE MUSEUM.

enough to cover freight and waste. Truckmasters were carefully chosen, and were encouraged to give free presents from time to time when it was desired to gain friends. Four bushels of corn and a gallon and a half of rum, for instance, were given to one party of sixty Indians in the hopes of using their influence with others. The result of such policy was almost twenty years of peace from Lovewell's War until the outbreak of the War of the Spanish Succession in 1745.

SETTLEMENTS HAD BEEN beginning to creep back from the coast to the lower river even before the short period of hostilities known as Lovewell's War, whose culmination for the colonists in those parts was the destruction of Norridgewock. Arrowsic Island was inhabited, as we have seen, and Fort Richmond was actually constructed as early as 1719. A more determined effort was made by Dr. Noyes of Boston, who established a settlement at Small Point, south of Arrowsic, which he, misleadingly as it turned out, christened Augusta. Here he built a stone fort which was widely reputed to be the best in the East, but which was swept away by the Indians in the course of Lovewell's War. Dr. Noyes was chiefly interested in the immense wealth of the Kennebec in fish. Trout were abundant at all times, but in addition the river swarmed with fish running inland from the sea. Smelt could be caught through the ice. Alewives appeared in the brown flood waters of spring, with shad following them by thousands in mid-May. Salmon were so abundant that a hundred years later agreements between servants and masters used to include the stipulation that the household should not eat salmon more than five times in the week. Jonathan Winslow, who was born by the Cobbossee in 1761, recorded catching sixteen fine salmon on a Sunday morning before breakfast. The most magnificent fish of all was sturgeon, which sometimes weighed as much as eight hundred pounds. For some years Dr. Noyes sent vessels through Merrymeeting Bay to fish for these on still summer nights by the light of torches, and he is estimated to have sent some thousands of barrels to the English markets.

Ten years after Dr. Noyes' time, fifteen hundred Irish Protestants were persuaded to establish a township called Cork on the Kennebec near the mouth of the Eastern River. However, the wilderness and the rumors of Indian raids discouraged them, together with the slackness of the government. Not only could they obtain no special protection, but the garrison of Fort Richmond was steadily being reduced, until a few years later it had sunk to ten soldiers. The Irish deserted by hundreds to Pennsylvania and New Hampshire, where the climate was easier and the location less exposed. In a very short time their clearings by the Eastern River had grown up to wilderness again.

During all this while the owners of the Plymouth Patent had been steadily increasing in number as each man divided his portion among his heirs. They never met as a group, did not all know one another, and had made no effort to protect their property from the encroachments of more active proprietors. The patent itself was actually lost, and though efforts had been made to look for it at various times, it could not be discovered. The Indian wars, which had discouraged the owners, had at least done them the service of preserving their property more or less intact. However, Maine trade was in fish, fur, and lumber, all of which were capable of quick revival, and as the Indian gradually ceased to be a menace, traders, or even settlers, were soon at work again. The conclusion of the Spanish War was a crucial moment for the proprietors, and fortunately for themselves, they saw it as such. At some time during its course, their interest had been stirred.

A certain Samuel Goodwin, who had inherited a twenty-fourth share of the Kennebec Purchase from his father, was the first to concern himself seriously about his rights. After spending considerable time and money in a search for the patent, he found it in the hands of Samuel Wells, one of the commissioners on the boundary question between the Plymouth Colony and Rhode Island. Wells himself had no manner of right to retain the document, which he had sought as evidence and obtained by some trick from an "ancient woman" who had long concealed it in the hope of turning it to good account. Some similar idea appears to have been in the mind of Wells, who was eventually forced by a court order to surrender it to Goodwin. He, meanwhile, had not been idle, but had persuaded a number of wealthy men to buy shares in the territory in the hopes of using their capital to exploit its valuable land. Among these men were William Bowdoin, Florentius Vassall, Thomas Hancock, and Silvester Gardiner.

THE FRANKFORT SETTLEMENT

SILVESTER GARDINER was not present at the first meeting of the Company called by Goodwin at the Royal Exchange Tavern in Boston on the twenty-first of September 1749. Only nine proprietors appeared, but these chose a clerk, appointed a committee, and agreed to push on development actively. Before the end of the year they had decided on a survey of the patent, together with a special plan of a township near the Cobbossee. The Plymouth Company was speedily incorporated, and two Portsmouth lawyers were appointed as counsel, since it was foreseen that much litigation would be necessary to establish the boundaries of the patent. A third lawyer was asked to prepare papers presenting the original grant from the Council of Plymouth, together with the various Indian deeds which had later accumulated. In case of dispute about the latter, Goodwin was authorized to lay out not more than fifty pounds in obtaining additional Indian deeds to the tract from the coast as far north as the Wesserunsett River. Meanwhile, Florentius Vassall, the Company's agent in London, was to lay all papers before the proper authorities and to

SEAL OF THE Kennebec Purchase Company consisting of an anchor and codfish within a circlet with a motto which translated into English means "The King never gave anything in vain."

present a petition from the proprietors for a separate county in the Kennebec valley with its own center of local government.

The assertion of legal rights was a slow business, especially as several companies claimed the coast, the shores of Merrymeeting Bay, and the mouth of the Sheepscot, in which they were supported by various Indian deeds. In the event, the Plymouth Company was pushed back from the coast as far as the south end of Swan Island, though it retained a right of entry up the channel and across Merrymeeting Bay itself. Meanwhile Samuel Goodwin went up to the Kennebec with a surveyor to examine the situation there and make a plan of the Kennebec Purchase as a whole.

It happened that towards the end of 1749 there had been a quarrel between a group of Indians and some white men near the mouth of the Sheepscot, not six months after a treaty of peace had been signed at Falmouth. One Indian was killed, and three colonists were arrested for his murder; but, whether by connivance or mismanagement, they escaped. Thereupon the Kennebec Indians, reinforced by those who had retreated across the Canadian watershed to the St. François settlement, sent down a hundred braves in the succeeding summer to take revenge. Falling on the fort at Richmond, which was garrisoned at the time by only fourteen men, they delivered a violent assault. Fortunately they were unaware of its weakness, and the next night Samuel Goodwin with his surveyor and six other men whom he had collected in a hurry were able to enter. Discouraged by these reinforcements, the Indians abandoned the siege and contented themselves with sending out parties against the scattered settlers of the neighborhood. James Whidden, who lived on the river in Swan Island, was surprised by about twenty Indians very early in the morning before his household was properly awake. He and his wife were aroused by screams and rushed down into the cellar, where they hid in their night clothes until the savages had plundered their furniture and gone. His two sons and two servants were carried into captivity, as were his daughter, her husband, and their seven children, the youngest only eight months old. One of Whidden's sons died of the treatment he received, but the other was eventually restored to him, though broken in health. In 1751 the poor man was still petitioning the government to help him recover the rest of his family. "With great concern of mind he understands," he wrote, "that great care and pains are taken by the French, to whom they were sold, to initiate his grandchildren into ye Romish Principles, and by all the motives of charity and compassion to their souls as well as bodies he is obliged to pray and seek for their liberty and redemption."

These experiences convinced Goodwin and the Plymouth Company that it was absolutely necessary that Fort Richmond should be moved higher up the stream. They set on foot a petition to this effect, while continuing to press their legal claims and to come to terms with squatters. These were informed that they might be confirmed in possession of their lands and houses if they would apply within nine months, but that they could retain no right to mill privileges and mill streams without paying for them. In the meantime, the chief concern of the Company was its own plan for starting a settlement by the Eastern River.

The succession of wars in Europe had by now dispossessed thousands of people along the borders of Germany and France. In particular French Hugenot refugees, who had been expelled from their country by the revocation of the Edict of Nantes in 1685, had been driven from their new homes by French invasion and were crowding further east, or into the ports of Holland. Various emigration agents, some of them on commission, were busy collecting settlers from among these on behalf of American proprietors. Henry Luther, a councilor of Frankfort am Main, was in touch with the authorities of the province and put forth various schemes, which cost him considerable time and money as it turned out. He and an agent, Joseph Crellius, now persuaded a group of these French and German speaking exiles to enter into an agreement with the Plymouth Company, which was looking for settlers. A site was marked out by the mouth of the Eastern River opposite Swan Island, which the Company gratefully christened Frankfort in the councilor's honor.

SILVESTER GARDINER, though he had only recently appeared at the meetings of the Company, was now appointed one of a committee of three to draw up the conditions upon which land should be given. This group agreed that a hundred acres should be granted to each settler, provided that he build a house thereon at least eighteen by twenty feet and eight feet high, that he clear five acres, and that he undertake not to sell to any but settlers as long as there were less than fifty families in the town. The first immigrants arrived in December, an awkward season, but the Company decided to charter a vessel and transport them from Boston as soon as a group of twenty had been collected. Meanwhile it undertook to furnish provisions for six months if the settlers would give bonds for them payable in twelve months after their departure from Boston. This arrangement, though perhaps inevitable, meant that the settlement started under the handicap of a considerable debt. Nor was this all. A vote of the Company on December 18, 1751, speaks of "such of the Germans as arrived in the ship Prisillah, John Brown master, and have not paid their freight." It later appears that these "Germans," as the Plymouth Company called them, having lost all their possessions in the course of the late troubles with France, had mortgaged their lands in advance to purchase their passage.

This situation caused much difficulty later, but in the meantime the Plymouth Company was optimistic and active. Mr. Peter Wild, who was at first intended to go up to Frankfort with the settlers as interpreter, was dispatched to Europe as another recruiting agent. He was instructed to travel through Germany and Holland, the populations of which were swollen with war refugees, and to offer any of these a hundred acres of land contiguous to the inhabitants already settled. Silvester Gardiner, who was already investing more liberally than the others, sent August Sumner to London and Rotterdam on the same errand at his own expense, and even dispatched a man to Quincy to see if he could entice away some of the foreign artisans, particularly the glass workers from there. The Company actually began to believe that they could have two hundred families settled in Frankfort by the end of the second fall.

Their first task in view of the late Indian troubles was to build a defensible house, on which they had fifty men working in a reasonably short time. Silvester sent up eight brass cannon and some ammunition, and he later undertook to purchase them firearms at twenty shillings each. This fort, named Fort Shirley, stood a little higher up the river than Fort Richmond, and on the opposite or eastern bank. Its main feature was a palisade of logs ten feet high and two hundred feet square. On two opposite corners blockhouses were built with an upper story for the cannon, while in the center was a barracks sixty feet long and thirty-two wide with magazines and storehouses attached. To erect such a fort was a large undertaking, especially for men who were artisans and townspeople, not woodsmen. Samuel Goodwin, who was to command here, had to employ professional carpenters to help, while the Company found it necessary to supervise the construction of fifteen or twenty huts for the settlers as well. However, by the middle of 1753, Fort Shirley was so far along that the Company thought it time to supply Goodwin with "one Barrel of Rum to treat the Indians that go to Frankfort, to make them *easy*." This was satisfactory, but it was discouraging to be informed that the whole building was overlooked by a hill, and that it would not be safe without another defensive house on top of this.

Such difficulties as these made little impression on the optimism of the Company, which now granted a township on the Cobbossee of twenty-one thousand acres to Ephraim Jones

HOUSE NEAR Dresden Mills, built by Dr. Gardiner and inherited by his son John. MAINE HISTORIC PRESERVATION COMMISSION.

and a couple of partners on condition that they should have a hundred settlers on the land within three years. They even made similar offers to Henry Luther in Frankfurt am Main, to an agent in Rotterdam, and to Gershom Flagg, a builder and glazier employed in Frankfort, who later bought a small share in the Company.

MEANWHILE IT SHORTLY became evident that Frankfort would not be self-supporting within the time that the proprietors had allowed. Provisions had to be supplied for twelve months instead of six, and regular trade with Boston would need to be established as soon as possible. Silvester thereupon built a sloop at his own expense, intending it to make regular runs up the Kennebec, except from December to March when the river was frozen. During this period he felt it would be necessary to use the Sheepscot, and he petitioned for a lot of four hundred acres there, on which he agreed to settle a family and build a convenient storehouse for trade. His first sloop was lost with all hands in a March storm, but another, *The Kennebec*, made regular runs up the coast both winter and summer on Silvester's business, going one December not merely to the Sheepscot, but clear north to Newfoundland. The possession of this sloop practically meant that Silvester controlled communications between the Frankfort settlement and the Company in Boston, and that little was done without coming to some arrangement with him. Major Goodwin, though he resided at Fort Shirley and continued to direct affairs at Frankfort, made his visits to Boston in the sloop, and relied on Silvester to hire skilled labor for him, spend money, and find new settlers.

Already in 1752, Silvester was asked by the proprietors to invest about eighteen hundred pounds on their behalf in supplies needed for Frankfort during the next six months. It is interesting to see that his list includes not only flour and meal, but meat and the inevitable rum. For clothing, nothing is needed but men's shoes, but the settlement asks for a vast assortment of ironwork, such as staples, hinges, padlocks, shovels, axes, and other tools. These form the bulk of the list, but other necessities for a pioneer village are: one flag, two drums, four grindstones, and a doctor's box. This last item seems to have been useful, since in the following year when Goodwin was asked to get the Frankfort men to work on a road to Sheepscot for the winter trade, the necessary supplies for his roadmakers seem to be: one barrel of rum, a hundred pounds of bread, two hundred pounds of cheese, and the doctor's box refilled. A few years later Goodwin was obliged to send a boat with six men clear down to Falmouth for a doctor to dress John Spearin's foot, which had been cut by an axe. Additional requirements for Fort Shirley in these unsettled times include a half barrel of good pistol powder, a hundred pounds of lead bullets, and five hundred good flints.

All these requirements do not seem to have been foreseen by the proprietors, who appear to have thought that one of Goodwin's earliest acts would be to build a sawmill, and that this would mean the export of enough board to pay for all supplies. About four miles up the Eastern River it is joined by a small tributary, now called Mill Brook, or sometimes Gardiner Stream. A large lot here was granted to Goodwin in partnership with three of the earliest settlers, who undertook to erect a sawmill within the first year, and a gristmill by the end of 1754. This proved impossible, since all hands were employed on Fort Shirley and on the huts during the first building season. Goodwin now took over the concession alone but failed again for lack of skilled carpenters and a mill wright. In despair he sold the lot to Silvester, who with his usual energy found men, sent them upstream to work, and erected not only the mills and dam on Gardiner Stream, but a small garrison house with a palisade to protect the mill workers. These mills were

GRISTMILL at Dresden Mills, built by Dr. Gardiner in 1753.
MAINE HISTORIC PRESERVATION COMMISSION.

SAWMILL at Dresden Mills, built by Dr. Gardiner in 1753.
MAINE HISTORIC PRESERVATION COMMISSION.

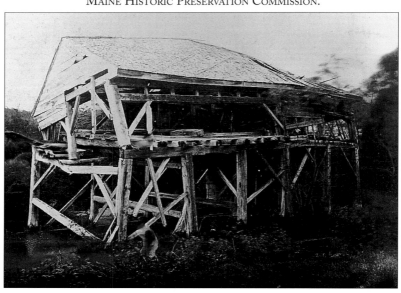

small sheds covered with shingles, the grist mill tiny, and the sawmill two stories high and somewhat larger. However, they served their purpose, and presently home-grown corn was being ground and *The Kennebec* was returning to Boston with its first load of Frankfort boards. Silvester went up to the settlement himself for a month or so over this business, and no doubt found that his fluent French gave him a considerable advantage in dealing with some of the settlers.

South of the Kennebec Purchase, the coast and islands were rapidly filling up, while by the mouth of the Sheepscot new groups of farms had appeared. As high up as Swan Island, James Whidden, undeterred by his misfortunes, accepted a grant of three hundred and twenty-five acres from the proprietors. Some parts of Frankfort were already higher upstream than Fort Richmond, to the perturbation of the Indians, who were concerned for their hunting grounds and restive at the uneasy truce between the English and the French. The conclusion of the Spanish War had satisfied neither combatant. The English were furious at the surrender of Louisburg in the peace treaty, while the French still claimed to the Kennebec, and were actively building a line of forts between the St. Lawrence and the Ohio. Settlements were pushing up the Chaudière from Quebec in menacing fashion, and the French government would by no means consent to release the captives taken in recent Indian raids. All in all, the situation was a tense one, and Captain Lithgow, the able truckmaster at Fort Richmond, had a hopeless task, even though the government sent him up several hogsheads of bread and barrels of pork as Indian presents. Meanwhile, the Plymouth Company, even more ineffectively, informed Lithgow that he was "appointed to carry on the settlements at the Kennebec," and requested him to keep the Indians quiet. Relations between individual settlers and Indians were no better than before, witness the following letter received by Silvester from Frankfort in 1753.

"There has been a very Bad affair happen'd here (as I'm inform'd).

"There are Two Indians killed on Montinicus Island by the man that was Order'd from it a few Days Ago.

"One Wright came up & informed Capt Lithgow of it & Said he knew the Two men that saw it Done — & helped to bury them there, & their Guns, but he wou'dn't tell their names — the Indians are ignorant of it at present But when they know it, they will revenge themselves, I am afraid, & we may Look out, for we are but Weak. If this be true, I think, Such Villains ought to dye without pity."

G OVERNOR SHIRLEY now appointed a commission to meet with the Indians at Fort Richmond and listen to their complaints. They behaved with some dignity, asserting not without reason that their fathers had never intended to deprive their descendants of the hunting grounds. They admitted the validity of the Indian deeds when pressed, but added threateningly that they had given the French permission to live and hunt on their lands in order that these might give them stores when they were at war with the English. All in all, though an Indian treaty was signed, it seemed to very little purpose, especially considering the events of the succeeding year.

Early in 1754, Captain Lithgow forwarded information to the governor that the French were reported to be building a fort at a "noted carrying place of the Indians" on the Kennebec. Shirley reacted promptly, sending up two officers with an armed guard to explore the river and bid the French remove themselves in the King's name. He added some fussy instructions about acting with great discretion, and ordered the expedition to get back before the ice on the river broke up. Presumably these officers set forth, but the weather in February must have discouraged them from making too much effort. At any rate, they came back without either discovering any

Colonel William Lithgow (1715–1798), a
political rival of Dr. Gardiner. Portrait by Joseph
Badger. Gift of Mr. and Mrs. Ellerton M. Jetté,
Colby College Museum of Art.

French or disproving the reports of their presence. Sixty Indians had appeared at Fort Richmond in a truculent mood and threatened the garrison with an attack from the French in the spring.

Silvester's account of what followed was given to the British government twenty-five years later at a time when he was particularly anxious to recall his services to them. According to him, Governor Shirley planned to erect a new fort at Ticonic, thirty miles up from Richmond, with the intention of restraining the French, making a jumping-off place for future attacks on Quebec, and rendering the timber of the East more readily available to the government. This would involve a subsidiary fort at Cushnoc, fifteen miles lower, since schooners would have to be unloaded there and supplies transshipped into boats before they could proceed upstream. Since the General Assembly opposed the suggestion on account of its expense, Shirley began to confer with Silvester as a representative of the Plymouth Company. Silvester, who agreed with the governor's policy and thought that the company should bear part of the burden of protecting their own property, brought it to consent to build the fort at Cushnoc, for which he promised to advance the money. This plan was adopted. The province erected the Ticonic fort, and the Plymouth Company that of Cushnoc, for which they borrowed the money from Silvester and never, as he complains, repaid him.

THERE IS NOTHING actually improbable in Silvester's version of this story. Shirley was intimate with Silvester, who was his family physician, and the governor's daughters are known to have called on Mrs. Gardiner. As Shirley showed now and Silvester later, they both had the same broad, imperialistic point of view on British politics. It is true that the Assembly's records do not show that it raised any objection to the Ticonic fort on account of its expense, but rather that it gave the gov-

His Excellency William Shirley Esq.[r]

Captain General and Governour in Chief &c. of the Province of the Massachusetts Bay in New England and Colonel of one of His Majesty's Regiments of Foot.

GOVERNOR WILLIAM SHIRLEY (1694–1771), a political supporter of the Kennebec Purchase Company.
SOCIETY FOR THE PRESERVATION OF NEW ENGLAND ANTIQUITIES.

ernor carte blanche to erect a fort wherever he pleased. However, in the letter that Shirley addressed to the Plymouth Company after the Assembly had passed this vote, it is evident that his plan had already been discussed with them in detail. He offers to build his own fort at Ticonic, provided that the Company will put one up at Cushnoc of hewn timber not less than ten inches thick and containing quarters and storehouses of prescribed dimensions; "and build a blockhouse," he continues, "of twenty-four feet square, at two of the opposite angles agreeable to a plan exhibited by you to me for that purpose, and furnish the same with four cannon carrying ball of four pounds." It certainly seems possible that Shirley, having privately consulted members of the Assembly about his plan for a fort at Ticonic, found that it would be unacceptable because of the expense of a subsidiary fort. He may then have made an arrangement through Silvester Gardiner, who induced the Company to submit the plan to which Shirley refers. The amended proposal would have been formally submitted to the Assembly, and when it had been passed, the governor would have made this offical proposition to the Plymouth Company.

It is fair to say that Silvester, though in large matters a truthful man, was not above some small unscrupulousness in presenting the facts of a case so as to serve his own interests. He certainly implies that he agreed with Shirley on the importance of opening the timber lands of the East. He may have, but only in a sense, since Shirley and the British government were undoubtedly thinking of mast pines available to them. Silvester was well aware of this mania on the part of the British government, and he was happy to take advantage of it when pressing his claims to gratitude later on. His own attitude, however, is well expressed in a petition of the Plymouth Company in 1771, in which they complain that they have given away eight thousand pounds as a company, and that individuals have invested considerably more. In spite of these heavy expenses, they have so far had no return, and meanwhile their woods are being stripped by the government for masts in a fashion they consider ruinous. A man who would in these circumstances suggest that he had supported the policy of the government might also be capable of exaggerating the amount he had lent to the Plymouth Company. Since Silvester averred that he had their bond, he undoubtedly did; but there is no real proof that he advanced the entire cost of the fort, while there is some slight suggestion in the Plymouth Company's records that other proprietors were concerned in it as well.

WHETHER THEY CONTRIBUTED to the cost or not, four other men were certainly joined with Silvester as a committee to take care of the building of Fort Western at Cushnoc for the Company. Moreover William Bowdoin went east that summer to superintend the work, while Silvester stayed in Boston and took Bowdoin's place as moderator at the Plymouth Company's meetings. The construction of this fort was quite elaborate, since the timber had to be prepared at Frankfort under the protection of Fort Shirley and towed up the river from there. The Company made it even stronger than their agreement called for, with walls twelve inches thick instead of ten, and sentry boxes of oak plank in the two corners that did not contain block houses. Their barracks and storehouses were almost twice as large as Shirley had agreed on, and there were two sets of palisades, one joining the buildings, and the other outside it, thirty feet distant, surrounding it on all sides except that bounded by the river. If Silvester lent the Plymouth Company money for all this, he must have been willing to invest a good deal in the patent at this time.

Governor Shirley's proceedings were still more elaborate than the Company's. He went down from Boston with a force of eight hundred men under General Winslow, and he did not arrive in Falmouth until June. Meanwhile, he sent two expedi-

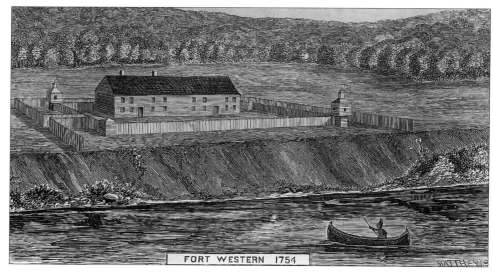

FORT WESTERN 1754

VIEW OF Fort Western in present-day Augusta.
NORTH'S *HISTORY OF AUGUSTA.*

PLAN OF Fort Western in present-day Augusta.
NORTH'S *HISTORY OF AUGUSTA.*

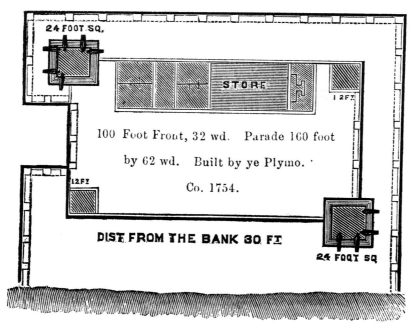

tions up the Kennebec, the first with instructions to discover if the French were building a fort and to approach as near as possible without hazard. The second under Major Goodwin was to go to Ticonic "to view the lands thereabouts, and particularly observe what timber may be there suitable for building a fort." If Goodwin met Indians, he was to press on without offering violence, unless in self-defense. News had naturally got about of Shirley's intentions, and on his arrival at Falmouth he was met by a deputation of Kennebec and Penobscot Indians, who had come to make their objections to the fort he proposed to build. Shirley once more showed them the Indian deeds, and they gave in and signed the treaty he proposed to them, though the Assagunticooks, who were also concerned, held out and sent no emissaries.

Shirley now marched with his eight hundred to Ticonic, sending five hundred up the river to look for the French, who were at least proved never to have been there at all. The remaining three hundred were kept busy hauling cannon in scows from Cushnoc, making a road for wheeled carriages which could be used to bring up supplies when the river was impassible, and building a blockhouse. Shirley himself, who was no organizer in spite of his grandiose plans, soon went back to Boston, after having arranged a whaleboat express from the fort to Falmouth which should accomplish the journey in twenty hours. Winslow completed the blockhouse, four small barracks around it, each opposite one corner, and part of a star-shaped palisade. He then turned the fort over to Captain Lithgow, who was to be stationed there with eighty men, and marched away. Lithgow, who was an able and active officer, thought little of this magnificent effort, and never ceased to complain until he had moved most of the buildings and turned the fort into a conventional oblong one with two blockhouses plus a row of barracks and storehouses along the sides of the stockade. Even then he said the fort was commanded by a hill and not defen-

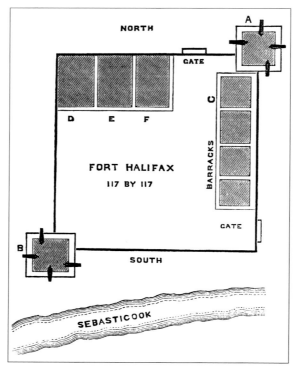

PLAN OF Fort Halifax in Winslow.
NORTH'S *HISTORY OF AUGUSTA.*

sible against a French attack with cannon unless a strong redoubt were built there also.

The half-finished Fort Halifax, produced by an expedition of eight hundred men, is a sad contrast to the Company's
Fort Western, larger, much more secure and comfortable, and
needing a garrison of no more than twenty to guard its supplies. To be sure, the protection of the governor's force was essential to the builders of Fort Western, and the permanent
residents of Frankfort had time to prepare much of the wood.
Still, the governor's abilities as an organizer were not equal to
the breadth of his vision, and the first winter of Fort Halifax
was in consequence a precarious one.

In November, the Province sloop which supplied its eastern forts had just been loaded when Shirley received word from Lithgow that a garrison party of six had been attacked by Indians while getting wood. A man had been killed and scalped, and four others carried away, only one escaping to tell the story. The House, falling into a panic at the news, suggested vast reinforcements which were shown to be impracticable on account of the accommodations at the fort. It then recommended that forty men be sent up to strengthen the garrison, four hundred and sixty from the independent companies to the eastward to be held ready to march, and that the redoubt on the hill should be strengthened immediately. Meanwhile they sent up twenty double beds and forty single blankets, which

VIEW OF Fort Halifax in Winslow.
MAINE HISTORICAL SOCIETY.

they considered sufficient to keep forty men warm in the depths of a Maine winter.

It is clear from the nature of these preparations that what the Province expected was not an Indian, but a large-scale French attack. Such fears were strengthened by a letter received by Silvester within the course of a very few weeks.

"De Loutre expects war in the Spring or Summer as he says,—They say he is gathering the Indians together.

"I suppose if he expects a French war, they will not begin Hostilities before. I hear they expect a number of Large and some small Canon—also two or three hundred soldiers.... I hear the French are very Vext at the Forts up Kennebec River—One of them told me it was only 37 or 40 Leagues from Quebec.... They report here that a Canada Mulatto named Picort shewed Gov. Shirley the way to the River Chaudière, and that there is a Number of Indians hunting after him to put him to Death."

This gossip sent down from Canada by a ship captain gives a fair picture of the rumors that were flying about at this time among French and colonists. Shirley's dispositions in this emergency show the same hearty good will and poor execution that he had demonstrated in the preceding summer. Of the forty recruits voted by the Assembly for Fort Halifax, only nineteen appeared, and these not till February, when they helped bring up some desperately needed stores.

No ATTACK MATERIALIZED, which was just as well, since early in January Lithgow wrote to the governor in real desperation. Scarcely thirty men out of his eighty were well enough to cut and haul fuel, and even these could hardly struggle through three feet of snow without snowshoes. "Our being in a manner naked," he said, "it is out of our power, were we in health, to keep scouts abroad, or even to send a guard with these men who haul wood, neither can they carry their arms with them, being hard put to it to wallow through the snow with their sled loads of wood." He went on to point out that it was very bad that the barracks had not been properly completed and that more supplies had not been sent up before the winter came. "If it was bad carrying up ye stores then, I aver it's ten times worse now, and I fear will continue so this winter, for I doubt ye river above Fort Western will be hard to freeze on account of the strong current that runs there, and as to the cut road being any service, it would take fifty men and ten yoke of oxen two days to brake, and after it was broken it would choke up with ye first wind that blew; some of ye gullies now are drifted ten or fifteen feet deep with snow." All in all, he could only suggest that the independent companies collect cattle and oxen to haul supplies from the river mouth to Fort Western in sleds and carts on the ice. Thence they would have to be carried up by men on snowshoes, and when these had beaten a road, his invalids might stagger down to Fort Western, where they would at least be out of his way. Meanwhile he had but four weeks' bread and one barrel of rum left in his storehouse. He had been down in person to Fort Western and procured some leather and two shoemakers, but the ice on the river had been so treacherous that he was hardly able to make the fort.

Shirley, whose intentions were good, replied soothingly to this catalog of distress and sent up a sloop of supplies. Shoes, blankets, bedding, stockings, and provisions of all sorts had to be dragged on hand sleds up the river to Fort Western and carried up from there on the shoulders of the men of the independent companies. The fort was relieved, but Lithgow now began to press for alterations in the spring. Either it must be rebuilt completely, he declared, or a wall must be erected between it and the hill which commanded it, consisting of two walls of timber with a core of earth in between. In any case, the whole shape of the fort must be changed, and he needed four hundred and fifty tons of timber, forty or fifty thousand shingles, and forty thousand bricks or equivalent stone, together with oxen for hauling and hay to feed them.

The governor, still conciliatory, promised timber and help, adding that he had four flat-bottomed boats armed with swivel guns ready for bringing up stores, and had ordered two more. In view of Shirley's previous record for inefficiency, it is not surprising to find that though Lithgow needed eight such boats, only four arrived, two of which though specially built were too large to be used on the river. However, the required fortifications, together with storehouse and officers' quarters, were somehow completed that summer. By the end of the second winter, Governor Shirley was actually raising the possibility of a small expedition based on Fort Halifax against the French settlements along the Chaudière.

While Fort Halifax was undergoing these privations, James Howard in the Company's Fort Western had a garrison of only twenty men and no difficulties of supply. He, too, was afraid of the French and anxious for cannon, but his chief fear was that the Indians would cut off a convoy to Fort Halifax and leave him short of men. He pointed out that they could easily secrete themselves in a gully no more than a hundred and fifty yards from the fort, whence they could watch what went on and intercept any party sent out. This never happened, however, and the superior strength of Fort Western was sufficient to defend its stores in spite of its tiny garrison.

Forts Western and Halifax served their purpose in protecting the settlements lower on the river from any large-scale attack. Indian demonstrations were confined to burning a few houses on the outskirts of Frankfort, and on the whole the French and Indian War passed the Kennebec by. The forts never did become jumping-off places for an expedition against Quebec, and the only indication that such a route to Canada was used lies in a story told by Silvester of a notable service he rendered to the British government. Wolfe being before young man's misfortune, rode directly to the neighbours, who very expeditiously rose and drew him up. He was presently put to bed, and is now perfectly recovered.   *Attested by us,*

     John Hart,   *Robert Sherwood,*
     Wm Wise,   *John Sherwood.*

Plan of Fort HALLIFAX.

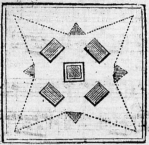

THE above fort was built under the direction of *Wm Shirley,* governor of *New England.* It is situated on a fork or point of land formed by the meeting of the rivers *Kennebeck* and *Sebastoocook,* the latter of which empties itself into the former, at the distance of about 3 quarters of a mile from the falls at *Taconnet.*—This spot is 37 miles higher up the river *Kennebeck* than the old fort at *Richmond,* which old fort is about two miles above *Swan* island, on the West side of the river, and about the same distance below fort *Frankfort,* built on

Plan of Fort FRANCKFORT.

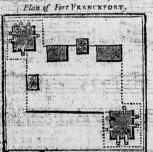

the opposite shore; the last of which is not less than 24 miles from the entrance of *Kennebeck* bay, and both upon the *Plymouth* company, who have the possession of this northermost boundary of the province of *Massachuset's* bay. So that the whole computed distance of this new fort from the *Kennebeck's* mouth is about 61 miles, the utmost extent, to which it was

adviseable or safe to carry a fort up that river, at first, as it is not quite 50 miles from *Penobscot,* and but 31 from *Norridgwalk* by water, and 22 by land.

The only known communication which the *Penobscots* have with the river *Kennebeck* and *Norridgwalk Indians* inhabiting it, is thro' the river *Sebastoocook,* by means of a carrying place which they cross within half a mile of *Taconnet* falls; and their most convenient passage from *Penobscot* to *Quebec* is thro' *Kennebec* to the river *Chaudiere.*

But as the river *Kennebeck* is not navigable for sloops beyond *Cushenock,* that is, about 43 miles high, and the navigation between that and *Taconnet,* being 18 miles, is, for much the greatest part of it, so incumbered with shoals and rocks, and strong currents occasioned by frequent falls, that the transportation of bulky and heavy stores appeared impracticabe, till a house of hewn timber, ten inches thick, 100 feet long, 32 wide, and 16 high, for the reception of the provinces stores, with conveniencies for lodging soldiers, picketted in at 30 feet distance from every part of the house, with a block house of 24 feet square at two of the opposite angles, mounted with four cannon, was built at *Cushenock,* which will not only serve to lodge the public stores, but add to the defence and protection of the river, and greatly encourage settlements upon it : And to make it still more beneficial a road of communication between *Cushenock* and *Taconnet* has been cleared for wheel carriages, whereby the transportation of stores by land from fort *Western* at the former, to fort *Halifax* at the latter, in the space of one day, will be rendered practicable, and the want of a convenient carriage by water supply'd

Plan of Fort WESTERN, *built in* 1754.

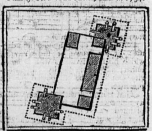

Fort *Hallifax* is capable of entertaining 400 men ; and when garrisoned with a hundred, is of sufficient strength to withstand any assault, which may be reasonably expected to be made upon it, either by *Indians* or *French* with small arms. And upon considering the difficulty which the *French* must have to transport cannon or mortars by land to attack it, there is but little danger of their attempting to do that soon ; and there is no doubt but it will effectually answer the service for which it is designed, in every respect.

PLANS OF THE Forts on the Kennebec River from the *Gentleman's Magazine* (London, 1755). The accompanying text describes the readiness of the forts to withstand assaults "either by Indians or French with small arms." MAINE HISTORIC PRESERVATION COMMISSION.

Quebec, an urgent express for him arrived in Boston from General Amherst. Silvester took one messenger on board his vessel and had reached the mouth of the Kennebec in sixteen hours. Arrived there, he went up to Fort Western and got Captain Howard to send his son, the only man who knew the Indian route, to take the messenger up river and across to Quebec by way of the Chaudière. Silvester gave them a letter to Captain Lithgow, who of course knew him well, requesting him to furnish supplies for the pair from the stores at Fort Halifax. This messenger was the only one of three to reach General Wolfe and was, Silvester maintained, instrumental in bringing him victory. Whether this be true or not, such promptitude and efficiency are characteristic. As for the use of the route, only one year later an English officer of engineers named Montresor did undoubtedly come down to Fort Halifax from Quebec by going up the Chaudière and across to Moosehead Lake, and then returned to Quebec along the Dead River. Both routes were passable to canoes, he declares, though there were beaver dams, in one case as much as ten feet high, and many falls. Montresor had Indian guides, of course, but so must Howard and the messenger have done; and at this late stage of the war it is possible that they would not have been molested. In any case, after the conquest of Quebec, the work of the two forts was really over. In 1762, the combined forces of both of them in government pay consisted of one lieutenant, one armorer, two sergeants, and thirteen privates.

WITH THE DESTRUCTION of French power in Canada, the Indian menace rapidly diminished and the way was open for a peaceful development of the lands of the Plymouth Company. There was one more raid in 1762, when Ezra Davis near the Eastern River heard a scream from his little son Thaddeus, followed by an Indian warwhoop. Rushing to the door of his house, Davis tried to close it, but not before a shot had been fired which killed his mother-in-law, who was lying sick in bed. About seven Indians attacked the door with their tomahawks, but disconcerted by Davis's stout resistance, they soon retreated, taking with them the eight-year-old Thaddeus, who was never heard of again.

This tragic episode was the last flare-up on the Kennebec. Decimated by war and disease, the Abenakis had in a short time sunk into insignificance. Jacob Bailey, the clergyman at Frankfort, declares a few years later that the Norridgewocks had only about fifty warriors left all told. They used to come down to the seashore at a certain season to feast on shellfish; but though this gathering was a tribal custom, Bailey thought it worth recording that in the preceding summer he saw as many as thirty of them at one time. Bailey made some effort to teach them, but was repulsed, and it is fair to say that neither he nor his fellow colonists showed the sympathetic understanding of Father Râle. Râle describes with much appreciation their fine, white teeth, black and white shell beads, and long, loose, red and blue mantles. His successor, Bailey, is content to dismiss them as "very savage in their Dress and Manners." He adds with some asperity: "They have a great Aversion to the *English* nation, chiefly owing to the Influence of Roman Catholic Missionaries, who instead of endeavoring to reform their Morals, comply with them in their most extravagant Vices, and teach them that nothing is necessary to salvation, but to believe in the Name of *Christ*, to acknowledge the Pope, his holy Vicar, and to extirpate the English, because they cruelly murdered the Saviour of Mankind."

$\mathcal{F}$ACTIONS IN
POWNALBOROUGH

IN 1760 WHEN THE British were at last in possession of Canada, a sloop with twelve passengers set out from Falmouth at that very season of the year when the small New Plymouth shallop had first gone adventuring down the coast of Maine. It beat up the same narrow channel past Arrowsic, lately incorporated into Georgetown, and ran through Long Reach on the incoming tide while a few scattered maple branches on the headlands were beginning to turn red. Across Merrymeeting Bay lay the Kennebec Purchase, comprising Swan Island, the Eastern River settlement, and the wilderness above. In Frankfort, a few log cabins were giving way to clapboard, while the stout buildings of Fort Shirley, garrisoned no longer, were to be converted into a jail. The township had been enormously enlarged, and it now ran eight miles up the river bank and clear east to a settlement on the Sheepscot, so that the eighty families by the Eastern River formed little more than half of its inhabitants all told. Out of compliment to the governor it had been rechristened Pownalborough and was to be the shire town of a new county, Lincoln. Above Pownalborough lay Gardinerston, extending five miles along both banks of the Kennebec through unbroken forests of magnificent hemlock, oak, or pine. One the western side, the Cobbossee Contee Stream foamed down from the hills to form a little inlet in the narrow, fertile plain through which the Kennebec runs.

The Falmouth sloop turned in by the Cobbossee to anchor, and the eight men among the passengers took axes and prepared to go ashore. As the leaves fell, four little huts, unfloored and propped on logs, were being hastily roofed with strips of spruce bark secured by long poles strongly fastened down. Each had a blank hole for the doorway, and at least one other not so much for air as for the escape of smoke. The women and the two six-year-olds, Thaddeus Davis and Sarah Winslow, might stop up cracks or pile boughs against the outside to keep out wind and snow where the ground was so uneven that there was space between the bottom logs and the earthen floor. Branches or reeds must be cut for bedding, and the stores or simple treasures disembarked.

There was plenty of firewood that winter for the hauling, not only green logs, but the uncollected windfalls of generations as well. The smoky little huts were warm enough, but dirty and crowded. The women must have welcomed signs of spring in the chilly floods of melted snow, a sharp snapping of ice in the river, and the melancholy hooting of wild geese in the dark. Spring came, and presently dried out as woodcutting went steadily on. Soon *The Kennebec* might be expected with Dr. Gardiner and a fresh store of provisions. Down by the Cobbossee the men were at work on a dam.

This township by the Cobbossee Contee had long been recognized as one of the best sites for development that the Plymouth Company owned. In the early days of Frankfort, when the Company had optimistically hoped for two hundred families in that settlement by the end of the first two years, it had not seemed unreasonable to insist that Ephraim Jones plant one hundred by the Cobbossee within three years as a condi-

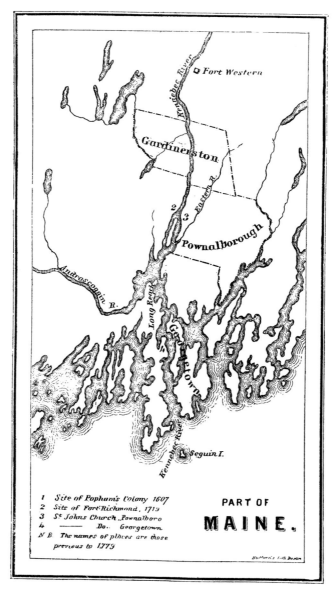

MAP SHOWING boundaries of Gardinerston and
Pownalborough on the Kennebec River prior to 1779.
BARTLETT'S *FRONTIER MISSIONARY*.

tion of his grant. As the difficulties of the Frankfort settlement became more obvious, and even a sawmill by the Eastern River could not be constructed till 1754, Jones and his partners abandoned their undertaking in pure despair. Indian troubles were brewing, and until Fort Richmond could be moved, it was useless to ask settlers to venture so far upstream. The Company made a few more offers of the territory to various people, still insisting on a hundred settlers, and was steadily refused. In 1754, however, when Dr. Gardiner was approached by Shirley on the matter of building Fort Halifax, he immediately perceived the advantage this would be to peaceful developments on the river. Though war was about to break out, Silvester persuaded the Company to grant him twenty-one thousand acres on the banks of the Cobbossee as part of his share in future divisions of the Company's land.

SILVESTER'S PROCEEDINGS in developing his township were very different from those of the Company in settling Frankfort. Instead of collecting a miscellaneous group of European exiles unused to the climate and inexperienced as wilderness pioneers, Silvester had selected two New England millwrights, a wheelwright, a carpenter, and four other men. He sent this small body up to the Cobbossee to work for him on wages, with the option of settling on the land there if they liked. They were to stay a year at least, cut logs, dam the Cobbossee, and erect a grist mill for the benefit of future settlers. The Great House was also to be built, not as a fort, but as an inn where Dr. Gardiner and William could stay, with a surveyor, and any other person who had business in those parts. For the establishment of such a nucleus, Silvester was prepared to pay in cash and supplies, or else in land. James Winslow, the wheelwright, got ninety acres of good land across the river which had been cleared after some fashion by the Indians. He raised a shack for his family and went off to work at his trade on some mills being erected down the coast near Damariscotta. Mrs. Winslow and little Sally rowed over the river day after day for manure from the Great House farmer, dressed their land, sowed it, and together harvested some forty bushels of corn.

Once the mill and the Great House were up in Gardinerston, Silvester began to offer lots of five to ten acres near the mill and the river, and to lend money for supplies and buildings on the security of the land. This policy attracted plenty of settlers and worked well enough with industrious people like the Winslows. More shiftless families failed to repay Silvester, who in time repossessed their land. In fact, so often did this happen that only eleven families in the township owned a clear title when Silvester's grandson and heir came of age in 1803. Naturally the land had been cleared after a fashion, and those that were turned off did not fail to complain that the value of their improvements had passed into the Doctor's hands. Since they made no effort to replace valuable timber, or the provisions and tools Silvester had supplied them on credit, this exchange was by no means totally unfair. Still, Silvester was never entirely popular in Gardinerston, where his enemies could slander him behind his back all year while he only came down for a month or two in the summers. Meanwhile, the settlement grew fast, and in little more than three years after the first arrivals, a hundred and eighty people were busily establishing themselves.

Experiences in supplying Frankfort had taught Silvester that a pioneer settlement was far from self-supporting, and that to buy necessities, it must develop trade. How much more clearly he saw this than his partners may be illustrated by the fact that his grist mill was the highest one up the river for more than twenty years, and settlers from thirty miles above at Norridgewock were forced to bring their corn down river in canoes to get it ground. Not content with this achievement, Silvester went on building, and in a few years he had completed two sawmills, a fulling mill for cloth, a potash works, a wharf, a store,

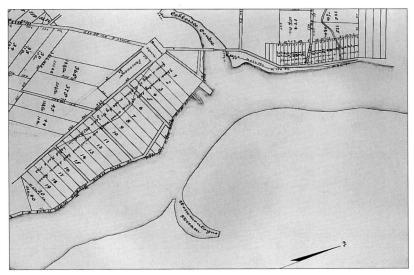

DETAIL FROM the Solomon Adams Survey of Gardiner, in 1808, which incorporates the earlier survey of lots in downtown Gardiner by John McKecknie in 1763 for Dr. Gardiner. The 1763 survey has been lost. CITY OF GARDINER.

POST OFFICE built in 1763 by Dr. Gardiner at the foot of Vine Street in Gardiner. It was demolished in 1882.

HANSON'S *HISTORY OF GARDINER.*

and a few small frame houses in the town. Little wonder that by 1764 several vessels were loaded in the river for Europe, besides *The Kennebec* and other coasters which were carrying on the Boston trade.

The Kennebec Purchase land was filling up, and to encourage settlers the proprietors announced themselves ready to grant away one-third of their best land along the river, and the whole of the outermost section, ten to fifteen miles from the stream. Meanwhile they made a number of divisions among themselves, in which Silvester acquired land across from the Cobbossee, and north and west of the piece by the stream which he already owned. His chief interests were thus in Gardinerston, but he also took two-thirds of Swan Island, four hundred acres in Pownalborough, and several tracts elsewhere. His policy in such a case was to clear a farm, build a house himself, and establish a tenant. Eventually half a dozen two-story clapboard structures with long roofs sloping to a single story behind were scattered from the very edge of Merrymeeting

HOUSE BUILT on Swan Island between Dresden and Richmond by Dr. Gardiner and inherited by his Dumaresq descendants. MAINE HISTORIC PRESERVATION COMMISSION.

Bay to the banks of the Cobbossee. All in all, Silvester owned about a hundred thousand acres, on every part of which he left some evidence of his improving hand.

IT WOULD BE A MISTAKE to suppose that Silvester looked on the Kennebec as a place from which he hoped to squeeze a fortune without regard to the welfare of the settlers of his land. One of his most pressing concerns had been to establish a minister among the people of Frankfort, who though religious refugees in the beginning, seemed likely to sink in a few years to an almost savage illiteracy and ignorance of those very beliefs for which their forefathers had left their homes. Pownalborough, though now eight years old, was for the most part miserably poor. Log cabins seven feet high and generally without chimneys were still the usual habitations. Children went shoeless and half clad, even in winter, and slept on heaps of straw. In spite of the abundance of salmon, wild duck, and other game at various seasons, whole families lived on roasted potatoes for months on end. If these failed, they took to dried moose meat or actually wandered down to the mouth of the river as soon as the ice broke up, to camp there living on clams and ready to swarm aboard the first coaster of the season and beg for supplies. Part of this distress was due to the load of debt with which the settlers had started, part to the war which had consumed both stores and energies, and much to the high price of those articles which the settlers did not produce for themselves. A pair of shoes, for instance, cost fifteen dollars, or in the local currency three thousand feet of boards. Butter for those who owned no cows was two hundred and fifty feet of boards a pound. Even game meant the expense of powder and shot, while farming and logging demanded tools. Small wonder that the Frankfort colonists were poor, and that numbers of them had lost courage and sunk to shiftlessness, squandering what little they had on the settler's only pleasure, rum.

Rum was the curse of the Maine settlements, not only because it was a cheap pleasure, but because a stimulant of some kind was really called for by the intense physical discomforts under which the settlers had to live. Wood must be chopped at twenty degrees below zero or hauled through five or six feet of snow. Plowing, planting, and hoeing were made intolerable by swarms of black flies and mosquitoes from the undrained forest swamps. Loads must be carried on men's backs over pathways where the use of wheeled carts was quite impossible. Rocks and tree stumps encumbered the little clearings. Such daily demands on physical strength produced a craving for liquor, which led in many cases to habitual drunkenness. Rum was cheap and was so universal a drink in this part of the province that wages now and for many years later were partly paid in it. For instance, in 1742 when Fort Richmond was being strengthened, the laborers working on it were paid in cash and some supplies, including rum. To less than a quart of milk, each man consumed two mugs of flip and two shillings and eightpence worth of straight rum.

I N SUCH CONDITIONS as these, many Frankfort settlers, though respectable people at the start, had ceased to give their children any kind of education in letters, morals, or religion. Those who felt their degradation were perfectly aware that the community could not support a minister either then or for many years to come. Meanwhile, the Jesuits, who were still active on the Kennebec both before and after the French and Indian War, had been making efforts to entice the people away from Frankfort to their own centers of influence and had alarmed some settlers of Huguenot ancestry who were strongly anti-Catholic. In this situation, Frankfort and Georgetown, though twenty miles apart, were induced to petition the Society for the Propagation of the Gospel to send them a missionary between them. Silvester Gardiner was active in persuading the Lutherans that the Church of England was very similar to their own persuasion, as indeed in many respects it was. The Frankfort settlers, who could not read English, were unable to satisfy themselves about doctrinal points as they would have wished. Some, however, had consulted their ministers before leaving Germany and had been advised to attend the Church of England services if it were possible. In the upshot, Frankfort and Georgetown did address a petition to the Society for the Propagation of the Gospel in 1754, and it was granted. Owing, however, to the difficulties of the scattered mission, it was impossible at first to get a clergyman to stay. Not until 1760 was Pownalborough fortunate enough to receive a missionary of indomitable spirit whose work in the Kennebec continued for nineteen years.

Silvester and Major Goodwin had first propounded this arrangement and talked with the Frankfort leaders into acceptance of the English church. Both were prepared to contribute towards the establishment of a clergyman. Major Goodwin took him into his house. Silvester later set him up in the abandoned Fort Richmond, and finally induced the proprietors, some of whom were unwilling, to grant land for a church and parsonage house. He got up a subscription in Boston to help with the building, and contributed liberally towards the fund himself. He even had a well-known sermon on the English prayerbook printed at his own expense and distributed to such parishioners as were troubled with theological doubts. Major Goodwin and the younger Hallowells were Episcopalians, but other proprietors were hostile or indifferent, and on the Kennebec the parson was always considered peculiarly Silvester's creature. Dr. Gardiner had even discovered him, a young man named Jacob Bailey, educated at Harvard and already licensed as a Congregational minister, but becoming interested in the Anglican faith. Silvester, attracted by his situation, lent Bailey theological works and learned to appreciate something of the young man's unusual quality. He introduced him to Henry Caner, rector of King's Chapel, and got up a subscription to pay his expenses to England when he decided on ordination. About Christmas, 1759, when Bailey came down to Boston to collect letters of recommendation before departing for England on this errand, Silvester was very ill, and could not see him. "I perceived, however," declared the young man, "that the Dr. took notice of my affairs in the intervals of his disorder." All was arranged through the young James Gardiner, and Bailey embarked on an armed ship for England with letters to various bishops and to the Society for the Propagation of the Gospel.

JACOB BAILEY was born in 1731 in the settlement of Rowley, Massachusetts, a small Puritan community which was narrow, bigoted, and backward. Anyone who knew more than his neighbors, or set out to be more virtuous or more polite, was either shunned as odd or branded with the names of hypocrite and upstart. Recreations were confined to "training night" and "lecture night," each followed by mugs of flip at the tavern. "Every man," says Bailey, "planted as many acres of Indian corn, and sowed the same number with rye; he plowed with as many oxen, hoed it as often, and gathered in his crop on the same day as his grandfather. With regard to his family, he salted down the same quantity of beef and pork, wore the same kind of stockings, and at table, sat and said grace with his wife and children around him, just as his predecessors had done before him."

In such a society the lot of a boy like Jacob Bailey who had an insatiable thirst for knowledge, was extremely hard. He felt himself so conspicuous that he was actually afraid to walk down the street in broad daylight, while if he saw a woman coming, he either climbed a fence or ducked behind the nearest bush to crouch there trembling until the dreadful creature had passed by. From his earliest years he was busy from dawn to dark on

THE REVEREND JACOB BAILEY (1731–1818), rector of
St. John's Church in Pownalborough, now Dresden.
BARTLETT'S *FRONTIER MISSIONARY.*

his father's farm and got little education, but his ambition was so compelling that he trained himself to snatch an hour from his sleep every evening in order to do some studying. He had few books, if any, and was forced to take up his time in writing on any subject that he could find. By the time that he was ten years old, he had composed in this way what he later imagined would have been enough to fill several volumes. A curious visitor then happened to pick up one of his scattered pieces of paper and took it to the minister, who in his turn was sufficiently interested to go and pay the author a visit. "I esteemed our minister, in that day," says Jacob, "such a great man, that thousands would not have tempted me to come into his presence." The minister had to be content with talking to the boy's father, whom he actually persuaded to let Jacob come to him for free lessons. Poor Jacob crept out of the house after a sleepless night and made his way over to the minister's. In spite of his burning desire for knowledge, he had to walk backwards and forwards about ten times before he could summon the courage to go up to the door. Here his heart failed him again, but fortunately he perceived that one of the neighboring girls was staring at him, and concluding the minister was the lesser of two evils, he hastily entered.

After this unpromising start, young Bailey never looked back, and by the age of twenty he had gained enough knowledge and self-possession not merely to enter Harvard, but to recommend himself to a number of people, including Sir William Pepperell and the Wentworths, who were asked to contribute small sums for his support in college. For some years after his graduation in 1755, he earned his living by teaching school and was licensed as a Congregational preacher. In 1758 he was taken by some friends to an Episcopal service in Portsmouth, and was immediately interested. In fact, he says he should have fallen asleep from the heat and the fatigues of his journey, had not the novelty of the service kept him awake. That very same evening he had a long discussion with his hostess about church ceremonies. In less than two years he was on his way back from England with Episcopal ordination and his appointment as missionary to the church at Pownalborough in his pocket.

In person Jacob Bailey was below middle height and considered himself a weakling, though his hardy upbringing and incessant activity suggest that he did not lack endurance. His features in the only profile we have left of him are chiefly remarkable for a large nose and an extremely obstinate chin. His sermons were rational, rather than fervent, but there is no doubt that his convictions, even his prejudices, went very deep. As a representative of Silvester on the Kennebec, his resemblance to his patron was almost too strong. Less irascible, but equally persistent, he was, like Silvester, very much a partisan. The good that he did in Pownalborough was enormous, but he lacked the faculty of appreciating virtues in the opposition. Thus it is hard to say whether the feeling against Silvester on the Kennebec was heightened by the conduct of Bailey, or whether opponents of Bailey were inspired purely by hatred of Silvester. To some extent both men were caught up by forces beyond their control which from the very close of the French and Indian War were beginning to lead the country towards revolution.

IT WAS FORTUNATE that Jacob Bailey was young and energetic, since a less persistent man might easily have despaired about the state of the Pownalborough mission. Among the settlers there were Christians of eight different denominations, many of whom had not been baptized, could not read or write, and had the haziest notions of Christine doctrine. Such people had no decent clothes to come to church in, and partly for that reason, but mostly out of sheer idleness, were unwilling to make the effort. The parish was scattered, and there was no church building. Services were held on the upper floor of the new courthouse, which overlooked the river and was convenient for Frankfort settlers, but at the extreme end of the township from those by the Sheepscot. There was no parsonage house, and though Goodwin took Bailey as his guest for a while, at the end of his first year, he married and needed a residence of his own. As a temporary measure, Silvester then established him in Fort Richmond, which besides being dilapidated was on the opposite side of the river from the courthouse and the whole of his parish.

These difficulties in Pownalborough itself were bad enough, but they were as nothing to the discomforts endured to carry on services twenty miles down the river in Georgetown. Every third Sunday, Bailey undertook this journey by canoe and on foot, encumbered by his books and his habit, and often alone. Once late in November, after paddling for eight hours down the river without anything to eat or drink, he was forced ashore by a severe thunderstorm and had to spend the night in the woods. At other times, he had to make his way through snow several feet deep, or was tormented by heat and maddened by armies of flies and mosquitoes. When at length a separate mission was established at Georgetown, new demands on Bailey's strength were made by the growing settlements on the Cobbossee and around Fort Western. Bailey considered Gardinerston a settlement of bigots and strong anti-churchmen, but this did not prevent him from approving enthusiastically Silvester's plan for building a church there and endowing it for the benefit of the ungrateful people.

In a couple of years the whole moral tone of the Pownal-borough settlement had begun to be different. The Society had sent out Bibles for those who could read, catechisms for instruction, and prayer books. The tract issued by Silvester was also in common use. Bailey had started a free school for the children, but found that few lived near enough or could be spared from their work by their parents. When he moved over the river to Richmond, he was obliged to his regret to drop the whole project. However, he soon had fifty communicants and wrote to the Society that it gave him great satisfaction to find "Industry, Morality and Religion, flourishing among a People, till, of late, abandoned to Disorder, Vice, and Profaneness."

ONE OF THE MOST attractive qualities about Bailey was the way in which he rapidly identified himself with the Kennebec and began to talk of Pownalborough as home, not with despair, but with pride. The violent extremes of climate, he said, made people more lively than in the rest of New England, and he loved to boast of their improvements. The banks of the river, he wrote, began to present a most beautiful mixture of contrasting scenes as shipbuilding multiplied, wharves were constructed, and vessels were loaded. On shore one might perceive a gloomy forest "with all its native horror" broken up with clearings green with grass and corn, or beautified by an increasing number of "commodious dwellings." To these attractions he himself made one valuable contribution. His garden, first at Fort Richmond, and later at the parsonage house, was the envy and wonder of the entire neighborhood. Every kind of fruit or vegetable commonly grown in New England was tried out there. His flower garden, which was bright and pretty from the time of the earliest crocus to the latest, hardiest aster, was an attractive example of that pride in appearances which the miserable settlers needed to relearn.

THE PARSONAGE in Pownalborough, now Dresden, where the Reverend Jacob Bailey resided and planted his famous gardens. BARTLETT'S *FRONTIER MISSIONARY*.

For all these reasons Bailey was popular with his congregation, though he had little material support from them to add to the fifty pounds a year granted by the Society. However, they did their best. One year when the parson lost twenty sheep by the wolves and his horse and winter provision by bad weather, they set up a subscription to help him. It was not their fault that his desk was rifled while he was away in Georgetown and the whole result of their effort destroyed. For the building of a church and parsonage house they mainly relied on the energy of Doctor Gardiner, who procured them a hundred acres of land from the proprietors, provided a model and plan of the church for discussion with the vestry, solicited subscriptions in Boston, set up nails, and hired two carpenters for seventeen pounds thirteen shillings and four pence, half a quintal of fish, half a hundredweight of bread, six pounds of butter, and, sad to relate, five gallons of rum.

While all these improvements were going on in Pownalborough, it would be a mistake to attribute them entirely to Bailey's influence. Most were due to the peace and to the judicious encouragement given by the proprietors to industry. For instance, in 1760 Jacob Bailey's brother was proposing to come to Pownalborough and establish a brickmaking business. Silvester immediately saw him, discussed prices, and promised him all the assistance he could, writing enthusiastically to Jacob that six hands constantly employed could not make enough bricks for the Kennebec's needs in the following year. In a few years Pownalborough was even prosperous enough to have acquired a schoolmaster, George Lilly, who built himself a one-story log house out of the timbers of the old Fort Shirley. This had no cellar, but was floored, had a fireplace, and contained no less than twelve panes of glass in its windows. The town was not able to afford contributions for the assistance of Lilly, who taught the children of the poorest free. Not very much later, Pownalborough could boast a doctor, though it must be admitted that Robert Taggart was a farmer in his spare time and that his training does not seem to have been scientific. His unfailing remedy in difficult cases was to flay a black cat and wrap its reeking skin about the unhappy patient.

Such increasing indications of wealth were due in part to the peace and in part to a very radical change in the character of the town. Pownalborough in 1760 had become the shire town of a very large county whose population was growing rapidly. This brought not only a courthouse and sessions, but resident lawyers. Bailey, in fact, was not the only educated man in Pownalborough besides Major Goodwin. Two or three other people who arrived at about the same time were equally ready to assume leadership, but in a very different fashion.

B Y FAR THE MOST interesting character among the Pownalborough lawyers was a Harvard classmate of Bailey's named Jonathan Bowman, a nephew of Thomas Hancock and his agent in the Kennebec territory. When court officers were being appointed for the new county, Bowman was a candidate for registrar, but was opposed by a group of the Plymouth Company proprietors headed by Silvester, who was anxious to secure a man with Episcopal connections. To his disappointment the Hancocks were successful, and Bowman duly became registrar and clerk of the courts for Lincoln County. He settled in Pownalborough, built himself a comfortable frame house, and employed a sloop in trade with the West Indies to supplement his income as a lawyer. Presently he became one of the largest employers of labor in the settlement and a lawyer with whom it paid to be on good terms. Though it seems unlikely in view of his character that he forgot Silvester's opposition or was unaware that this had in the first place been prompted by Bailey, he was far too prudent to engage in a hasty quarrel to the detriment of his business. It was to his interest to buy boards from Silvester in exchange for a cargo of West Indian sugar or molasses, to make some attempt to join Bailey's congregation, and in general to adapt himself to the position of things around him. Such considerations had less weight with Silvester, who was willing enough to do business, but whose real interests could not restrain him from rushing into a dispute with the entire Hancock connection.

By 1760 the boundaries of the Kennebec Purchase had been more or less clearly defined, but there still remained some disputed areas, notably in Georgetown and on the Sheepscot. In addition, there was a good deal of confusion existing inside the boundaries of the Purchase as a result of hasty surveys, destruction of boundary marks as the land was cleared, and the rapid shift of population. In the frequent lawsuits that arose in these years, Silvester was invaluable to the Plymouth Company. His pugnacity, his persistence, and the wide experience of legal proceedings he had gained from his trading ventures soon

RESIDENCE OF Jonathan Bowman, attorney and opponent
of the Reverend Jacob Bailey. In 1762 Bowman
commissioned Gershom Flagg to build this Georgian-
style house in Pownalborough, now Dresden.
MAINE HISTORIC PRESERVATION COMMISSION.

made him the champion of the Plymouth Company's interests on every occasion. Silvester enjoyed a noisy quarrel with plenty of discussion and abuse, in which any trick was good enough as long as it was legal, and any argument was fair in support of a cause he knew was just. This sort of thing was all very well while the Plymouth Company acted as a body, but the moment it began to divide lands among its own members, Silvester's methods were bound to cause trouble. Meanwhile, the death of Thomas Hancock in 1764 removed a colleague whom Silvester could not fail to respect and left his affairs in the hands of young John, whose vain, touchy disposition was offensive to an older man and whose abilities had not yet been proved to the world in general. In 1765, Silvester opened fire on the Hancocks by forbidding two men to cut hay on land that they had received from Thomas, and by later entering into a lawsuit with John over its possession. Four years later he tried to evict someone else from land bought from John Hancock which he claimed as his own. It would not be fair to suggest that Silvester did not necessarily have right on his side in such disputes, but it is at least relevant to point out that the Hancocks were only one of three groups of proprietors with whom he quarreled. Moreover the last case actually concerned the Hallowells, his own daughter's relatives by marriage.

This breach with John Hancock over a few fields marked for Silvester, though he did not know it, the end of his undisputed power in the Kennebec Purchase. Jonathan Bowman was a formidable enemy, the more so because he was the exact opposite of Silvester in every way. In person he was tall, spare and impressive, with commanding features. He dressed in black with neat silk stockings and shining buckles, said little in company, but coolly demanded deference from others, and usually got it. He was a man more feared than loved, cautious, intriguing, and once offended, quite implacable. He began his campaign against Silvester by trying to undermine the cause which he had most at heart, the power of the Episcopal church in Pownalborough.

In justice to Jonathan Bowman it may be said that his opposition to Jacob Bailey was not solely inspired by malice. When a few educated New England lawyers took up their residence in Pownalborough and found that the Episcopal church service was the only one performed in the entire area, none of them liked it, but each in his own fashion made the best of a bad situation. Charles Cushing, the sheriff, who was another classmate of Bailey's at Harvard, swallowed his prejudices and even became a church warden, reasoning that any form of religion in Pownalborough was better than none. Bowman's attitude was more uncompromising, but his wife was an earnest member of Bailey's congregation, and he did occasionally make some effort to attend the services. Here, however, his snorts of indignation at various parts of the ritual offended Bailey, who felt that he was trying to make the women giggle. For a few years he contented himself with such demonstrations, and with putting into the collection soap, scraps of paper, news letters, or playing cards instead of money. Once he got hold of some of the Common Prayer Books and erased a few sentences in the service which he considered contrary to Scripture. All this was annoying, and perhaps ungentlemanly, but some sympathy must be felt for Bowman when it is considered that very few of the congregation had been brought up as Anglicans, and that he saw them being converted by force of circumstances to a worship that he considered blasphemous or silly.

After Silvester's quarrel with the Hancocks, Bowman's persecution of Jacob Bailey became increasingly virulent and personal. One of his first acts was to convince Charles Cushing, over whom he had much influence, that it was better to drive Bailey from the parish than to compromise with him. Accordingly, the two made common cause, and commenced an active persecution. Large droves of cattle began to break down

Bailey's fences and trample his garden. It was at this time that Bailey's desk was rifled while he was at Georgetown, and the subscription list got up by his grateful parishioners was abstracted and published with invidious comments. As a result, the parson felt obliged to forego the money, though it was in fact no more than his due. Great efforts were made to prevent people from going to church. Bowman forbade his own servants to do so and employed a mixture of persuasion and threats on other people. When Bailey lived on the western side of the river, people detained every boat they could to prevent him getting over to church. One Easter a gang broke two locks to get at his canoe and carry it off, supposing it the only one fit to launch on his side of the river. These acts did not deter Jacob Bailey, who was fully as obstinate, sustained by a clear conscience, and in possession of one great advantage. He was still the only clergyman in the town, and likely to remain so, since it was only the fifty pounds granted by the Society which enabled the people to support a missionary at all.

In these circumstances, it is not surprising that it took Silvester a number of years to persuade the proprietors to grant a hundred-acre lot for church and glebe. His persistence was finally rewarded, however, and in 1769 it became obvious that unless the opposition took immediate steps, a church and parsonage house would very shortly be built. Bowman countered by getting up a petition for a grant of land for a Congregational church, which he persuaded quite a number of people to sign. Bailey exposed his methods by remarking that eighteen of the signatories had actually petitioned the Society for the Propagation of the Gospel for a missionary in 1754, four were church communicants, and twenty-four owned no lands and had been bullied into signing because they were either servants or dependent on charity. The number of churchmen who signed this paper is evident that Bowman had made a systematic attempt to tamper with Bailey's congregation. In fact, he approached the Lutherans and tried to persuade them that the beliefs of the English church were not as close to their own as those of the Congregationalists. Since these people were still unable to read theology in English, they were quite at a loss on being asked to choose between Bowman's and Bailey's versions of what the doctrines of the Church of England actually were. Bailey had to send an innkeeper named Francis Rittal, who was one of their leaders, up to discuss the matter with the rector of Trinity Church in Boston, whose word on the subject the congregation was induced to accept. This result somewhat nullified the petition of Bowman, who nevertheless persuaded John Hancock to offer some land and was busy soliciting subscriptions, being evidently of the opinion that every penny he received for a Congregational chapel was a penny less for the church project. How little he was in earnest, and how impossible it was to establish a minister may be seen from the fact that it was twenty-two years after Bailey left before the town could afford to do so, and that then it only succeeded by taxing all residents, irrespective of denomination.

Silvester Gardiner was aware of Bowman's attacks on the church in Pownalborough, but as long as they were theological or personal, he was content to leave the controversy in Jacob Bailey's hands. Bailey, though not such an eager fighter as the doctor, had plenty of spirit and defended himself voluminously in sermons or letters, not scrupling to describe his troubles as due to "the merciless rage," as he would "presume" to say, "of the vilest miscreants on earth." Suddenly, however, Silvester was drawn into the quarrel by a move of Bowman's which must have given that astute lawyer intense satisfaction. Bowman became aware that a small part of the land granted to the church by the Plymouth Company had been claimed under a will of which Major Goodwin was executor, and that the disputed corner actually included the ground on which the church and parsonage house were to be built. Somehow he persuaded

Goodwin to let him handle this situation, and once he had obtained a right to act, he waited until the church and parsonage house were completed, and then entered suit. He won his case, and informed Bailey that unless he were paid the value of the land in cash, he intended to take possession immediately.

Poor Bailey wrote off in haste to Silvester for guidance, who replied that it was an "infamous falsehood" to suggest that he was going to be turned out by force. "Your enemies know your weak side," he wrote most unfairly, "and throw out these things on purpose to plague and worry you. If you would take no notice of them, but treat them with the contempt they deserve they would leave off." To these unsympathetic suggestions, he added the advice that Bailey should do nothing at all, but that if an execution were served on him, he should go into the lodgings with his family, leaving all his possessions behind him. "They and all their coadjutors can never make the land … a part of Maj. Goodwin's estate, more than they can prove the same to be green cheese." He therefore begged to hear no more about the affair until Bailey was carried out of the house by the sheriff, in which case he would of course see justice done, though in fact such a thing could certainly not happen.

This was all very well for Silvester, a hundred and sixty miles from the spot and secure of his own roof above his head on Marlborough Street. A few days after receiving this advice, Bailey was notified by Bowman that he intended to take possession within twenty-four hours according to due forms of law. He added that in case of any opposition, Sheriff Cushing would be empowered to raise the whole force of the country to assist him. "I have," he said, "no Inclination to injure you in the least degree." He therefore advised him to give up in a peaceful and amicable manner, and by no means to embroil his rash supporters in a conflict with the forces of the law.

Thus forced to make a decision, Bailey yielded. When the sheriff actually appeared he consented to take a lease of the parsonage house for six months from Bowman, which that astute gentleman was glad to get as an acknowledgement of his rights. In Bailey's view, it would be hopeless to appeal in a part of the world where all the officers of justice were dissenters, and besides, he was by no means sure that Bowman's claim was not legally valid. In fact, he blamed the Doctor for erecting the church and house on disputed land, especially as some rumor of trouble had leaked out at the time the buildings were being started. He now saw nothing to be done but to compound with Bowman for money, which his six-months' lease gave him a little while to raise. If the Doctor would only "compose himself to reason," the matter might be settled on these terms.

Silvester, who had never composed himself to reason with an adversary in the course of his life, was determined to force Bailey to pursue the case at law. Turning savagely upon him at the next Episcopal convention, he accused him of conduct amounting to sacrilege in that he had relinquished property belonging not to himself, but to the church. He intended, he said, to get up a petition to the Society for the Propagation of the Gospel asking for Bailey's recall, and he wished the assembled clergymen as a body to affix their signatures. Poor Bailey defended himself as best he could, but several clergymen who, as he bitterly says, had no understanding of the law or the circumstances were violent against him. Fortunately he had some supporters among the clergy and was backed by his wardens and vestry, who would not hear of going to law and promised to support him by a counter petition to the Society. In the upshot, the clergy were divided, and no formal complaint was made. Later, a more accurate survey of the ground in question proved that the church and parsonage house were not included in the land claimed by Bowman after all. This happy solution to the question put an end to the quarrel. Dr. Gardiner settled matters with Bowman, while the loyalty of the people to their pastor seemed to have been only strengthened by his troubles. In that very year he baptized forty-nine people, twenty-one of whom had belonged to the families of rigid dissenters, and he had besides five new communicants, all educated Presbyterians.

Silvester's behavior in this affair presents his character in its most unattractive light. Apparently he was wrong about the law, and in any case nothing can excuse his virulent attack on poor Bailey, who had spent nearly a year's salary which he could ill afford, and who had acted throughout with the consent of his vestry and wardens. It is true that Bailey's own attitude in the affair was irritating. He did say that Silvester ought to have known better than to erect the buildings on this piece of land, and he offered to compound for money, which could hardly have been raised without a handsome subscription from Silvester's pocket. Still, Bailey's untiring efforts in Pownalborough had earned him the right to more consideration. The fact is, the Doctor had recognized the malice of Bowman's proceedings and had made up his mind on no other grounds that his own cause was just. This being so, he had no respect for contrary opinions, and no scruples as to method. If to regain the parsonage he must ruin the parson, Silvester was evidently anxious to do it.

Bowman was defeated on the parsonage issue, and the church's position for the moment seemed stronger than ever. However, he must have enjoyed the confusion while it lasted, and he was not the man to let another opportunity slip when it arose. Taking advantage of a law passed by the General Court in the following year, Bowman and Cushing called a parish meeting at a time when the two wardens and Major Goodwin were absent. Nothing was said about its not being an Episcopal parish meeting, but when the church members did attend, they were told by the moderator that they had no right to vote. They therefore offered to withdraw, provided that the meeting would undertake not to tax them for the establishment of the Congregational worship. This being one of the real purposes of the assemblage, their request was refused. However, they made such a good case for themselves that when they withdrew, a good many others went with them, and only eight people were rel among themselves, so that the whole business ended in confusion. To promote a rival religion in Pownalborough was proving hopeless. Bowman's only chance, which he was not slow in taking, was to change the grounds of his attack from religious ones to political.

While the church in Pownalborough was going through these convulsions, Dr. Gardiner had been proceeding with his plans for one in Gardinerston. Here he gave the land himself, paid for the building, and endowed the church with an income of ten pounds a year. His son William, who was living at the Great House, added the final touch of a gilded salmon as weathervane to commemorate the Indian name of "Cobbossee Contee." Bailey dedicated this church in 1772 and wrote to the Society recommending that they extend some help to Gardinerston. The people, he says, were of New England stock and various denominations, but a number who had moved up there from Pownalborough had been formerly under his care. Settlement now extended forty-five miles up the river from Pownalborough and included four hundred families, among whom there was no ordained minister of any sort. He himself could do no more than perform occasional services, which his increasing congregation in Pownalborough demanded most of his time. "I am obliged to remark," he added with great generosity, "that we are indebted to the care and vigilance of this gentleman (Dr. Gardiner) for the redemption of our parsonage at Pownalborough, and its present establishment upon a sure foundation." Such willingness to forget grievances for the sake of a good cause deserved a better reward than Bailey's sufferings during the years that followed.

SEVEN

*L*EGAL TROUBLES

FOUR YEARS AFTER the end of the French and Indian War, the Plymouth Company had already given away two hundred thousand acres and spent nearly four thousand pounds on defensible houses, not to mention other investments which various individuals had made. As a result, the Kennebec Purchase was filling rapidly, and all sorts of difficulties between the settlers and the Company had begun to multiply. Georgetown and Pownalborough were summoning town meetings to combat a petition "which silvanus gardener Esqr have put into the general court." It appears that when the Company attempted to prosecute various people for stripping the land of valuable timber, it was forced to send its representatives and lawyers all the way down from Boston to Pownalborough at considerable expense. When these arrived, however, Pownalborough judges had refused to conduct the trials because they themselves were interested parties and no fair jury could be appointed in the region. Silvester was making an attempt to have land cases transferred to another county, but was frustrated by a counter petition from Lincoln, whose citizens were proud of their privileges. Pownalborough courthouse

POWNALBOROUGH Court House on the Kennebec
River in Dresden, was constructed in 1761 by
Gershom Flagg. It was identical to the Great House
which Dr. Gardiner built at the corner of Water and
Church Streets in downtown Gardiner.
MAINE HISTORICAL SOCIETY.

was fairly small, and it was still reached from the river landing
by a winding trail marked with blazed trees. Such as it was,
however, the citizens were already looking upon it as a bulwark
to protect them from their absentee proprietors.

One of the difficulties of the Plymouth Company in
maintaining its rights was that a great deal of its valuable timber was readily accessible from the river. There were so many
small tributaries of the Kennebec with plenty of water power
for a sawmill that they were a perpetual temptation to needy
settlers. The Pownalborough courts could not in decency set

aside the law, yet in dubious cases the attitude of the jury was plain enough. There was plenty of land for all, they felt, and it was hardly fair that a company which had bought the area for a fraction of its value should interfere with an enterprising man's attempt to earn his living. Silvester could combat this feeling, but he could not quell it. Indeed, his methods were such that he often stirred up a strong personal resentment against himself.

ONE OF SILVESTER'S most marked characteristics as a businessman was his enthusiasm for new faces and new plans. Instances of this can be found in his partnership with young Jepson in Connecticut, his patronage of Jacob Bailey in Boston, and his arrangements to send the latter to England. Silvester eagerly assured Bailey's brother, who certainly never did make a success, that he could easily employ six men without satisfying the Kennebec's need for bricks. Young James Flagg, son of one of Silvester's fellow proprietors, had opened a store and a warehouse in Pownalborough. Silvester encouraged him, sent him up supplies on credit, promised him land, and entered into his plans for moving to Gardinerston and branching out into shipbuilding. In all these cases, and many others, he talked largely. Without precisely promising anything, he certainly drew a rosy picture of the future. What these inexperienced young men did not realize was that Silvester was attracted by their plans and not by their personalities. When they failed, the Doctor had no sympathy, but was as energetic in abuse as he had been before in encouragement. Bailey was attacked before the convention of his Episcopal brethren. Jepson was the victim of a protracted suit in which the Doctor seems to have been right, but to have magnified a mere muddle into deliberate dishonesty. As for James Flagg, he was not merely sued, but bombarded by appeals and pamphlets afterwards.

In his relationships with his tenants, Silvester often fared no better than with his associates. Thomas Dinsmore, who settled on Silvester's land on Swan Island in 1765, found two or three acres roughly cleared with a tumbledown shack without door, floor, or chimney, which he put in some sort of repair and inhabited for five or six years. Silvester supplied him with draft oxen and tools on credit and helped him out with some supplies while his children were young. In 1770 Dinsmore's land reverted to Silvester, to whom it was mortgaged, as payment for the above services. Silvester now proposed that Dinsmore should stay on the farm as his tenant, promising to give him an eight years' lease and to build him a decent house. This was done, but Dinsmore, who did not read very well and had not listened carefully as William Gardiner read the lease to him, was outraged to find that the Doctor had driven a harder bargain than he thought fair. In the first place, Dinsmore, though he might in general clear his land, was not henceforth to cut any pine or white oak whatsoever. In the second place, though Silvester would build him a house and barn, the hauling was to be done by his own oxen and chains, since he had not yet paid Silvester for them.

THE HOUSE AND BARN were built in time, and Dinsmore himself dug a well and added a storehouse. Dinsmore's lease expired in 1778, and two things at once became apparent. In the first place nothing could persuade him that the farm on which he had struggled for thirteen years, the first six in a hovel, was not his for life and his sons' after him. Secondly, it is clear from his testimony, prejudiced though it is, that Dr. Gardiner in a moment of expansive planning had encouraged him to suppose that he never would be turned off. Thomas Dinsmore Junior had even convinced himself that the Doctor had promised every son of the family a hundred acres, "'for,' said he, 'I've Land enough.'" The actual words of Silvester thus quoted carry conviction. Yet from the Doctor's point of view, he had made a suggestion, not a promise, and one which would naturally depend on the course of future events.

It appears that Silvester had performed quite large services for Dinsmore, who took them as a matter of course and felt free to be perfectly ungrateful. The same thing is true of others. "David Welch," says Silvester, "became my tenant—very poor had a large Family of young children which obliged me to supply him with Stores of almost every kind otherwise he must have suffered greatly." Silvester hired two men in Boston and sent them down to help Welch with the draining of his great meadow, yet Welch felt injured that he was asked to take a spade and pitch in with the work himself. This attitude partly reflects a general dislike of the proprietors and a popular impression that mere occupancy gave a right to the land. Furthermore, the harsh conditions of life, and the sudden, ruinous catastrophes caused by weather, wild beasts, or fires induced settlers to demand help almost as a right from a rich proprietor who could survive such accidents.

In January of 1770, the ice of the Kennebec and the Androscoggin was broken up by a sudden thaw. Great blocks came thundering down with the current, and as sometimes happened, they jammed across the stream from bank to bank until the water rose with sufficient strength to sweep the obstacle away. On this particular occasion an unusually high tide coincided with the break-up and raised the waters to an unprecedented height. The great falls of the Androscoggin were entirely leveled by ice, which was computed to be packed forty feet deep below them. Three mills were carried away at Brunswick, and two others on the Androscoggin partially destroyed. Silvester's storehouse was swept away from Gardinerston and deposited on the back of Swan Island with its contents presumably ruined. His potash works were jammed into the back of a settler's house. "They paddled a Cannoe up over your

Great Dam being all still water," writes John McKechnie, Silvester's surveyor, "and the water was near over the Grist mill roof." Such losses, though serious to Silvester, were by no means ruinous. Henry McCausland, whose house was swept downstream, was in far worse case. He was one of the original settlers of Gardinerston and had started out in one small cabin for two families, and without either chimney or floor. To be houseless now after ten years of struggle was a terrible blow. Silvester was expected to help the McCauslands as a matter of course. He undoubtedly did so, yet where such demands are made, there is often dissatisfaction, either with the service rendered, or with the amount of gratitude expressed.

Such ill feeling on the part of his tenants did not concern Silvester greatly, even assuming that he noticed it. While conducting his own affairs in Gardinerston, he had undertaken for the Company one of the most difficult pieces of negotiation that it had to handle. The Sheepscot River, which runs parallel to the Kennebec on the east, is less than fifteen miles away and was therefore included in the Kennebec Purchase. However, its separate mouth had for a long time afforded entrance to settlers whose claims were based on Indian deeds. Some of these were quite old, so that the land had been sold or parceled out among several heirs. In 1750 when Samuel Goodwin first went up to the Kennebec with his surveyor, he had approached the settlers on the Sheepscot, who had indignantly held firm to what they considered their rights. None cared to repurchase their land, while if they were tenants, they did not wish to be in the position of owing rent to two landlords at once. By the end of the French and Indian War, the boundaries of the patent had been fairly well established in some places, but there remained a large amount of disputed land on the Sheepscot. Silvester now undertook to develop this area on the Company's behalf and to account to it for the proceeds. He gave two bonds of twenty thousand pounds in earnest of his intentions and began to survey the land and call on the inhabitants to take fresh titles.

Silvester could hardly have devised a better method for making himself personally unpopular in Pownalborough. The west bank of the Sheepscot was actually included in the town's boundaries, and its settlers very nearly equalled in number those of Frankfort itself. Many men had bought their lands in perfect good faith and had been there for a generation, or even more. It is true that Silvester did not try to extort money from such people, except for mill privileges, but he did intend to assert control over the settlement in general and to upset mortgage arrangements or payments of rent. Some of the settlers gave in, though resentfully. Others resisted. Prominent among the latter was Jacob Averell, one of the tenants of Deacon Whittemore, an absentee landlord who claimed an extensive tract on the authority of Indian deeds.

J ACOB AVERELL HAD BEEN assistant to one of the early surveyors on the Sheepscot, on which he had settled in 1738. When Samuel Goodwin came over to claim the land for the Plymouth Company, it was Averell who took the lead in persuading his neighbors to have nothing to do with him. He was a dramatic, obstinate man with a certain eye for strategy, which led him to score a success against Silvester in the early moves of the game. Hearing, or affecting to hear, that the Plymouth Company had marked down a certain stream as a site for a sawmill, he wrote off in all haste to his landlord promising to get there first and erect a mill himself if Whittimore would send him up "an hundred pounds in Rhum meloses Corn or meal and pork" to pay his men. By the time that Dr. Gardiner paid his annual visit to the Kennebec in 1760, construction on this was well underway. Silvester sent over to the Sheepscot, asking Averell to come in and see him, and when he received a flat refusal in answer, he lost his temper in characteristic, but regrettable fashion. Averell, to whom the messenger evidently reported, says "He called me knave and rouge and protested to sue me forthwith."

Silvester returned to Boston and, having recovered his self-command, wrote Averell a temperate letter of advice from thence. He was sorry, he said, that the rain had prevented him from making Averell a visit as he had intended. He was also distressed to hear that wood was being cut to build a sawmill on the Plymouth Company's land. He felt it right to inform Averell that this would certainly result in a lawsuit, and he advised him as a friend to give up the project.

Any effect this reasonable letter might have had on Averell was completely spoiled by Silvester's previous fit of temper. He bade the Doctor defiance dramatically, and said he was ready to defend his cause in each successive court of law up to the King himself. He accused Silvester of being in league with all the Irish in the settlement, apparently because he was confused about the difference between Catholic and Episcopalian. Later on Major Goodwin brought over a gang of men to block up the road he had made to his mill, and Averell swore that one of the workmen was a "Roman Irish man" and had vowed to kill him. In short, Averell was completely intransigent and revelled in the quarrel. Meanwhile his neighbors, who had shown signs of coming to terms, were persuaded to hold out by his successful defiance.

SILVESTER'S CHIEF DIFFICULTY in this whole negotiation was the practical certainty that the Pownalborough courts would not uphold his case at law. If the Plymouth Company could not prosecute trespassers on land that was indisputably theirs, it was hardly likely that they could enforce their rights to a tract held on the authority of Indian deeds dating back several generations. Averell and his friends maintained that the Indians did not know what a mile was, which made it meaningless for them to grant away fifteen miles on the bank of any river. Rivers were their highways, each one opening up a separate area. Thus all that an Indian chief could grant would be halfway from one river to the next, which would push back the Purchase boundary at this point to a line less than four miles from the Kennebec's eastern bank. Such arguments may not have been valid, but they would have had weight in Pownalborough, to which a great deal of the disputed land belonged.

Undoubtedly Averell had relied on the strength of local prejudice to prevent the Doctor ever winning a case against him at law. The event proved that he had underrated his formidable opponent. Doctor Gardiner had discovered that though an action for trespass would be tried in Pownalborough, a suit under a writ of tover would be heard in Boston. In other words, if he started an action to recover the value of something wrongfully appropriated by Averell to his own use, he might have the advantage of a court whose prejudices, if any, were on his own side. True, several lawyers whom he consulted advised him that an action for trover did not properly lie against Averell, who was guilty merely of trespass. This did not prevent Dr. Gardiner bringing an action for trover and forcing Averell and several of his friends to come up to Boston at their own expense. The moment that he got them there, he pressed for a postponement, and was granted it. Averell had to pay his way back home, with the prospect of coming to Boston again at some time in the future. Backed up by promises of aid from his landlord, Whittimore, he returned for the second trial, only to find that the Doctor was asking for another postponement. In despair at the thought of a third trip, he came to terms with Silvester, who offered to sell him the land outright at eight shillings an acre. The suit was therefore abandoned. Averell's neighbors fell into line, and the control of the Sheepscot passed into Silvester's hands. It is notable that nearly thirty years later an action against the Plymouth Company was pressed home, and the Draper estate, to which Averell's land belonged, was transferred to its original owners. The unfortunate Averell, who had paid Silvester in full, now found his title worthless and was pressed by his old landlord for an accumulation of back rent.

For the time being, Silvester had won his case on the Sheepscot, and surveys were pressed on vigorously, despite the ill feeling that his conduct must have aroused in Pownalborough. It was perfectly obvious that he had won his battle not because of the justice of his cause, but because of his superior ingenuity and greater financial resources. As a matter of fact he shortly afterwards brought another action of trover against a trespasser, and lost it. He thereupon put in his petition to the General Court to get land cases transferred to another county. At the same time, he got two legal opinions about bringing the trover question before the King in council. Both lawyers were against an appeal, and his petition to the court was dismissed. After that time the wonder is that Silvester could show himself in Pownalborough at all without a riot.

Such actions on Silvester's part may have made him unpopular on the Kennebec, but they were at least invaluable to the cause of the Plymouth Company. As if to show that no particular group of supporters was necessary to him, he now proceeded to quarrel with several of the individual proprietors. From the moment that the Company had started to divide up its lands, it was inevitable that some conflicts should arise, and Silvester's temperament was not suited to settling them amicably. His quarrel with the Hancocks and Jonathan Bowman was an example of the difficulties caused by rough-and-ready surveys. His dispute with James Flagg, which was far more complicated, brings out some of the problems of developing an area like the Kennebec without being constantly on the spot.

James Flagg, like Jacob Bailey, started his career as one of Silvester's protégés. In 1761 he was up on the Kennebec with his father, Gershom Flagg, the builder, and they were engaged

GERSHOM FLAGG (1705–1771), building contractor for
the Kennebec Purchase Company and one of its lesser
proprietors. WADSWORTH ATHENÆUM, HARTFORD,
CONNECTICUT. THE ELLA GALLUP SUMNER AND MARY CATLIN
SUMNER COLLECTION FUND.

in planning a store and warehouse to set the young man up in
trade. Silvester, who had put his own son William in a store in
Gardinerston a year or two earlier, was interested in helping an
intelligent and educated young man. Young James Flagg was
very plausible, and Silvester discussed possibilities with all his

usual enthusiasm. He had an idea that shipbuilding might be one of the next logical industries, and he knew a shipwright whom he wanted young Flagg to meet in case the two might consider a partnership. For the time being, he was happy to supply stores on credit and would take payment in boards when Flagg had collected them. After one season in Pownalborough, young Flagg did decide to go for shipbuilding. Silvester persuaded him to move to Gardinerston and promised him a five-acre lot for himself, another for his partner, and eight more to be at his disposal for any respectable workmen he might import. While they were about it, Flagg had better have a power of attorney to deal with these five-acre lots, so that he could dispose of them at discretion without needing to refer to Boston. Moreover, he might collect the rent for Silvester's two sawmills, which were naturally paid in boards, and thus combine it with those owed for supplies to the mills and lumbermen in general. It might be as well for Flagg to act as a supervisor for the mills, whose lessees, Henry and James McCausland, did not always have money enough to keep them in good repair. Flagg might freely supply them with anything that was needed up to the value of five pounds.

ALL THESE COMMISSIONS are ample evidence, not merely of Silvester's eagerness to encourage a deserving young man, but of his distrust of the abilities of his own son William. He had already found that William was a failure in trade at Gardinerston. At this time the young man was mainly acting as his father's errand boy, going down to Hartford with instructions when Jepson failed to execute a commission, taking possession of lands whose mortgages had fallen in, and conferring with the surveyor. There was no real reason why William should not have supervised the mills, or had Silvester's power of attorney if his father had trusted him. As it was, he was simply passed over for the new favorite, and it

Mr. Jepson,   Boston 4 Mar. 1762

I am this moment favourd with yours ⅌ Lowder. and am greatly surprizd at the construction you put on the Dirĕctions I gave you ⅌ him; as I think nothing can be plainer. and which I beg you would follow literally, which is this; first take Leverets & Daniel Hubbards Note of hand for £200 payable by the 20ᵗʰ May next. then take Daniels' bond for£ 1281. 12. 3 (which makes the whole he owes me) payable any time within 4 Years with interest annually; then take Danˡ. Hubbard & his fathers Mortgage of the house & Land where Daniel Lives together with mia's Lott (the incumbrances first being taken off) as a Col- -lateral security for the said £ 1281. 12. 3. without having any regard for what it will really fetch: as I take it as a Collateral security. I beg for any directions I shall hereafter give you, you would

follow

Litterally. without paying any regard to any general conversation passing that has between us: and if you shew any Lawyer the Letter I wrote you ⅌ Lowder he can not hesitate one moment about the true meaning of it. I am for , Your obliged & very hble servant

Silv. Gardiner

LETTER FROM DR. GARDINER to William Jepson in Hartford, Connecticut, instructing him to enforce strictly a pharmaceutical contract. GIFT OF MYLES MARTEL, GARDINER LIBRARY ASSOCIATION.

must be admitted that his apparent ignorance of Flagg's later proceedings seems to justify Silvester's lack of confidence.

Running a country store in a new settlement cannot have been easy, especially for a young man inexperienced in business and unacquainted with the people with whom he was dealing. Logging and sawmill gangs were paid in supplies, most of which they actually consumed while they were working. In other words, it was necessary for James Flagg to give extensive credit and hope at the end of the season that there would be sufficient boards to pay him back. He had neither Silvester's obstinacy, nor Jonathan Bowman's understanding of human nature, with the result that he was very shortly burdened with a number of bad debts. There was nothing to be done but to make Silvester wait for his money, which he was quite prepared to do, since his own experience in supplying small-town doctors had taught him about some of the troubles that must be encountered. The situation seemed fair enough to Silvester in Boston, but William on the spot should have understood it better. In a small settlement like Gardinerston there was no excuse for William not knowing that some things were going on which would make his father very uneasy. He ought to have discovered, for instance, that Flagg was charging people higher prices for supplies than he was actually putting down to the Doctor's credit in his books. He should undoubtedly have notified his father that quite expensive repairs were being carried on at the mills, and that Flagg was employing his own debtors on the work, withholding their wages to pay himself, while of course the Doctor would be asked to refund the whole amount. Even when a big repair bill did go in to Silvester and he realized how far young Flagg had exceeded his instructions, William was no help. Silvester told him to present Flagg a bill for all the supplies so far received, and to see that he paid it. William found he could collect nothing, and he did not even notify his father that such was the case.

In this dispute with the Flaggs, as in so many others, it was not so much what Silvester did as his method of doing it which got him into trouble. First he encouraged young James a little too heartily and allowed him to involve himself in shipbuilding before he had sufficient capital to pay for materials and workmen. He had slighted his own son William, and possibly made him jealous, as it is difficult otherwise to conceive why he was not more alert. As soon as trouble arose, Silvester reversed himself completely and presented young Flagg with a bill for over seven hundred pounds, which he must have known could not be paid immediately. He then went up to the Kennebec with the intention of making other arrangements for distributing his stores. He found another agent and agreed to send up a sloop of provisions from Hartford, where a captain was ready to transport them in return for a full load of boards. Having done this, it then occurred to Silvester that young Flagg might be able to pay him some boards at any rate, and he hastily wrote up to the Kennebec, suggesting that he start to collect them before the sloop arrived. Flagg, who had been first dazzled by too eager patronage, then stunned by the large sum demanded all in one lump, was now thrown into confusion by this new approach and seems to have been genuinely uncertain whether the promised stores were consigned to him or not. He hoped so, as he had a ship half finished and no other way to buy supplies or pay his men. When they arrived for the other agent, his failure was certain, and his bitter disappointment after so many bright promises made him resentful. He paid Silvester nothing. Silvester swore out a suit against him, and in 1765 Flagg's property was attached and he himself arrested with a demand for a bail of seven hundred pounds.

In view of the fact that Jonathan Bowman went bail for Flagg, it is hard to doubt that some of his later actions were guided by that astute gentleman's advice. The first move was to enter a counter-suit for breach of contract, maintaining that

JAMES FLAGG (1731–1773), son of Gershom
Flagg, fierce political antagonist of Dr. Gardiner.
Portrait attributed to Benjamin Blyth.
PRIVATE COLLECTION.

Silvester had made a verbal promise to send up the stores to Flagg, and offering as supporting evidence that unfortunate letter about collecting boards before the sloop should arrive. Issues were by now so confused that both parties agreed to submit their conflicting claims to a group of referees. These in due course delivered a most surprising judgment, awarding Flagg damages of several hundred pounds. Assuming that the referees were honest in this matter, which is by no means certain, the explanation apparently is that James Flagg, or possibly Bowman, had skillfully taken advantage of the Doctor's peculiar character.

DOCTOR GARDINER HAD a good case, and he had backed it up by numerous depositions, which he had taken in front of a justice of the peace after inviting Flagg to be present, and during which he had ostentatiously warned the witnesses not to tell any untruth, even to do him a favor. When he came to the hearing, however, he was asked if all points at issue between the contending parties ought not to be submitted to the referees. He agreed, and enlarged his complaint to include the mill rent and some ship's rope, for which he claimed Flagg owed him. Flagg, thus permitted to enlarge in his turn, put in two more demands for heavy damages. In the first place, he declared he had been held for excessive bail, and that this had destroyed his credit in the community and was part of a deliberate attempt to ruin him. In the second place, the Doctor had out of sheer malice encouraged the McCausland brothers to enter suit against Flagg for having so weakened the dam during his mill repairs, that it had collapsed during the next flood season and ruined them.

It is evident that these unexpected charges coming at the last minute threw Silvester completely off balance and destroyed his control over his temper. The referees complained that he began to treat his bare assertion as though it were proof, and that his virulent abuse of young Flagg in court was ample evidence of his malice. Even his own counsel was forced to make excuses for his violent temper and to admit that the people of the Eastward hated him "as they did the devil." The Doctor lost his case, as the referees showed some unfairness in refusing to let him collect evidence in rebuttal.

The hearings in this case had been extremely public, since they had been held in one of the popular taverns and attended by a large number of the acquaintances of both parties. It was not to be supposed that Silvester would have any intention of sitting down under such a defeat. No regard for his old friend Gershom Flagg, who had at first been genuinely shocked to learn that his son was deeply indebted to Silvester, would now prevent the Doctor from charging headlong into battle. A little pamphlet entitled *Doctor Gardiner vs. James Flagg* appeared giving Silvester's side of the case, and it was followed by a long supplement to the *Boston Evening Post* strongly condemning the conduct of the referees. Silvester also set up what his enemies described as a "canting petition to the general court," which they declared was supported by "plenty of whisperings, squeezings by the hand, and some say, good dinners." This petition failed, and another pamphlet shortly appeared to usher in an application to the superior court. Flagg was goaded into producing *A Short Vindication of the Conduct of the Referees in the Case of Gardiner vs. Flagg*, which Silvester in another pamphlet immediately replied might better have been denominated "a harsh, rude, and unchristian invective against Doctor Gardiner…. One might as soon expect," he added, "to see all the fables of Ovid's Metamorphosis converted into realities, as his suppositions into truths."

The interminable arguments of this case reveal that, active and energetic as the Doctor was, it was impossible for him to run three businesses in different parts of the country without some confusion. Not only did he not prevent James

Flagg from exceeding his instructions with regard to mill repairs, but his correspondence shows that he was ignorant at the time of what was happening and was actually encouraging the plausible young man to go ahead. His habit was to trust no agent, but to hedge his associates around with explicit instructions. On the other hand, he rather liked these to be exceeded at discretion, though he refused to accept responsibility for a failure.

I N SPITE OF ALL THESE TROUBLES, it was evident that the settlements on the Kennebec were succeeding, partly because the time was ripe for them, but partly because of the intelligent and active way in which Silvester had fostered their interests. He was not afraid of investing his money heavily in his enterprise. When he needed winter supplies for the Kennebec and Jepson's arrangements with the master of a sloop broke down, Silvester sent William to Hartford and bought a sloop and cargo of provisions outright. When the McCauslands complained that the sawmills needed repairs which they could not pay for, Silvester was willing to put them in order. When the dam was carried away, he was able to collect a large gang of men and set them to work as soon as the water was low enough to undertake repairs. In return for these services, he had some grateful dependents and close associates, in spite of the misunderstandings that made him unpopular. Bailey's congregation had reason to be grateful to him. The McCauslands, though they took the Revolutionary side, refrained from direct action against their patron. Among the proprietors, the Hallowells remained especially intimate with him, even though they owned some land on the east side of Gardinerston and might easily have come in conflict. In fact, Briggs Hallowell, one of Robert's brothers, did mortgage his land to Silvester and did petition the courts for annulment of the judgment that Silvester had obtained against him during the seige of Boston. However,

Briggs was the only Hallowell to take the Revolutionary side, and he seems to have been read out of the family and to have died in poor circumstances. Silvester's mortgage was eventually upheld, and the money was paid in to his estate some time after Briggs Hallowell's death. Whether Silvester himself ever had the use of it is doubtful. The time had come when every unguarded word or arbitrary action was to be visited on Silvester after a fashion which he had never considered possible in his days of prosperity.

EIGHT

REVOLUTION

IN 1771 ANNE GIBBINS GARDINER, who was fond of flowers, went out into the fine garden behind her father's old house in Marlborough Street, in which she had been brought up. Perhaps she felt the heat. At all events, when she came indoors, she sank into a chair, bent forward her head as though to smell what she had picked, collapsed, and died. Silvester was evidently attached to her and must have missed her exceedingly, but he was not the man to put up with the discomforts of loneliness if they could be remedied. A year or two later he married Mrs. Abigail Eppes, a youngish widow with three half-grown children of her own.

The new Mrs. Gardiner was a woman of much energy and spirit whose vivacious, cheerful manner concealed a determination to have her own way. She was very popular in her own circles, being fond of society, an excellent hostess, and a strong Tory. Silvester evidently married her for love, and was much influenced by her, somewhat to the annoyance of the Doctor's children, who felt it ridiculous that their father while well on in his sixties should be so fond of a woman over twenty years younger than himself. This discrepancy did not trouble

ABIGAIL (PICKMAN) (EPPES) GARDINER (1732–1780),
second wife of Dr. Gardiner, portrait by John Singleton
Copley. BROOKLYN MUSEUM OF ART, DICK S. RAMSAY FUND 65.60.
PHOTO BY DEAN BROWN.

Silvester, who found her youthful cheerfulness a stimulus and
who spoke of her after her death as: "She whom my Soul loved
and in whom were all my Joys." Perhaps Silvester's children
were jealous of the fact that he took young William Eppes as
an apprentice and that the two growing daughters came to

make their home with their mother. At any rate, there was a slight coolness, and the new stepmother made it clear that visitors were not welcome in Marlborough Street except when they were asked.

The daughter who felt her changed position most strongly was naturally Abigail, who had been mistress of the house after the death of her mother, and how now found herself pushed aside by a youthful stepmother who was much more attractive to society than she was herself. Abigail soon found the situation intolerable and accepted the hand of Oliver Whipple, a young man of good family who had recently set up a law office in Portsmouth, New Hampshire. Though Abigail did not scruple to tell her father at a later date that the happiest days of her life were those spent with her "dear mother," the second Mrs. Gardiner, it was evident that her choice was really influenced by a desire to have a house of her own. Whipple does not seem to have married for love either, but to have hoped he could live on Abigail's money and avoid the necessity of work.

The unfortunate pair soon found that they were in almost every respect entirely opposite. Socially the advantages were all on the side of the husband, since Abigail was plain, stupid, and by no means easy in temper. Oliver Whipple was a tall, good looking man with an expressive countenance and a dignified, but perfectly agreeable manner. He had literary tastes and produced some rather indifferent verse, his pleasure in which would have been quite excusable if he had made a real profession out of anything else. His poems hymned such figures as Commerce, Culture, and Progress in orderly couplets in which rivers were reduced to "meandering rills" and the wide lands of the Ohio valley to gentle "Meads." In short, Whipple was a dilettante and a sentimentalist, but not without charm, a quality which his wife entirely lacked. In religious matters, there also was an irreconcilable difference. Abigail was an earnest churchwoman, rather self-righteous, but passionately devoted

SILHOUETTE of Abigail (Gardiner) Whipple
(1750–1827), daughter of Dr. Gardiner.
PRIVATE COLLECTION.

to the doctrines of the Christian faith as she understood them. On her very deathbed she had herself lifted up to put her mark on the covenant she yearly sealed with her God "in the presence of God the Father, the Son, and the Spirit, and in the presence of all the elect angels." In contrast, Oliver Whipple was a Mason; actually Grand Master of the Masons of New Hampshire.

Such being the characters of husband and wife, there was inevitably conflict between them. It tended to crystalize itself around the fact that Abigail, who was the stronger personality, expected her husband to amount to something or at the least to be prudent in managing their money. When it became evident that he was not going to live up to her hopes in either respect, they might actually have parted, had they not both desired Silvester to adopt their son, his namesake, for his chief heir. When the child was not specially preferred in Silvester's will, this disappointment was open and obvious, Abigail even going so far as to break off relations with the more favored Hallowells. Some money was left to Abigail, of course, but it dwindled under her husband's management until her constant recriminations became unbearable to him. Finally they actually dissolved their marriage by divorce, only to find that this arrangement suited them no better. Whipple was unwilling to support himself if it could be avoided, while Abigail found young Silvester an even more incompetent administrator than his father had been. Eventually the pair remarried, he hoping to have something to live on, she to have a man in charge of what money she had left. When all was finally spent, there was nothing more to keep them together. Abigail went to live with her married daughter, and Whipple was forced to obtain a clerkship in Washington and tie himself down to regular work for the rest of his life.

THIS MARRIAGE BETWEEN Abigail and Oliver Whipple took place in 1774, only a few months before the outbreak of hostilities between the British troops and the patriots. It is easy to see from the list of those who called to compliment the bride that the influence of Silvester's new wife and his own behavior had isolated him from most of his friends who were not Tories. True to his conviction that he had a right to express his opinions as he pleased, Silvester put his signature to the loyalist addresses to both Hutchinson and Gage. The unwisdom of such honesty was not apparent to him, not could he ever be brought to see that there was anything blameworthy about his conduct during the seige of Boston itself.

At the outbreak of hostilities, Silvester looked upon himself as a non-combatant, partly because the British were conducting their operations with regular troops, but partly also because he was very nearly seventy years of age. He considered himself sufficiently occupied with the personal problems that this mad outbreak of rebellion had brought upon a peaceable man. Silvester had by now almost retired from practice as a physician, and his very large income was nearly all derived from trade. Even his retail sales in the drugstore depended upon regular imports from England, which immediately became difficult to keep up, since the shipping space was commandeered for war supplies. Meantime his investments in Hartford, Middletown, Newport, the Kennebec, and elsewhere were heavy, and it was impossible to find any method of collecting outstanding debts. In a word, Silvester suddenly found his income reduced to a hundred pounds or so from the rents of his houses in Long Lane and Marlborough Street. Two of these he let to British officers, apologetically making his financial position clear, yet to no avail, since it was nearly five years before he received the payment due for one of them. Nor was this all. As Silvester's income vanished, prices went up and the size of his household increased. William Eppes, it is true, had taken service with the British, but his elder sister, who had recently married, had fled from the rebels with her husband, and both were now permanent visitors at Marlborough Street.

In these difficult circumstances there was little for Silvester to do but to collect such debts as might be owing to him in Boston. Briggs Hallowell, who so bitterly complained that Silvester had seized upon him when he happened to have business there, may have been the victim of the Doctor's panic and his determination at least to save what he could. Meanwhile Thomas Ainslie, an old associate, had taken refuge in Quebec. Silvester wrote to him for barrels of wheat and any livestock, since the Gardiner household was reduced to salt beef or pork from the military stores. Unfortunately, the purchases of the government had swept Canada clear of wheat, and the best that Ainslie could do was to find two sheep, for which he could not without General Robinson's permit get shipping space. General Robinson being one of Silvester's tenants, the Doctor probably got the permit and in time the sheep. At all events, Ainslie was able to send a box of drugs and a muff for Mrs. Gardiner about a month later, though it was evidently not possible to procure more food.

ALL THESE PURSUITS were fairly harmless, though they did involve constant association with British officers, applications for permits, and so forth. Two actions of Silvester's appeared more questionable, and aroused a great deal of feeling against him later. He publically congratulated the soldiers for a small victory on the islands in the harbor, and was considered to have been exulting over the slaughter of his countrymen. On another occasion, he showed his sentiments by sending his carriage to help home wounded soldiers from the battle of Bunker Hill. Considering that Silvester was a surgeon and his duty was to save life, his last action seems rather more praiseworthy than not, but these were curious times. At least no one cast it up against him that he had tended wounded soldiers in person, though it seems most probable in the circumstances that he did.

Within a few weeks from the nineteenth of April, the whole character of Boston society had undergone a change. Even in the Tory stronghold of the King's Chapel, pews fell empty, and certain familiar carriages were missing from the Sunday parade. More than half the congregation now wore scarlet coats, while here or there new, anxious faces denoted Tories who had fled from outlying towns with what they could carry and were wondering how they could afford the rising cost of food. Over two-thirds of the town's regular inhabitants had left, and the greater part of those that remained were disaffected. Meanwhile over ten thousand common soldiers were enjoying the cheapness of New England rum and were to be found drunk in all quarters of the town in spite of horrifying punishments. A diet of salt pork and beans soon became so monotonous that the bells were actually rung to celebrate a successful foray which had brought back large numbers of sheep and cattle. Before the year was out, hay was so scarce that carts and carriages were vanishing altogether, while horse meat was appearing on the table of those who could afford it. Coal was almost unobtainable at any price, and wood far from plentiful, even though about twenty buildings were torn down during the winter for fuel. Smallpox had broken out all over the town, and there were other sorts of sickness brought on by insufficiency of fresh provisions.

Amid all these privations, the plight of Tory merchants like Silvester was truly pitiable. Anxious about the fate of friends or relatives elsewhere in the country and inflamed by hideous stories of persecution, they were at the same time cut off from most of their normal employments and had little to do but worry or listen to gossip. Silvester at least was needed as a physician, but he was getting too old to go the rounds of his patients as he used to do, while his stepson and assistant, William Eppes, had left him to enter the service of the British. He was far too intelligent not to see that the British conduct of the war was all wrong, even though it never occurred to him or to any of his friends that the Colonies could actually win it. As the seige wore on, all these things became more and more depressing, and Silvester was upheld only by his natural obstinancy and by the valiant spirit of his wife.

There were a great many gentlemanlike officers in the town with nothing much to do, and some of the Tory ladies found themselves with time of their hands. The result was, parties were frequent. The British, who did not share Bostonian prejudices against the theatre, set up a stage in Faneuil Hall and enlivened the winter by producing various topical dramas. Among these was *The Blockade of Boston*, in which General

Washington had just appeared with a large wig, a rusty sword, and an orderly carrying a gun about seven feet long, when a regular sergeant rushed on the stage and cried out, "The Yankees are attacking Bunker Hill." As soon as it was realized that this was an actual alarm and not part of the play, there was shrieking and fainting among the ladies of the audience, many of whom were combining the novelty of a dramatic performance with the pleasant task of keeping up their spirits. Among this group of women, Mrs. Gardiner was exceedingly prominent. Though her husband's preoccupation and straightened means evidently prevented her from entertaining as elaborately as she would have liked, her lively social gifts made her in great demand. Silvester's children later blamed her for making herself conspicuous at this time in Tory circles, though in fact it is

"A View of the Town of Boston With Several Ships of War in the Harbour," engraving by Paul Revere for the *Royal American Magazine*, 1774.

probable that Silvester's own want of tact had already offended the patriots beyond hope of forgiveness. Silvester himself never reproached her, but continued to find her good spirits a source of help and consolation in evil times.

No ONE CAN HAVE been more dismayed by the cutting off of communications with Boston than William Gardiner, who had been for many years before the Revolution his father's personal representative upon the Kennebec, living first in the Great House in Gardinerston, and later in a small cottage of his own nearby. He was a handsome, mild-mannered man, whose apparent laziness was a mask for a real timidity in dealing with people. His father, who reposed small confidence in his judgment, never trusted him with a general power of attorney, but was perpetually sending down instructions about specific tasks, which were frequently unpleasant. William was to draw up a lease for Thomas Dinsmore. He was to present James Flagg with a bill and see that he paid it, to foreclose the following mortgages, or to repossess certain lands whose settlers had deserted them. William seems to have got in the habit of putting off any job which involved an unpleasant interview in the hope that his father would forget about it if not reminded. When Silvester came up in summer and inquired into the state of affairs, he manifested as William politely put it "great uneasiness." In other words, Silvester abused his son, who let the storm roll over him and did exactly the same thing next time. In these circumstances, it is not surprising that Silvester entrusted agencies to James Flagg and other people when they should properly have belonged to William. He remained his father's errand boy, and was also allowed to supervise the surveying and to act as Silvester's representative on social occasions.

Whether it was a cause or a result of this treatment, William Gardiner never quite seemed to grow up. He had not married, though he had been fond of girls as a young man and ready to steal out of the house to a party without his parents' knowledge. An elaborate practical joke on the inhabitants of the Great House in Gardinerston gives a fair idea of William's childishness and of the nature of his humor. It seems that he carefully laid a light train of gunpowder through the entire house, in each of the entries, up both flights of stairs, and into every room to which he had access without being discovered. He then commenced rolling a canon ball across one of the upstairs floors. The inhabitants, awakened in the middle of the night by a sound resembling an earthquake or the thunders of the Last Judgment, rushed out of doors. William immediately lighted the gunpowder, and the whole house was filled with a satisfying flash of home-made lightning. After this incident, it is not surprising to find that when the British surveyor for mast pines came up the river and was met by William, he was led into a swampy part of the woods and attacked by such clouds of mosquitoes that he and his host were literally driven out again into the open.

Such a son, though by no means satisfactory to Silvester, suited him far better than the downright John, who was exceedingly like himself. William never opposed or argued, and if he did not agree with his father on important points, he preferred to make a pretense of doing so. Silvester, for instance, built the church at Gardinerston, while William gave it a bell and a gilded weathercock and showed himself perfectly ready to act as its patron. Yet he seldom seems to have appeared in Bailey's congregation, though he was personally friendly, and when John brought his eldest son up to the Kennebec in 1784, William got into a theological discussion with the young man and displayed such free-thinking sentiments that his brother roundly declared him unfit company for respectable people. John was far more liberal in his ideas than his father, and his condemnation of his brother would have been as nothing to that expressed by Silvester if he had ever been favored with Willliam's opinions. Not only was William weak enough to get on with his father, but he was also in his own mild manner very much of a gentleman. Silvester appears to have thought with some justice that if he himself made the fortune and set up the estate, William would be able to preside over both in an ornamental, if not precisely a capable fashion. This he might well have done in easier times, but he was not the man to handle the Gardiner property in a period of revolution. The best that can be said for his conduct is that he had an impossible task, and that to let things slide as he did was a lesser mistake than to take sides with Silvester and Bailey.

Revolutionary ferment in Maine was slow in arising, chiefly because the grievances of this part of the country did not really concern England at all. Most of the trade being coastal traffic with Boston and elsewhere, customs duties were not a real burden. Taxes seemed inconsiderable, and Pownalborough never complained of them until after the outbreak of war. British agents laying claim to mast pines were resented, it is true, but being confined to unoccupied lands, they could not trouble settlers as much as they did proprietors. Nor was it until the Indian menace had receded completely that people felt free to take an interest in weakening the established forms of government. As late of 1765, while Boston was in an uproar over the Stamp Act, people were laboring over fortifications in Gardinerston, and the Winslows were fleeing across the river to safety with a dark cloak thrown over their little son to make him invisible against the ground. This proved to be the last Indian scare on the Kennebec, but there is no doubt that its memory played a part in keeping the settlements loyal.

On the other hand, it is evident that by the time the Boston Tea Party and its attendant troubles threw the whole country into an uproar, there was just as much enthusiasm on the Kennebec for the patriot cause as there was everywhere else.

The reason for this change may partly be found in the constant arrival of new settlers from Boston and elsewhere. It is also true, however, that the various strains and resentments which had developed since 1760 were easily capable of taking on a political side, even though their origin had been legal, religious, or personal. Jonathan Bowman found an opportunity to destroy the influence of the Episcopal church and drive out Jacob Bailey. Silvester's debtors or tenants might hope that a change in political power would give them undisputed possession. Squatters and would-be exploiters of timberland could side with the cause of the free, enterprising citizen against absentee government. John Hancock, Gershom Flagg, William Pitts, and other proprietors of the Kennebec Company found it no hardship to be free of the dominance of Silvester, in spite of the problems that his absence from their midst might entail. Thus though the disputes in the Kennebec settlements appear to change suddenly in character, actually this is not so, since every man with a grievance looked on the Revolution as a chance to redress it. If Silvester, the dominant proprietor on the Kennebec, had been a Congregationalist and a Patriot, this situation might never have arisen. As it was, each man found a peculiar opportunity to mingle pure love of his country with his personal advantage.

THE FIRST OPEN RIOTS on the Kennebec occurred in September 1774, in connection with the closing of the port of Boston and the consequent "Solemn League and Covenant" sent out by the Committee of Correspondence to the provincial towns. This document, which bound its signatores to refrain from importing or using British goods, was the first definite issue to separate Patriot and Tory in the County of Lincoln. Jacob Bailey, whose opinion of the Boston Tea Party riot appeared to coincide with Silvester's, was unalterably opposed to the Covenant. Not only did he use his influence as parson against it, but he induced his churchwarden, Major Goodwin, to employ the authority of the Plymouth Company in his support. The consequence was that a very few of Bailey's congregation signed the document, which was not adopted in Pownalborough. On the other hand, Bowman got everyone he could to sign the Covenant, and was actually said to have threatened his wife with a separation unless she would cease to listen to the parson and fall into line with his own views. Feeling ran so high that the owners of the grist mill in Pownalborough refused to grind for non-signers, though they were forced to give in when they realized how many these actually were. Far more seriously alarming were the riots which started in Georgetown and raged up and down the river for over a week. Obed Hussey, who lived on the north side of Pownalborough, had a hundred and fifty pounds of tea thrown into the Kennebec, all except two pounds which his housekeeper had managed to conceal in the haymow. This being somehow discovered, the mob attacked the hay, which was soon following the tea downstream to teach its owner a lesson.

ON THE UPPER REACHES of the river, where James Howard, commander of the old Fort Western, was a strong adherent of the patriot party, the riots soon reached formidable dimensions. William Gardiner, who was mentioned as an especial object of hatred, did not wait to be visited in Gardinerston, but fled down the river to Bailey's parsonage, where he spent the night. Here he found himself no safer than before, since another group was moving up the river from Georgetown, and Bailey himself, Major Goodwin, and Francis Rittal, the Lutheran innkeeper, were apparently all on the danger list. However, the mob was still twelve miles away, and had stopped frequently as it progressed in order to partake of liquid refreshment. Indeed, there seemed to be some doubt as to whether it would ever sober up enough to get any further.

After attending service next morning, William judged it safe enough to go home. However, that very same evening he was either warned by a neighbor or alarmed by the shouts and singing of the Gardinerston mob, which was advancing towards him along the bank of the river a hundred and fifty strong. William fled up the Cobbossee in a canoe, spent the night in the woods, and finally made his way across to the Androscoggin and eventually to Falmouth.

Meanwhile, about midnight the rioters surrounded William's house and demanded that he admit them to search for tea. One of his Hazard cousins from Narragansett, who happened to be visiting him, now came out and started to parley. After some discussion, the crowd was brought to consent that none but five chosen delegates should be permitted to enter. When the door was opened, however, others soon pushed in after their leaders, and in a very short time the whole house was overrun. There seemed to be nothing to do but to bring out some rum, which Hazard did, with the result that the men became completely unmanageable and stole his very shoe buckles, presumably right off his feet. Next they began to call for "Black" or "Mahogany" Jones, the Company's surveyor, who was a bigoted Tory and had refused to sign the Covenant. When Jones came out to them, they presented him with the document again. He tore open his shirt and cried out that they might stab him to the heart if they pleased, but that nothing should induce him to sign that accursed paper. They were not quite ready to go the lengths that he suggested, but they tied him to a rope, threw him in the river, dragged him about a little, pulled him out, and repeated the performance a number of times. As Jones, who was a violent and obstinate man, really did prefer death to giving in, they left him alone after a while, for which piece of forbearance they must in the next few years have been heartily sorry. By now they were so completely drunk that they were fighting among themselves. This broke up the party. Some remained to sleep it off, but most returned in the direction from which they had come.

On the next day the riots reached Pownalborough. Major Goodwin, the intended victim, was suddenly taken ill on hearing of the rioters' approach. Men forced themselves into his bedroom, seized him by the arms, and threatened to drag him out of the house in spite of the outcry raised by his wife. His daughters, who ran in to help their father, were driven screaming down the stairs, half dressed as they had risen from their beds. When it came to the point, however, the mob was not quite ready to make sport with a sick man, though some grumbled that it was all a pretense on their victim's part. Finally they let him alone after forcing him to make a recantation of the address to General Gage which he had signed.

The crowd next began an advance in the general direction of the parsonage house, shouting and discharging their muskets. While Bailey escaped to the house of a friendly parishioner, some of his supporters staged a diversion which saved his house from being plundered. The suggestion was made that all go down to the courthouse, where the court was then sitting, and make sure their magistrates were true and honorable men. Here, after several harangues, a paper was drawn up in which the gentlemen of the court engaged not to act under the alteration of government enjoined by the recent act of Parliament. This being signed, the rioters began to disperse after having raged up and down the river for nearly a week without having discovered much tea, or added any signatures to the Covenant.

It is interesting to see how this affair unreels itself like a film in extraordinarily slow motion. The Gardinerston and Pownalborough riots took nearly a week; this is not entirely owing to the fact that many of the rioters went home in the early hours of the morning to sleep off their debauch and reassembled for more mischief towards the end of the following afternoon. In a straggling town like Pownalborough, where forty acres was a small farm and where roads were still woodland trails, the only methods of getting about were on foot and by canoe. This meant that it took a very long time for a crowd to collect and that once assembled, it might take several hours to reach the place where it had decided to go. Rum and speeches consumed more time and caused a good deal of noise, with the result that shouts or the discharging of muskets gave the victims plenty of warning, even if some friend did not come in to tell them that it was time to be off. Thus the only people caught seem to have been Goodwin, who was too ill to be moved, and Jones, the surveyor, who was evidently too obstinate a man to turn his back on a mob. No one was tarred and feathered in Pownalborough or ridden out of town on a rail, yet this cannot be put down to any particular moderation on the part of the people. Pownalborough was not done with riots yet, and evidence shows that the only difficulty in conducting a lynching was the very serious one that a victim was by no means easily caught.

Ineffective as these riots were after a fashion, they were certainly terrifying, and their result was to leave the leadership of the Kennebec Tories to Bailey alone. Goodwin, who was by now an elderly man, was evidently unequal to so much excitement, nor were his Tory principles stronger than his attachment to the country which he had helped to build. Though a churchwarden, he was a friend of Bowman, and while positive and blustering in manner, he was in fact easily led. For some time at least, he kept up his membership of the church and his personal friendship with the parson, but he ceased to throw his influence into the scale against the revolutionary movement. Soon it even appeared that he preferred putting himself at the head of the rioters to becoming their victim, and one of Bailey's narrowest escapes was in an affair that was sponsored by Goodwin.

William Gardiner's reaction to these troubles was exceedingly similar. So nervous was he that he had fled from his house for the first time some while before the danger was acute. When the mob actually arrived, he went clear down to Falmouth, whereas Bailey merely concealed himself for a couple of days and returned home the instant the coast was clear. When William reappeared in Gardinerston, he was evidently anxious to avoid offense. Indeed, in the following June after hostilities had broken out, we find him on the Committee of Safety and actually petitioning the Provincial Congress for powder for the protection of the town in its "Infant and defenseless state."

Jacob Bailey, who was of a far different calibre from either of his patrons, now found himself in an exposed position from which he could not in all honesty recede. Some fifteen years before, he had gone all the way over to England for his ordination ceremony, which had included a solemn oath on his part of allegiance not only to the English church, but to the King of England who was its head. Very naturally he felt that the taking of this oath had put him in an entirely different position from a man who had merely been born one of the King's subjects. Not only so, but he was the missionary of an English society, while his fathers in God, so to speak, were the English bishops. These connections were of such a special and sacred kind that the whole idea of revolution appeared to him wicked. Thus he was not only bound to allegiance himself, but he felt if necessary to give a right direction to his people. His sermons in 1774 include such subjects as: "caution against those who spread unauthorized opinions," "love of our country," "persecutions that holy men have suffered," and "danger of being connected with persons of vicious character." Petty persecutions naturally increased as his conduct gave more and more offense, yet it is a tribute to his real influence for good in the settlement that many of his congregation remained obstinately faithful even after the outbreak of war.

For a few months the inconvenience of assembling in large numbers, together with the small achievement of the September riots, kept the people along the Kennebec at home. The first fresh point of issue was the order of Thanksgiving sent out by President Hancock and the new Provincial Congress. Bailey refused either to read this proclamation or to open the church for the occasion; while Bowman, who as a relative of Hancock's was especially interested, determined that the celebration should be held. Fortunately for his purposes, there was a young man in town who had spent a year or so at a theological seminary and was now a schoolmaster. Bailey's account of this gentleman is that he was very young and of notoriously bad character, having been expelled from Harvard. In fact, there is some suggestion that he was also turned out of the Providence seminary for stealing the president's horse. However this may be, he had recently undergone a sudden conversion which went along with tremendous zeal in the cause of liberty. He was thus a very suitable person to set up as a rival to Bailey, and from this time on for several months he officiated regularly at the courthouse. It immediately followed that men could not excuse themselves for going to church by saying that there was no other form of worship available. Members of Bailey's congregation were denounced as enemies to their country and so fiercely threatened that they were forced to go occasionally to meeting in the hopes of avoiding trouble.

WHILE THIS STATE OF things obtained, Major Goodwin, who was apparently anxious to be forgiven by the popular party, made the suggestion that New Year's Day should be the occasion for erecting a Liberty Pole. The best place for this, he thought, would be in front of the church. However, as the vestry opposed him, people were induced to choose another spot. This celebration being formally announced beforehand, every patriot was expected to attend, and one cannot but admire the courage with which the parson and about twenty of his followers stayed away. Bailey's absence was fortunate, since Jonathan Bowman had provided a good deal of rum, which was consumed with such inflammatory effect that someone suggested the parson be dragged down to consecrate the pole by prayer. If he refused to do so, he was to be whipped around it. This notion was rejected by a small majority in a heated discussion, and the meeting dispersed after listening to a number of speeches which Bailey described with some justice as "the most horrible effusions."

THIS WAS NOT the end of the Liberty Pole affair, since a few nights later it was secretly cut down, and popular indignation accused Bailey of having a hand in it. He denied it vehemently, but feeling was so high against him that his friends were seriously alarmed. When therefore Sheriff Cushing sent him the recent votes of the Provincial Congress with an order to read them in church the next Sunday, he was repeatedly urged to give way. He consented to read a request for donations for the relief of distress in Boston, but he suppressed another order for the enlistment of Minute Men, which action brought him almost as much odium as if he had entirely refused. Meanwhile, he found himself in trouble with the Society for the Propagation of the Gospel on account of this tiny concession, and he was forced to excuse his action as best he might.

The news of the Battle of Lexington came to the Kennebec as a confusion of the wildest rumors. Two thousand British had been beaten by fifty Continentals. The entire British army had been surrounded by fifty or sixty thousand Continentals under arms. All the Tories were to be massacred except the clergy, who were to be sent to perpetual slavery in the Simsbury mines. People were running around in groups shouting, "Let us fight! Let us fight!" and were answered by a cry of, "Let us first murder the Tories.... not a devil of them shall continue to breathe another day." At the parsonage, Bailey was insulted and threatened, while an attack was made on his servant. Meanwhile another rumor shortly began to spread that British men-of-war and transports had landed a thousand men on the coast to plunder and destroy. Everyone rushed to arms and assembled at the courthouse. So great was the confusion that the Committee of Safety, which was headed by Bowman, was actually alarmed by it and took measure to induce the more disorderly parts of the mob to disperse. These made an effort to assert themselves by planning the lynching of a prominent member of Bailey's flock who was someone's personal enemy. He, however, as usual had time to escape, and the disappointed rabble consented to go home, after being assured by the Committee that all traitors should be immediately disarmed.

While matters were in this state, and more or less orderly groups were patrolling the roads or searching the houses of Loyalists for weapons, a further sensation was caused by the arrival of Bailey's brother-in-law from Marblehead. The Reverend J. Wingate Weeks, who was also an Episcopal clergyman, had recently been expelled by Patriot mobs from his parish. He now chose this minute to arrive with his wife, his eight children, and his furniture to take refuge with his relations. All was immediately in an uproar. The rioters reassembled at dawn by the courthouse and marched down to the landing place to prevent him from bringing his goods ashore. Another outbreak seemed inevitable, but fortunately the committees of several neighboring towns happened to arrive at this moment for a conference on the state of public affairs. It was agreed that the fate of Mr. Weeks should be left to their united determination. After being rudely questioned for above an hour, he was finally permitted to land his furniture at the expense of putting his name to an "ignominious paper." Weeks's account of his situation in Pownalborough was given to the Society for the Propagation of the Gospel. "I am now stripped of the comforts and conveniences of life; my wife and a family of eight helpless children are obliged to seek shelter in a wilderness, the horrors of which they had never seen or felt before. And even there they have not been suffered to remain in quiet. Their happiness has been often interrupted by insults, and by the snapping of a loaded gun at Mr. Bailey and me, while walking in the garden."

Weeks is dramatizing somewhat, and yet there is no doubt that Bailey's life was more than once threatened. As a group was marching down the road past Pownalborough church, a man named Harvey loaded his musket and leveled it at the parsonage house, where Bailey with several children was to be seen looking at them through the window. Someone asked Harvey what inducement he had to behave in this fashion.

"This is a —— nest of Tories," replied he, "and I am going to blow as many of them to the —— as possible."

At this he pulled the trigger several times, but as Bailey said, "it was Providentially prevented from going off, notwithstanding it was never before or after the experiment, to miss fire."

Fortified by this evidence of divine protection, the parson stuck to his post, though he was no longer able to receive his salary from England and did not know how he should live. During the summer his enemies shot seven of his sheep and one of his heifers at a time when it must be remembered that he had ten extra mouths to feed. Fortunately Mr. Weeks departed before winter, but Bailey's need was by now so great that he was forced to sell what livestock he had left, until by spring he owned nothing but a single cow. Even his vegetable garden was ruthlessly trampled. Meanwhile the assistance of his own parishioners was largely cut off by a tax laid on the town for the support of a Congregational minister. Taking advantage of the ignorance of many of Bailey's foreign-born congregation, the collectors were ruthlessly seizing cattle and precious equipment in lieu of cash. A minister might have pitied some of the miseries that were caused for his sake, and have consented to wait and be paid by degrees in produce. There being, however, no minister in fact, the money remained in the hands of the collectors and was irrecoverable. In short, it was becoming evident that unless Bailey could find some relief, he would soon have the choice between leaving the country and starving completely.

These miseries of Bailey's were increased by the fact that every fresh development in the general situation found him in a particularly vulnerable position. Upon the publication of the Declaration of Independence, other Loyalists might at least keep silent, but Bailey was required to read the document in church. Wild threats were used to induce him, while more reasonable people assured him with every evidence of good faith that he would be the only clergyman in the country not to give way. Prayers for the King were a set part of the Anglican church service, and in normal times Bailey had no more right to omit them at pleasure than he had to decide to leave out the Creed or the Lord's Prayer. Every sort of pressure was now put upon him to do so, but his conscience was adamant. "Some of you perhaps expect that I should read a paper," said he, "but I cannot comply without offering the utmost violence to my conscience, and I solemnly declare in the presence of this assembly that my refusal does not proceed from any contempt of authority, but from a sacred regard to my former engagements and from a dread of offending that God who is infinitely superior to all earthly power." Such refusal could only result in his arrest, yet when his came, his defense of his position was so skillful, and his supporters still so numerous that the Committee found themselves at a loss and did not commit him for trial.

While Bailey was undergoing these difficulties, William Gardiner was busy ingratiating himself with his neighbors as best he might. Some time during the summer of 1775, it became evident that great things were about to happen on the Kennebec. Major Benedict Arnold of the Continental Army had been reading with much interest the diary of Montresor, that British officer of engineers who had come down the Kennebec from Quebec in 1760 and had returned by another version of the same route. Where one had ventured, many might follow. Montressor had traveled light with a couple of Indian guides in a canoe, who had probably been able to kill some game as they went along. To take over a thousand men with all their provisions and military equipment up this way to Quebec was a desperate venture, only justified by the value of the prize they might be able to grasp. As a matter of fact, Arnold lost a quarter of his men by desertion and another quarter by death. Yet arriving with only six hundred sick, ragged, and desperate men, he very nearly succeeded in taking the town and in exercising an incalculable influence on the entire course of the war.

PREPARATIONS FOR this expedition were on a large enough scale to occupy most of the attention of a settlement the size of Gardinerston. Two hundred bateaux were to be built there, which meant work for every carpenter on the river and endless demand for tools. A storekeeper who tried to hold out on the price of nails was judged unpatriotic, and soldiers broke in and took them from him without paying at all. It was late in September before the transports came and were received in Pownalborough with wild enthusiasm and the firing of salutes. James Howard, the commander of the old Fort Western, was famous for his hospitality; and according to a tradition which seems to be authentic, he acted as host at a tremendous banquet spread for the officers of the force and all the notable people of the district. The food consisted of bear meat, ten baskets of roasted green corn, quantities of smoked salmon, a hundred pumpkin pies, watermelons and wild cherries; and it was eked out by beef, pork, and bread from the military stores. Howard sat at the head of the table with Aaron Burr on his left, splendidly dressed for a wilderness adventure in black knee breeches, blue swallow-tailed coat with gilt buttons, buff vest, silk stockings, and silver buckles. Arnold sat at the other end, and in between were scattered Major Colburn, who had built the bateaux, Judge Jonathan Bowman, Colonel Charles Cushing, Major Goodwin, the recently converted Tory, and William Gardiner, Esquire. Drums rolled, salutes were fired, and toasts were called, while Bailey absented himself from his home for greater safety and other Tories thought it better not to be seen abroad. William, whose father was now closely besieged in Boston, and whose own political opinions never seem to have differed from Silvester's in the least, was climbing back into favor by his presence at this function. He probably told himself that it was more important to keep in with his neighbors than to protest against an inevitable course of events.

$\mathcal{E}$XILE

T HE EVACUATION of Boston by the British was brought
about quite suddenly by Washington's fortification of
Dorchester Heights, commanding the town and the
harbor. Actually the Tories had about a week in which to decide whether they would leave with General Howe, and if so to
make arrangements for their passage and for getting their families and their goods on board. General Howe had about thirteen thousand soldiers to remove, and he was naturally short of
shipping space, so that his generous offer to take with him those
Loyalists who dared not stay was by no means easy of execution. Room was somehow found for upwards of eleven hundred refugees, and space was allotted for carrying their
furniture at the expense of valuable stores of provisions and
other necessities. The whole period of the evacuation was one
of terrible confusion. Officers were trying to sell their personal
property, Tories to take measures for the protection of their
house until they should return, and townspeople to prevent
their goods being pillaged by the departing troops. Nothing
was safe that was left unguarded. Soldiers broke into the empty
houses of wealthy Patriots, drank their wine, smashed their

china, and made off with everything they could carry. Sailors, brought ashore to help in loading the ships, pilfered freely from the valuables of Loyalists as they were put on board, and plundered all parts of the town to which they had access. A gang of soldiers under General Howe's orders to seize goods that would be useful to the rebels in carrying on the war, perpetrated organized robberies under cover of their instructions.

There must have been many conferences among panic-stricken Tory families during these chaotic days, and at first Silvester Gardiner was determined to remain behind. Like many another self-made man, he put a high value on his property, and his experience of being virtually deprived of all that he owned in Connecticut and Maine had hardened his determination to hold on to what remained to him in Boston. Since he had not served the British directly, nor contributed any money towards the conduct of the campaign, he felt personally innocent of offense towards the rebels. His age he also trusted would be a protection. At least it was an additional motive for staying behind, as he really did not feel equal to starting life again encumbered by a family of ladies and with no other resources than what he could carry away with him.

Such arguments had very little weight with Mrs. Gardiner. During the course of the siege, the Patriots had uttered a number of virulent threats against Tories, which had been repeated with all the exaggerations of gossip in the circle of ladies to which she belonged. Silvester was certainly in danger, and she herself might hardly be safe when her conduct during the siege was brought to the rebels' attention. Silvester was too old to be a combatant, but neither could he have endured being tarred and feathered or hunted out of town by a drunken mob. Many a man more inoffensive than he had suffered such tortures, as was common knowledge. There was no knowing what wild deeds would be done when the rebels appeared in the town drunk with victory. A more violent partisan even than her husband, Abigail Gardiner would rather go to England, where decent folk were to be found, than live among such people. Nor did she fear a fresh start as much as Silvester, since her greater youthfulness and cheerful disposition induced her to make light of the privations awaiting them. The discussion between the two must have been prolonged, since Silvester was never an easy man to persuade. However, it soon became clear that all their friends thought it madness in Silvester to hold out. Robert Hallowell, who had been collector of customs, was taking Hannah, though she was expecting a child in a few months. The Dumaresqs were leaving also. In the end, there was nothing for Silvester to do but to fall in line.

O F THE DOCTOR'S two sloops, one at least was at this time in Boston Harbor, but either it had no crew, or Silvester was afraid that so small a ship would be snapped up by some privateer. At all events he with his wife and two stepdaughters accepted the accommodation provided by General Howe. Of what nature this was can only be guessed by the fact than an efficient and important man like Benjamin Hallowell, the Comptroller of Customs, found himself sharing a cabin which contained thirty-seven people. Masters, mistresses, servants, and children were forced to camp on the bare deck as best they could for six days and a half, with a high sea running to add to their miseries. Meanwhile, however, Silvester's immediate difficulty was to decide what could be taken and what must be left. Transport to the dock was almost unavailable, and possessions had to be watched every minute to protect them from looters. In these circumstances, there was no use in Silvester trying to move his stock of drugs, his library, or his expensive furniture, even supposing the ship had room for them. He took five hundred pounds in cash, which he happened to have by him, his silver plate, which must have been quite valuable, and very little else but clothes and personal possessions. His moderation was rewarded by receiving his goods intact at Halifax. This was not the case with more ambitious persons who had tried to bring china or other articles which could be easily damaged. However, of all the vast quantity of things Silvester left behind him, he never saw or owned a single piece again.

Halifax, Nova Scotia, in 1776 was a town of three or four thousand inhabitants, and consisted of a half a dozen parallel streets of grey wooden houses strung out along the side of a hill, whence they commanded a magnificent view of the town's extensive harbor. Founded in 1749 as a British counterpart to Louisburg, it had been hastily peopled by Irish dockyard workers and German refugees swept up by an unscrupulous emigration agent for a commission of a guinea a head. This unpromising mixture was combined with English fishermen and seamen, together with a fair proportion of New England settlers, who were now largely anti-British. In 1760, according to one account, one house in five was retailing liquor, as often as not without a license. This situation was fostered by the town being largely a naval base, which also accounted for the fact that it was perennially short of stores. Only four bakers and four butchers existed to supply the large quantities of salted meat and ship's biscuit that must have been needed from time to time. The fact was that the inland parts of Nova Scotia were as yet so sparsely settled that they hardly supported themselves, let along supplying Halifax with meat or grain. Even on the edges of the town, the half-burned stumps of trees were dreary evidence that the work of clearing for farmland was very little more than begun.

The climate of this unattractive town was damp and cold at most times, and in late March and April particularly unpleasant. Judge Oliver, one of the Tory exiles, declared it impossible to visit his next-door neighbor without taking a cloak, since even a cloudless sky afforded no guarantee that it would not begin to pour with rain within a few moments. "If anyone chuses to live there," he summed up the place, "he is welcome to do so, provided he will not compell me to live there too." Shelter for nearly fourteen thousand soldiers and refugees was simply not available. There were little more than a thousand houses in the town, and by no means all of these were in good repair. "The houses of Halifax," says Oliver, "seem to have been sowed like mushrooms in a hot-bed, and to have decayed as fast; for although they have been built but a few years, yet there are scarce any of them habitable." Silvester Gardiner is more concise, but equally frank. "Houses did I say," he exclaims, "they hardly deserve that name."

Naturally even houses of a sort, if obtainable, would have been better than none. As things were, there could not possibly be enough to go round. Prices shot up to fantastic figures for the most wretched accommodations. Cellars, stables, and unfinished attics were crowded with refugees. In many cases three or four families were obliged to lodge together in one room and to think themselves lucky that they were not in a makeshift tent on the Common, or even huddled under the shelter of an upturned cart. Food was almost equally unobtainable, so much so that at the end of a few months not a dog or a cat remained uneaten in the entire settlement. In an effort to keep alive, unfortunate refugees were forced to sacrifice the plate, money, or other valuables which they had relied on to support them until they could make a new life for themselves. Very few felt the least gratitude to the inhabitants of the town, whom they regarded as an inhuman set of robbers bent on making capital out of their miseries. In fact, the high prices were caused by scarcity rather than greed, and the inhabitants seem to have behaved well, especially considering that they had not invited the refugees and were in many cases not particularly in sympathy with their politics.

Silvester Gardiner was fortunate compared to many of his

friends. He obtained some sort of a house at a rent of fifty pounds per annum, though he complained it was a hovel which would not in normal times have been worth more than five. He was not a man to suffer in silence, and he relieved his feelings by exclaiming bitterly that people had "the conscience" to charge five times the normal price for firewood, and that the cost of meat and butter was simply exorbitant. At the end of six weeks his five hundred pounds had sunk to little more than four, and he was in a state very close to complete despair. God alone knew what he should do when his funds were exhausted! In the meantime he could only pour forth his bitterness upon the rebels, whose actions he said were a disgrace to human nature. "By this cursed rebellion," he wrote, "I am drove to this wretched place, and from a state of Affluence (could truly say I did not know a want) to a mere state of indigency." Some of the exiles were already making arrangements for their passage to England, but Silvester was unwilling to be forced to leave his native land. The severity of the winter in Halifax was more than he could face at his age in such a house, but he determined to wait through the summer and see whether the King's troops would not make good their footing in some place to which he might go.

THIS DECISION MADE, Silvester recovered a little of his energy and applied once more to Ainslie for assistance from Quebec. Ainslie was anxious to help, but though he got up at five in the morning to go out and scour the countryside for supplies, he succeeded in obtaining nothing but a dozen chickens, which he duly dispatched. Nevertheless, he assured Silvester that if he would only come and spend the winter in Quebec, he would find plenty of fresh provisions, all kinds of roots, and the best wines and rum on the continent. More he could not do, but he sent his regards to Mrs. Gardiner with the remark that if she had not lost her "ancient spirit," she would be an example to her countrywomen in distress and a real consolation to her husband.

By the end of the summer, the obvious move was to go to New York, where the British were firmly entrenched, and where things were more comfortable and cheaper. Silvester felt cheerful enough on his arrival to spend a little of his precious money refurbishing his appearance, which had evidently suffered under the primitive conditions of life at Halifax. One of his earliest acts was to buy a new bag wig, and to have his old one remounted with a new top, and both fitted out with fresh ribbons. Thus equipped, he sent to England for a few drugs and started up on a small scale in his business. Unfortunately the army was either importing its own supplies or getting them from established merchants who could deal in larger quantities. There was little demand for Silvester's wares, and though he eked out his resources by collecting a few outstanding debts and selling his silver, his means grew gradually more straitened as time went on. Arthur Browne, his English son-in-law, was generous enough to send him over some supplies, but Arthur Browne was not well to do and in any case could support him much more cheaply in England. After two years of New York, it was apparent that a move to England would be soon inevitable. The British Government was granting small pensions to ruined Loyalists, and Silvester's only remaining resource was to get over there and apply for one while he still had money left for the passage.

Silvester's flight to Halifax with the British army had undermined William's new position on the Kennebec by giving a chance to such people as wished to break up his estate. Property abandoned by its owner was for some time administered by the town to which it belonged, more because an empty house deteriorates and is liable to be looted than because there was any idea of confiscation. In the case of Silvester's Boston possessions, the town's course was perfectly simple, but his

Kennebec estate under William's direction was no more abandoned than it had ever been. The obvious course was to leave it alone for the present, but this was not quite satisfactory, owing to William's strictly limited powers. For instance, one of Silvester's last acts had been to lease the abandoned Fort Halifax to a man named Ephraim Ballard, who was known to be a Loyalist sympathizer. When the Kennebec found itself once more at war with a great power strongly entrenched in Canada, it could not fail to be extremely uneasy at seeing this fort in such hands. The committee of Winslow, in which township Fort Halifax now lay, suspected that it was state property and that the Doctor had no right to grant a lease. In the absence of his papers, however, they found themselves quite at a loss. Meanwhile debtors or personal enemies of Silvester saw their chance to even matters up. Claims began to be put forward which William, who was not quick to size up a situation, does not seem to have realized were politically dangerous. He resisted in an ineffective way, and made remarks about patriotic people which were easy to interpret as treasonable. When the situation finally brought about his arrest, he appears to have been outraged and surprised.

In 1777 an act of the Provincial Government requested towns to draw up lists of persons inimical to the States and to present them for trial. Those convicted were to be deported, under penalty of death if they persistently returned. William and Bailey both came under consideration at town meetings, but had enough supporters to keep their names off the list. However, the opportunity was too good to be missed by their enemies, who now put forward one of their number to swear out a deposition against William. Gideon Gardiner, who was a distant cousin, had originally been induced by Silvester to try his fortunes in the settlement. As usual, the Doctor had been over-optimistic at the start and had been induced to go surety for his cousin, who was much in debt at the time of his arrival.

When Silvester found himself forced to pay up, he was naturally furious and came down on Gideon heavily for payment. They had been partners together in a farm, or else Silvester had held a mortgage. In any case he then repossessed it and reduced Gideon, whom he described as a "villain," to the position of tenant. Gideon appears to have had some reason for thinking himself unfairly treated, and he had recently quarreled with William about lumbering some unoccupied land. He now induced the Committee to have William arrested and brought down to Pownalborough for trial.

Poor William defended himself with a good deal of spirit, which was the more necessary since the counsel appointed to assist him was too frightened to act. There was evidently a good deal of doubt as to what sort of a remark made a person clearly "inimical" to the cause of the States. As William had refrained from general expressions about politics and had confined himself to saying that Judge Bowman "wo'd in a little time be blacker than the Devil," or that North, another of his judges, "was a Joe Bunker justice," he had fair grounds for saying that treason could not possibly be proved. He pointed out that he had even contributed money to the support of the war, a part of his defense which he did not later pass on to his father.

ALL THESE PROTESTS were of little use. The jury had been packed, while three of the court were William's personal enemies and stood to gain considerably by his conviction. Jonathan Bowman was now judge of probate and had the care of forfeited estates. He eventually appointed Charles Cushing as agent, who in turn let the Cobbossee grist mill and double sawmills to Justice North. This latter gentleman was already freely exploiting Silvester's timber and had appealed to the Assembly to turn William out of the estate. His political opinions were so rabid that he had lately declared in open court that even to *think* the public administration unfair was a crime deserving transportation. Convicted by such judges, William was sent up to Boston, to be kept there in a guard ship until arrangements could be made to transport him to British Dominions.

There was no appeal from this sentence to a higher court, so that William's only recourse was to put in a petition to the Assembly. Here he was fortunate enough to have some friends. Even John Hancock, who had spoken violently against Silvester, bore no malice towards William. Moreover, if his statements were true, the trial was not only unfair, but illegal, since the jury had not been selected according to the proper forms. William was allowed to lodge in Boston on parole, shortly attended a hearing, and received permission to go back to the Kennebec in order to collect depositions. After another hearing, his case was reported upon favorably by the examining committee, but such was the pressure of business that it was almost a year before the matter was taken up by the Assembly as a whole. It then appeared that many of the papers had been lost, including statements from various people who had enlisted in the army and were not easily to be found again.

William's behavior in this accumulation of troubles was almost frantic. In truth, his position was difficult, for after having attempted to keep on terms with both sides, he now found himself popular with neither. Bailey, indeed, was generous enough to overlook shortcomings and write of William as a true Loyalist. None understood better than the parson the kind of pressures to which William had been exposed, and the hopelessness of expecting his behavior to be completely consistent. "No man among us has done more," he writes to a friend, "according to his abilities, to support the distressed friends of government." These excuses, however, did William no good with Silvester, who had not had the experience of living in an area governed by Patriots. In New York, the Doctor found himself a member of a very large refugee group which had nothing to do but to confirm its own prejudices by reference to *Rivington's Gazette*, a Loyalist sheet whose distortion of facts was notorious. He now therefore drove William frantic by declaring that his misfortunes were largely the result of his own folly. William hysterically replied that this accusation was a false as it was cruel, that enemies had misrepresented him to Silvester, that evil persons had suppressed his letters, and that most of his persecutions had been due to the enmity felt towards his father. He enclosed a detailed list of his legal expenses, bewailed the falling price of boards and the rise of taxes, swore he was subsisting on charity in Boston, and enumerated all the times he had been confined in jail or forced to be present at a hearing.

At the end of 1778 William got leave to go to New York, on the grounds that his father's papers contained some essential evidence. With typical inefficiency he arrived a week after Silvester had sailed for England, but Dumaresq, who received him not too cordially, was completely melted by the misery of his appearance. He reported that William looked thin and was very much altered, adding that he had been ill treated and deserved some compassion, since his sufferings were "fully sufficient for his past imprudence." William's own effusion to his father bears out his brother-in-law's account. He admits he burst into tears on hearing that Silvester had left, and then he proceeds to conjure up frightful pictures of his aged father crossing the wintry seas to destitute exile under difficulties such as few people had ever known. "Good God," he adds, carried away by this eloquence, "the scene makes my heart almost bleed."

Evidently this epistle softened the heart of Silvester towards him, while eventually his sentence was reversed by the Assembly in Boston, and he was enabled to return to his estate and even to recover it from the administration of Charles Cushing. He dared take no steps, however, to recover the value of farm implements sold by that worthy, or to check the depredations of Gideon Gardiner and other tenants. Enough rent came in to support him after some fashion, and he evidently still had many friends. These were so pleased to see him return that they even elected him a delegate to the Assembly, though he was objected to as a Tory and was not able to take his seat. William, whose one idea was to stay quiet and keep out of trouble, made no attempt to get this verdict reversed. Confiscation of his father's estates was probable, and in any case it was hard to see how he could control the situation for long, especially as he evidently preferred destitution to the consequences of trying to resist it.

SILVESTER'S DECISION to leave for England had been undertaken reluctantly, but the surrender of Burgoyne in the fall of 1777 and the alliance with France in the spring of 1778 had made it reasonably certain to intelligent men that the Colonies would eventually win the war. One of the early acts of the Patriots on occupying Boston had been to confiscate Silvester's supply of drugs for the benefit of the Revolutionary Army. "That theif Washington" was Silvester's outraged comment of this affair, but his indignation did not alter the fact that his drugs, and shortly after his sloops were pressed into the service of his enemies. His five Boston houses scattered along Long Lane and Marlborough and Winter Streets had been leased by the revolutionary government for its own benefit. His furniture, his fine library, his carriage and other personal possessions had been sold at public auction and were gone forever. In the fall of 1778 his name appeared on the list of those banished from Massachusetts, with a penalty of transportation for the first, and death for the second appearance. By this time it was also obvious that the states would soon resort to confiscation of Loyalists estates in order to help pay for the war. In this case, Silvester would lose his Kennebec property, his Boston houses, his real estate in Middletown and elsewhere, and even a chance to collect his outstanding debts. To stay in New York might mean to starve. It certainly would not assist him to recover the riches of which he had been robbed.

Hannah Hallowell, whose second daughter had been born during that dreadful summer at Halifax, had not been two years in England, and was settled in Bristol, where houses were cheap owing to the decline of its American trade. She was happy there amid a small refugee colony, and her husband was able to eke out his government pension with a number of little commissions which he earned not so much by his abilities, as by his unusually pleasant and sociable disposition. Hannah undoubtedly urged her father to come over, and Mrs. Gardiner was very ready to take this advice. However, in spite of his early memories of England and all his present connections with it, Silvester now felt not the slightest desire to spend his declining years in that country. He went because he had no option. He seems always to have disliked it, and he spent most of his time after the peace in attempting to get permission to return to Massachusetts.

Silvester left for England at the end of 1778, just missing a consignment of supplies from the Hallowells and another from Colonel Arthur Browne, both of which he instructed his friend Bartholmew Sullivan to sell in New York for what they would fetch. He had left with the same agent his stock of drugs, a few notes of hand from people who owed him money, and the duty of extracting from the British army the as yet unpaid rent of his Boston house. By these means he gained about a hundred and fifty pounds in remittances during the next twelve months, which appears to have been all that he had to live on, with the exception of such support as might be granted him by the British government.

The method established for gaining such relief was to submit a petition to Lord George Germain, undersecretary of state for Colonial Affairs. This petition, together with the depositions supporting its claims, was eventually taken under consideration by the Lords of the Treasury, who made an allowance of from fifty to two hundred pounds per annum as they thought proper. Silvester, who had taken the trouble to come exceedingly well recommended, was in high hopes of getting the largest sum, and promptly. What actually happened was that he was granted a hundred pounds, apparently as an emergency measure to take care of his needs while the government found time to consider his petition. Eighteen months then passed, at the end of which Silvester was very nearly desperate. About a quarter of what the government had given him had been expended in the process of pushing his petition, so far with no effect. Peter Oliver, who was in his debt, wrote from Birmingham to say that he had gone there for economy's sake and simply had not the money to pay anything, though he knew Silvester did not have sufficient to live on. Meanwhile John Vassall was pressing for a hundred pounds, for which Silvester had become surety in 1774. The unfortunate doctor had to submit to being abused as dishonest because he attempted to pay the Vassalls by transferring to them the interest he held on a mortgaged estate in New England, which was not itself confiscated, though his own property was, and by assigning to them a bond of the painter, Copley, on which he had tried in vain to collect himself.

B Y THE MIDDLE of 1780, Silvester was actually considering the possibility of sending Mrs. Gardiner and her unmarried daughter back to America in order that they might throw themselves on the charity of her relations. Her brother William wrote cruelly to her that she would never be allowed to return to her native land or to lie in the tomb belonging to the rest of her family. Nevertheless, the real drawback in this plan appeared to be that Silvester did not know where he could find the money to pay for their passage. Meanwhile of course he spared no pains to remind the government of his necessities. Count Rumford was interested in his case, and Sir William Pepperell was induced to speak to him and to Lord George Germain. Sir William's chief recommendation, however, was that Silvester write to Lord North, the Prime Minister, every two or three days, and he remarks that the letters cannot possibly be too pressing. Whether for this reason or for some other, the government did shortly thereafter make up its mind, and granted to Silvester an annual allowance of a hundred and fifty pounds. This, coinciding with a reduction in the size of his household which followed shortly thereafter, made Silvester's needs much less serious. He seems to have been able to live, if not with comfort, at least without major financial anxieties, from this time forth.

It was not to be expected that an intolerant, forceful man like Silvester would be content to come over to England without attempting to teach the English something about how to run the mismanaged war. Silvester was violently critical of Howe, whom he called "the Infamous Howe," and whom he declared could have finished the rebellion four times to his certain knowledge. He regarded the whole officer corps as dissipated and inefficient and was prepared to offer a plan that would reform these evils and introduce some intelligence into the conduct of the war as a whole. Count Rumford presented Silvester's suggestions to Lord George Germain, who went so far as to say he would be very glad to see them carried into execution. Probably the matter rested there, unless indeed the very submission of such a plan was enough to delay the Lords of the Treasury in considering Silvester's petition. Undoubtedly American Loyalist critics were not popular, and sensible as their remarks often were, they ignored one factor in the situation which automatically made most of their ideas impracticable. The British were fighting this war with a professional army, a highly complex organization, and the only thing of its kind that they had got. To suggest a radical change in the system of appointments or the equipment and training of the soldiers was at this juncture hopeless. In time the lessons of this war might take effect, but at the moment responsible ministers could only shrug their shoulders in angry fashion at the impertinent criticisms of people who had never managed the smallest expedition, let alone an army that was not fighting two nations at once.

These two pieces of important business naturally kept Silvester in London at first, where he might have remained among a number of his Boston acquaintances, had he not rapidly found that the capital was far too expensive for his limited means. Two weeks' lodging cost him five guineas, and though he moved immediately to somewhere else which only charged four, even this was considerably more than he could afford. Besides, he had to buy a new dress wig and silk stockings, since it was absolutely necessary to meet people who would recommend his case to the Treasury lords. The cost of food was also high, and as another London refugee put it, "truly one cannot breathe the vital air without expense." The Hallowells were settled in Bristol and wrote highly recommending that town. As its trade had been largely American, the war had brought depression and a fall in living costs, with the result that a number of American friends had gone to live there. The town itself was pleasant, its climate relatively mild, and its people, who were largely seafaring, were the nearest thing that could be found to New England merchants. In fact, as Governor Hutchinson had said, "you might pick out a set of Boston selectmen from any of their churches."

Silvester was persuaded to come to Bristol and to invest thirty pounds in the rent of a three-story house with garret and in the hire of a certain amount of furniture. The two main bedrooms, for instance, were fully furnished, whereas the hall seems to have had nothing in it but an oil painting in a gilt frame, and a meat hook with a line and two pulleys. Such as it was, the house was large enough for a the family, and if Silvester had been content with Bristol, he might have afforded to live there as well as anywhere. Unfortunately the climate, though fairly mild, is wet, and by the end of a couple of months Silvester had already caught two colds and was sunk in depression about his health, about his affairs, and about Bristol generally. Life seemed to be made up of paying taxes. There was a house tax, a land tax, a window tax, a poor tax, a bridge tax, a watch tax, and even a lamp and scavenger tax that had to be paid. Refugees are seldom popular with the people among whom they find their home, and though it was possible for an agreeable man like Robert Hallowell to be happy in Bristol, it was far more difficult for Silvester. He was not agreeable, but irascible and set in his ways, and he had arrived in the town at a time when the people were heartily tired of American exiles. The Reverend J. Wingate Weeks, Bailey's brother-in-law, who was now an exile in London, commented on the fact that people who had spent a few idle years at Oxford held a worthy American clergyman in open contempt. The same thing doubtless was true among doctors. At least it was notable that in all the years Silvester spent in England, there is no evidence he practiced his profession, whereas on returning to America at the age of seventy-eight, he resumed it immediately.

A MID ALL THESE minor calamities it was not the least that the spirits of Abigail Eppes Gardiner began for the first time to fail. She was troubled by a very violent headache, which her husband immediately attributed to the damp, heavy air. Neither of them could bear to stay in Bristol longer, and they shortly began looking around for a place which should if possible be cheaper and have a climate milder than Bristol, or at all events less damp. The seacoast town of Poole in Dorset, not far from the borders of Devon, is today little more than a fishing village, though its Georgian guildhall and a few eighteenth-century houses recall the fact that in Silvester's time it was a trading port of quite considerable wealth. It stands on the shore of a wide spreading estuary, some forty miles in circumference and almost entirely landlocked. Most of this is very shallow, with the result that the ebb of the tide converts it from a vast inland lake to a series of wide mud flats intersected by little rivers and haunted by herons, curlews, sheldrake, and gulls. The beauty of Poole lies in its coloring. Blue or grey water contrasts with bright yellow sand dunes, brown salt marshes, and vivid green splashes of weed. Inland, the low hills are yellow with gorse and rich purple with heather, the climate being so mild that some of the former is almost always in flower. Violets bloom here in Christmas week, while lilacs and golden laburnum come out in March. Here, if anywhere, Silvester might have found the air he craved for and the kind of people among whom he liked to live.

Poole owed his fortune partly to the safety of its harbor, but partly to the fact that the meeting of currents in the channel provides it with four tides in twenty-four hours instead of two. This gift of a double high tide, though not peculiar to Poole, is sufficiently uncommon to gave it advantage over other fishing villages further down the coast. Already in the seventeenth century Poole was important enough to be one of two towns that had held out for the Parliament when the forces of the King overran the West. In the eighteenth century, its official trade was chiefly with Newfoundland, wither Silvester also had sent *The Kennebec* from Boston. Newfoundland was merely a fishing center at this time, and almost all its supplies were provided by the merchants of Poole, who took back cargoes of fish and oil in return. The trade was profitable enough to support coopers, bread-bag makers, bakers, millers and various other artisans at Poole, as well as the merchants themselves, who lived in stately houses along a few streets running up from the wharves to the center of the town.

This, however, was only part of Poole's trade, the legitimate part. Another side to the town's activities, it was renowned as one of the greatest smuggling centers on the coast. In the middle of the century a gang of sixty smugglers had actually broken open Poole customs house in broad daylight to recover a couple tons of tea which the revenue officers had laid their hands on. They returned through Fordinbridge with their load and were watched by several hundreds, but only one had the daring or the spite to say that he could recognize any of the gang beneath their masks. The sequel to this affair was the murder of the witness, for which seven people were finally and with great difficulty brought to justice. In such a town the wisest part was to stay indoors after dark, and to ask no questions. Even people who were not involved in the trade, and these were few, were happy to buy tea, wines, or brandy from smugglers at a reasonable price. Silvester, who as a merchant had no use for import duties, was probably willing to accommodate himself to the situation and make no trouble. In any case during his first six months in the town, he had other matters of greater personal importance on his mind.

Mrs. Gardiner had felt better after the move from Bristol, and perfectly recovered her spirits. Nevertheless she began to complain of a slight weakness in her left ankle, though unaccompanied by pain and only noticeable if she attempted to walk too far. Gradually, this began to extend itself up her leg as far as the hip and to become more obvious, until she was positively unable to walk more than about a hundred yards. Silvester now became really worried and, though his finances were almost at their lowest ebb, he took her up to London to consult with the best physicians. No improvement ensuing, the pair next went to Bath, only to find that she grew worse more rapidly than before. Convinced once more, as he had been in Bristol, that this degeneration was due to the heaviness and dampness of the air, Silvester returned to Poole. Mrs. Gardiner was soon completely bedridden, and had lost her reason and the use of her whole left side. It was evident enough that she was not going to recover. In November she finally died, about two months after her husband received the pension that would have made such a difference to her life.

Silvester was really crushed by this blow. Not all his religious feelings, which had only been strengthened by his misfortunes, could console him for such a loss. Abigail's cheerfulness had been his greatest support in trouble, and her death by depriving him of the companionship of his stepdaughter also, had left him completely alone. She was the best of wives, he told those friends who offered consolation, and all his happiness in this world had been centered in her. Her loss was quite irreparable.

MISFORTUNES SELDOM come alone. It was during his wife's first indisposition that Silvester had received news from the Society for the Propagation of the Gospel of the arrival in Halifax of a little vessel of fifteen tons from the Kennebec, bringing Bailey and his family with the miserable remains of their household goods. Mrs. Bailey had nothing left to wear over her petticoats but a ragged baize nightgown tied round with a woolen string. Her husband's coat, a charitable gift, was so much too large that the waist was almost down to his knees, while its original blue color was nearly indistinguishable amid the patches, stains, and threadbare places which disfigured it. They had been taken to the house of Captain Callahan, an old friend and parishioner, where their little Charley, now two years old and talking freely, exclaimed at the sight of a loaf of bread on the table and asked their astonished hostess what it was. Their abandonment of the cause at Pownalborough, and their arrival in British territory without bringing so much as a verbal message from William were ample evidence that the last vestige of Silvester's influence on the Kennebec had been destroyed.

The silencing of William Gardiner had afforded an excellent example of the way in which the Revolution fused personal and patriotic grievances by offering a common method of redress for both. William's judges may have been prejudiced by self-interest, yet he was undoubtedly a Loyalist; and though he might be harmless personally, he was in a position to give help and comfort to those who were not. War had come upon Maine at an unfortunate moment. Settlements were still far from self-supporting and depended for necessary supplies on coastal trade. It was hard to prevent a man with a load of boards from taking it to Boston, and in the early days when that city was in British hands, Patriots at Georgetown went so far as to set up cannon by the mouth of the Kennebec in order to prevent ships sailing out of the river at all. This situation could not last, and throughout the war the Assembly was deluged with petitions such as that of Joseph Christopher of Pownalborough, who represented himself as "being under the most urgent Necessity for the Article of salt, having a Quantity of Alewives which are in a Suffering Condition for want of salt to Repack them." Trading permits were liberally issued to people whose patriotism was undoubted, and within six months commerce was proceeding on a considerable scale, if by no means as freely as before. When, however, the British retreated to Halifax, and the coast of Maine found itself in the front line of the struggle, the results were disastrous. Lincoln County estimated that of sixty coasting vessels owned in the area, forty-nine were taken or lost within three years. The export of masts and spars was finally forbidden, lest they be smuggled to the British or fall by capture into their hands. So desperate were matters that in 1777 when *The Gruel* was loading with spars in the Sheepscot about four miles above Pownalborough, Sir George Collier actually brought *The Rainbow* into the river and sent his boats up past the town to bring *The Gruel* out. The ship was seized and would have been taken, were it not for the fact that her sails were not aboard and it proved impossible to get her down the river before the Lincoln County militia arrived. This episode took place the week before William Gardiner's trial, and it undoubtedly influenced opinion, as the countryside was buzzing with rumors about who got word to *The Rainbow* that *The Gruel* was there. In fact, Pownalborough was in the midst of a spy scare, which though exaggerated was not unreasonable, considering the nearness of the British and the number of Loyalists with personal grudges against Patriot competitors.

THIS SITUATION RESULTED in the arrest of a number of other Loyalists in Lincoln County, who were saved from the consequences of the Transportation Act only by the trial of William and by the peculiar slow motion with which affairs proceeded in a frontier settlement. Owing to the difficulties of getting town meetings together, it had taken the townships a great while to make out their lists of Tories, with the result that the next trial was not held until November the fifth. The settlements, exhausted by the frequent calls on their time, had provided no jury. Since William Gardiner's appeal to the Assembly had already shown the weakness of the hasty and irregular methods previously employed to produce one, there seemed nothing for the court to do but to adjourn for a considerable time while jury lists were being made out. Six weeks later when it reconvened, Judge Howard from Fort Western suffered a terrible fall on the ice as he was setting out, and was unable to proceed. His unexpected accident prevented the justices from having a quorum, and the court was adjourned for the second time. The Transportation Act had not allowed for such dilatory proceedings and was timed to expire at the end of the year. As a result, a number of persons whom the public considered to be dangerous escaped these proceedings altogether.

In 1779 the British fortified Castine on the Penobscot and thence carried the war into Maine to such an extent that neither harbors nor inland settlements felt themselves safe. "Mahogany" Jones, the surveyor who had been dragged through the river by the Gardiner mob, had now fled to the British and was in command of a company of Rogers' Rangers. His knowledge of the countryside made him particularly dangerous to the Kennebec settlements, where he was regarded almost as an incarnation of the Devil himself. On one occasion he actually brought a party through the woods from Castine to Pownalborough, and very early one morning they surrounded the house of Charles, now General Cushing. Two men went up to the front door and began to knock until Cushing himself looked out of the bedroom window to ask who they were.

"Friends to the Congress," replied one instantly, "and we are arrived with an express from St. Georges, announcing that fifteen hundred British soldiers have landed at that place under the protection of three capital ships."

THESE TIDINGS BEING by no means improbable, the general hastily came down to the door with a candle in his hand and clothed only in a pair of breeches and an ancient plaid nightgown which was said to be entering upon its fifteenth year of use. The moment he appeared, his enemies seized him. The general resisted violently, and Mrs. Cushing, who had started downstairs, at the first sound of a struggle retreated hastily to the bedroom and put her head out of the window yelling, "Murder!" at the top of her voice.

Jones silenced her by horrible threats, vowing that he would have her scalped by his Indians unless she held her tongue. His men then made off with their prisoner, whom they hustled down to the bank of the river and into a canoe, by which they had come. Ten miles upstream they disembarked, and giving their captive a pair of shoes and stockings, they marched him off just as he was through the woods to the British stronghold.

This outrageous kidnapping of an important public figure from the very edge of the township was only the climax to a series of minor incidents which kept the populace in a constant state of alarm, and of indignation against those suspected of aiding in such affairs. The militia was called out so frequently and kept under arms for so long that farmers had not time to get their hay or winter provisions. As early as 1777 a good Patriot who was a Committee member from Machias wrote to complain: "my bread is Indian procured with great difficulty, my drink water, my meat moose, and my clothing rags, and many of these the dear partner of my misfortunes, who was tenderly educated, has been obliged to beg from those who could illy spare them."

Worse was to follow. In the next summer, the most severe drought on record ruined the crops, and in the following one a plague of caterpillars destroyed every green thing they could find. In 1779 Jacob Bailey, destitute himself, gives an extraordinary picture of the desperate state of the countryside. "Multitudes of people who formerly lived in affluence, are now destitute of a morsel of bread, and the remainder are reduced to a very scanty allowance. Several families in the lower towns and in the Eastern County, have had no bread in their houses for three months together, and the anxiety and distress which this occasions are truly affecting. Great numbers who inhabit near the sea coast, and even at the distance of twenty miles, after being starved into skeletons for want of provisions, have repaired to the clam banks for a resource; while others, who were prevented by their circumstances, or distant situation, from acquiring this kind of food, were still in a more calamitous condition. I have myself been witness to several exquisite scenes of anguish, besides feeling in my own bosom the bitterness of hunger ... I have walked abroad ... weak and feeble myself, in hopes to obtain a dinner among my more wealthy acquaintance, and have returned home disappointed of my expectations, and when in other places I have received an invitation to eat, have refused, because I could not find a heart to deprive a number of children of their pitiful allowance, who were staring upon me with hollow piercing eyes and pale languid faces." This account is fully born out by the petition to the Assembly of Elizabeth Lines of Pownalborough, whose husband was killed in the Continental army, leaving her without means and with the care of five small children. "I have applied to two of the Selectmen," she declares, "but can get no help there they say they have not Gott it neither can they Geet any, it is not to be had." Small wonder that the County of Lincoln was finally driven to petition for relief from its taxes and from requisitions of beef, clothing, and men for the Continental Army.

In times of such distress, feelings were naturally fierce, and it was not to be expected that an open Loyalist like Jacob Bailey should be allowed to carry out Silvester's work on the Kennebec without molestation. Though his friends in town meeting had carried the removal of his name from the list of traitors, there was a widespread feeling that he ought not to escape the Transportation Act. A warrant was sworn out against him, and early in September, 1777, he judged it best to go into hiding. For five weeks he concealed himself in his house without so much as putting his head out of doors. Finding, however, that his health was suffering under this confinement, he yielded to the persuasions of his friends, the more so as it was known that his enemies were about to make a determined effort to apprehend him. The road to his house was being watched, and two lads riding in his direction were fired at, evidently under the impression that one of them was he. On the fifteenth of October, therefore, Bailey left his house by a back way as soon as it was dark and was conducted by devious paths to the house of his brother Nathaniel, where he snatched a few hours' sleep. Before it was light, he went down the river with two lads who had engaged to take him to Brunswick by canoe. There was a thick fog that morning, which concealed their movements, and in due course the parson arrived at Bruns-wick, where a friend was supposed to meet him with a horse. However, there was nobody to be found at the local tavern which had been chosen as a rendezvous, and Bailey spent some extremely uncomfortable hours, conscious that he was exposed to the chance observation of any customer, and remembering with some anxiety that he had almost no money in his pocket. Eventually his friend arrived, and he got safely to Falmouth and in time to Boston, where he remained until the Transpor-tation Act expired at the end of the year.

WITH CONSIDERABLE courage, Bailey returned to his family at the beginning of 1778 and resumed his duties in his parish. In July, however, he fled once more to Boston to avoid arrest, leaving his wife to look after a baby boy and two little girls. In such want was she that sometimes for several days there was nothing to eat in the house but a few boiled vegeta-bles and a little milk and water. Indeed on some occasions the family was twenty-four hours at a time without any food at all, for Mrs. Bailey was determined to die rather than to appeal to people who might get into trouble for helping her. Meanwhile, her husband arrived in Boston looking more like a scarecrow than a respectable clergyman. His rusty black coat was white at the seams and in holes at the elbows. His old jacket flapped on his emaciated form, and his dirty yellow breeches made out of the coarsest ticking had a large perpendicular patch of a differ-ent shade upon each knee. His wig, which was about the color of an old, greasy blanket, hung lank abut his ears and was sur-mounted by a hat with numerous holes in the brim and a num-ber of careful darns. His friends were kind enough to present him with a new outfit and some small sums of money, but it was evident that he could not possibly remain at his post. He therefore drew up a petition requesting leave to depart for Nova Scotia, where he might be able to receive his salary from the Society and to obtain some other preferment.

This petition was presented to the Assembly by several of Bailey's acquaintances who were influential there, among them Pitts, James Bowdoin's brother-in-law, who was a strong Whig, but had no great opinion of Bowman and was aware that the magistrates were persecuting Bailey on account of his former connection with Dr. Gardiner. Secure in the knowledge that his petition would protect him from arrest for refusing the oath of allegiance, Bailey returned to his family; but his enemies were by now too angry to be satisfied with his peaceful departure. In October, while the County Court was sitting, he was indicted before the Grand Jury for preaching treason on the Sunday after Easter. Fortunately he was able to prove that the words objected to had occurred in the First Lesson, which was the regular portion of Scripture appointed by the Church for that Sunday. The indictment ended in laughter, but Cushing and Bowman sent up to Boston the deposition on which the complaint had been founded, hoping to cause Bailey's petition to be refused. As the Council had already heard Bailey's side of the affair, this malice was a failure, and in November the parson received official permission to leave.

His troubles were not yet over. It was already so late in the year that no arrangement for transport to Halifax could possibly be made. In fact, it was the following June before Bailey departed, and the magistrates during that time were not willing to let him alone. Charles Cushing had forbidden him to hold a Sunday service, and for a while he consented to refrain. After some weeks, however, he yielded to the entreaties of his congregation, being unable to stand by and see the young people relapse into irreligious ways simply because there was no form of public worship which they might attend. Cushing had in fact no authority to prevent him from preaching, since an oath of allegiance was not legally necessary to qualify him to do so. On the Sunday before Christmas, accordingly, there was a full congregation, and the matter was drawn to Cushing's attention by his seeing a number of people passing his house in the direction of the church. He immediately sent for one of the church wardens and charged him with the following message: "Tell the Parson that if he presumes to discharge his functions any longer, I will immediately commit him to prison, and that if he do not enter into a written agreement to forebear the exercise of Publick Worship, I will myself appear on Christmas day, attended with a number of resolute fellows, and drag him headlong out of the pulpit."

Bailey answered in a mild and conciliatory letter, in which he repeated that nothing but the season of year was preventing him from taking his departure. This being so, he felt his duty to look after his parishioners while he was still among them, and he hoped that Cushing would not insist in stirring up trouble during the few months that he was forced to remain.

CUSHING'S ANSWER to this epistle was to appear in person at Bailey's house on Christmas Day, as he and his friends were sitting down to dinner. A furious altercation ensued, and a fight between Bailey's servant and one of the High Sheriff's attendants. Services were now interrupted, but the parson continued to visit the sick, to baptize, and to bury the dead until two weeks before his departure. At that time Cushing actually appeared at a funeral with a group of men to arrest him, but failed because he had been given warning in time to make his escape.

Such were the conditions under which the most valiant of Silvester's agents took his departure from the County of Lincoln, never to return. His later adventures are of no concern to the Kennebec, though it is pleasant to know that he was happy and reasonably prosperous at last. He was appointed to the parish of Annapolis Royal in Nova Scotia, a settlement not unlike the one he had left, and in which his honest and persistent endeavors bore excellent fruit. He died in 1808, and though he was never in possession of a really adequate income, his overflowing hospitality and kindness of nature won him universal regard.

The removal of Bailey from the Kennebec meant the final disappearance of that Loyalist community which had existed for so long. Nathaniel Bailey moved into the parsonage house for a while, but the church was empty and abandoned. People began to take out the windows for their own private use, and this was the beginning of the end. In a few years both house and church were stripped and falling to pieces. No other Episcopal church was consecrated in Pownalborough until the end of 1852. Meanwhile, such malcontents as still existed were either driven out or roughly suppressed. General Wadsworth was asked to look into the matter of the grumblers on the Kennebec, and took several of them to Falmouth for court martial. All opposition to the government of any kind shortly collapsed. William Gardiner, who was looking passively on at the extensive damage being done to his father's lands, now began to realize that they were likely to be confiscated and lost to the family completely. In his despair, he considered fighting on this issue, but dared not actually do so and had not even the nerve to write to his father, lest his letters be intercepted and read. Matters took their course without him, and Bowman and Cushing, who could not but despise such an adversary, left him unharmed.

T E N

ℛETURN

THE SENTENCE OF perpetual banishment passed by Massachusetts on the Tories who had fled with the British was dated October 1778, and was very probably the final stroke of ill fortune which induced Silvester to abandon New York for England. Like all his other disasters, he received it with a fresh sense of outrage. As no Declaration of Independence had at the time been published, his sole offense in 1776 had been to retire from one part of the British Colonies to another. Even this he had only done under pressure of threats and because other Loyalists citizens had been lynched by the Patriot mobs. The injustice of banishment on such grounds was infuriating, and it was even worse to discover that the same facts were being used as a basis for a Confiscation Act. Silvester raged against retrospective laws that made a crime out of actions that had been innocent at the time they had been committed. In vain he appealed to the conscience of decent men and the justice of God. The Confiscation Act duly became law, and his property vanished from his control, apparently forever.

Silvester's position was particularly galling because there is no doubt that, had he been given the choice, he would have preferred to sacrifice his King to his country rather than the other way round. Like most people with violent opinions, he looked on himself as an eminently reasonable man. It never occurred to him that his exile was really due to the fact that he could not live quietly among people with whose views he did not agree. He condemned William not for his timid approaches to the popular party, but simply because he had not managed to keep out of trouble. When he received William's frantic letter from New York, he was quite melted by its effusions and made no more reproaches. Nevertheless his advice was that William should stay in his own country, obey what authority there was, and on no account try to follow his father. To his surprise, he received no answer from William, and he wrote again several times to the care of his friend and agent in New York. Yet though he was repeatedly assured that it was easy enough to forward letters to Boston, he never had the least acknowledgement that any were received. When New York fell to the rebels, Silvester was no longer even able to write. Occasionally he heard news of William passed on by other people, such as that he had been elected to the Assembly and was on very good terms with everyone. As time went by, however, even such items became infrequent, and Silvester found himself completely cut off from news about his family and estate.

I N THESE YEARS of frustration when Silvester's energies were repressed by poverty and his personal happiness was shattered by the death of his wife, it was natural for him to find consolation for his misfortunes in religion. He had always been devout, but now he became strict, devoting whole days together to study and prayer. He began to draw up a small devotional book, which was later published at his own expense under the title of *A Daily Companion to the Closet*. Not a trace of his accustomed fire is to be found in his answer to a letter from James Bowdoin asking for his help in some legal matter connected with the affairs of the Kennebec Purchase. "God grant us all grace," he writes, "to put an end to this devouring war, so contrary to our most holy religion, and unite us all once more in that bond of peace and brotherly union, so necessary to the happiness of both countries, which God grant may soon take place, and give us all an opportunity once more to greet one another as friends."

Such mildness falls sadly flat in a character whose greatest charm is its vigor, and it is somewhat of a relief to find that Silvester was not too old to revive when his feelings were strong. The Reverend Edward Bass of Newbury, Massachusetts, was one of the very few Episcopal clergymen who had omitted the prayer for the King and had allowed his church to be opened on special occasions appointed by the Congress for prayer or thanksgiving. The Society for the Propagation of the Gospel, which had expelled him from its ranks, found that his conduct was hotly defended by Bailey and others who understood how much good he was doing by remaining where he was. In the course of time the Society reconsidered its suspension, and Silvester was one of the gentlemen asked to give them his opinion. The Doctor did not hesitate. Mr. Bass had complied with treasonable proclamations after a fashion, and this proved him a traitor. As for his character in general, Silvester declined to recall that he had ever heard anything good about it whatsoever. Mr. Bass's position in the Society was not restored.

It was just as well that Silvester had preserved some of his old asperity, since it was less than a year before he found himself once more involved in the tangle of his American affairs. His second son, John Gardiner, attorney general in the Leeward Islands, had taken a strong anti-British attitude from the beginning of the war. So violent, in fact, were his feelings that he had accepted office under the French when they seized possession of St. Kitts on their entry into the struggle. Naturally he was unpopular with the British in the Islands, and when the provisional peace treaty made it obvious that these would eventually be restored, it became clear that John would be wise to leave before the transfer was made. John was now nearly fifty years of age and had not lived in America since he was fourteen. As long as he had been making a career for himself in England or was master of a small estate in the Leeward Islands, his interest in his father's American possessions had been fairly remote. When he was forced to sell his property in a hurry and return to his native land with a wife and three children, his position was different. John was disposed to hope that his own sufferings for Liberty's sake and the influence of his French connections would enable him to recover a portion of his father's estate. There was no tact in his makeup to induce him to proceed with delicacy, and in announcing his intended move to Silvester, he made perfectly plain the political position he was going to take up. "I am a staunch Revolutionary Whig," declared he, "and abhor all kingcraft and priestcraft." In case this was not strong enough for his father, he suggested that as he did not know his future address, letters should be sent in care of Governor Hancock. "Not one word of Politicks for God's sake," he added with belated caution, "as I know not yet the position of the people there."

WHILE SILVESTER was apparently reeling from the impact of this blunt epistle, John actually appeared in Philadelphia with French letters of recommendation and began to make himself known to the leaders of the American cause. Like his father, he had not the least conception of anyone else's point of view, and he now unhesitatingly unfolded to Silvester a detailed account of his position and his plans. He had been obliged to leave St. Kitts, he said on account of "a terrible paralytick affection in both my Hands and both my Legs and Feet together with a return of Blindness." In addition to these horrible afflictions, which do not seem to have prevented him from holding a pen, he had felt it wiser to get away from the Leeward Islands before the British flag should fly there once more. On arriving in America, he had been brought to realize that it was impossible for any Loyalist like his father ever to show his face in the country again. Indeed, if Silvester but knew the truth about the murders, rapine, and general devastation wrought by the Tories, he would even recognize the justice of his own exile. John's plan therefore was to petition the Assembly for a grant of some part of his father's estate to himself, though he assured Silvester that he would of course account for it faithfully during his father's lifetime. "I am going to see that man," he concluded with enthusiasm, "that has done his country such great services and who is allowed even by the Enemies of his Country to be an honor to human nature— General Washington."

It is difficult to decide how John could possibly have produced a more infuriating letter. His motive for leaving the Leeward Islands, though thinly disguised by an improbable account of his sufferings, was evidently his disloyalty to England. His assumption that Silvester never could return and his plan to seize the Kennebec estate for himself seemed outrageous, but hardly more so than his attempt to teach his father about Loyalist crimes or his enthusiastic praise of "that theif Washington." Silvester was roused to a pitch of rage entirely new in their relationship. "I have received your two most extraordinary letters," he replies, "and such insulting letters never before I believe flowed from the pen of one who was once a Son to him who was once Father. all those natural tyes that ever subsisted between us are now disolved, and I therefore forbid you on that or any pretence whatever to meddle or concern yourself with any of my Estate or affairs."

These thunders were wasted upon John, who could take up a quarrel with just as much spirit as his father, and who had besides a certain sense of humor that Silvester never possessed. He replied that he had no desire to remain in a family in which he was not wanted. If his father did not come round by the first of next May, he would change his name to Washington and see how Silvester liked that.

Some time before matters had reached this ludicrous stage, John's activities had succeeded in stirring up William. Silvester had written several times since the truce had been signed, and there was nothing to prevent William from sending him an answer but indolence, or the awkwardness of not having done so before. However, William no less than Silvester might have a good deal to lose by John's petition, since the truth was that though the other estates had been confiscated, a typical delay in Pownalborough had left the fate of the Kennebec property uncertain. Suit had been brought against the estate in September of 1781, when it had been continued to the next session in order that all parties might be notified. Next year, the court convened in June and pronounced the property confiscated. It was then discovered that the notices ran until the following September and that judgment had been improperly given. It was now too late to bring up the matter before June of 1783. By this time, the truce had put an end to the proceedings, and it remained to be seen what settlement the peace would bring.

While matters thus hung in the balance, William had thought of an expedient more devious than John's and equally unlikely to commend itself to Silvester. He had actually forged a grant from his father to himself of the Kennebec property, dating it in 1774. If this could be established as genuine, the estate could certainly be saved, but at the expense of passing it to William. It was not very likely that Silvester would be brought to consent to such an arrangement, and before it could be suggested, it was necessary to prepare the ground.

With such considerations in his mind, William addressed

himself to making his excuses at about the time that John was arriving in Philadelphia. His long silence, said he, was by no means due to want of duty, affection, or filial respect. On the contrary, he had bravely faced poverty, cruel treatment, and loss of friends in the hope of saving something from the wreckage for "the best and dearest of men." No tongue could tell what troubles he had encountered, nor how seriously his well-wishers had warned him not to write to a soul within the British lines. Others had done so, he knew, but he had stood in special danger, since life itself would hardly have gratified his enemies' malice. Naturally his father would not have wished him to take such an awful risk for the sake of putting a few words on paper. He now found himself reduced to miserable poverty and exposed to scorn and derision. The estate was overrun by squatters, and the woods had been terribly wasted, though the rise in the price of land might compensate for much if all went well. Nothing in life would give him greater pleasure than his father's return, but at present this was not to be thought of.

S ILVESTER'S ANSWER was so affectionate and so delighted that all awkwardness was at an end until William heard a rumor from Philadelphia that the whole estate was granted to John. The latter had been busy presenting his French letters of introduction with flattering results. He had spent four days with General Washington and was overwhelmed with civilities. In Boston, he was cordially received by Samuel Adams, John Hancock, and numerous others, with whom he took the earliest opportunity of discussing Silvester's affairs. His present scheme was to bring Silvester back to Rhode Island from whence he might ask leave to retire to the Kennebec estates. In the meantime, John went up to the Kennebec to look into matters himself and to discuss the situation with William.

Mild-mannered William was no match for his quick, loud, dominating brother. His fears of further prosecution were brushed aside, tenants were found for his mills, and all sorts of matters which William thought it safer to avoid were immediately investigated. John intended to petition for a part of the estate which he said had always been destined for him, and he was urgent with William to support him in this procedure. With growing unhappiness William was giving way on all points when Silvester's furious letter to John arrived. Unable to argue with his brother, yet not daring to take sides against his father, William compromised by writing distractedly. He had joined in no petition, not he; and without his father's permission he never would do so. Living at a distance from Boston and seeing nobody, he had innocently agreed to John's plan because he longed to see his father again. He had never really meant to support the petition, and would oppose it with hand, tongue, and pen. In any case, he was certain the estate would be lost, and he himself would suffer further persecution. After living for years in solitary banishment with no companions but "those who had flown goals, for the most abandoned crimes," after having been jailed and imprisoned "for years," and having suffered every conceivable hardship, he was now certain to lose what little remained. "Why was I born?" he queried frantically, "and for what! I must answer for wretchedness and misery."

T HE FIRST OF MAY being now close at hand, John, who really preferred "Gardiner" to "Washington," thought it best to have another paralytic complaint. He therefore wrote to his father that a stroke had deprived him of the use of his fourth and little fingers and of the lower part of his right hand. Being thus on the point of death, he summoned up what muscles he had left in order to address his "dear and ever honored tho' much misinformed Father," possibly for the last time. Since his intentions towards his dear parent had been perfectly honorable, he could only conclude that the disagreement between them was due to the slanders of William. "I always speak the Truth," he declared stoutly, "and I can always therefore stand the Test of Examination—He *cannot* speak the Truth on any Occasion, and therefore he will avoid the Light." His last entreaty was that when he was no more, his father would cease to load his memory with unjust reproach.

It must have been evident to Silvester, who was no fool, that his sons were fighting over his estate before he was dead. The circumstances were peculiar, it is true, and may afford some excuse, but the selfishness was plain enough. John, who had started off by insulting his father, was now excusing himself by hysterical complaints against William, who he declared was living in luxury off the rents of the Kennebec lands. William, who had been in no hurry to communicate with his father at all, was trying to give the impression that only an innocent being like himself could consider John honest. Silvester was lonely and old, and he was pathetically anxious to drop all reproaches in return for a little affection. Still the habits of a lifetime were such that he was disposed to insist on his rights as a father and to judge William and John by the eagerness they displayed in his service. William's protestations of love had moved him to such tender expressions as "dear child" and "deare billy," but he could not help seeing as the months went by that lamentations were being used to disguise a neglect of his Kennebec affairs. On the other hand, though Silvester had roused himself to quarrel with John in his old arbitrary fashion, he was forced to perceive that John was really active in preparing his return. Silvester wrote that he was tired and his poor eyes were weak. It was the nearest he came to appealing for sympathy, as opposed to reciting his wrongs.

While the future of the Kennebec estate still hung in the balance, Silvester was particularly urgent with William to prepare his defense. As he never tired of repeating, he had joined no association against his countrymen, given no money to the British cause, and broken no existing law. If these facts could

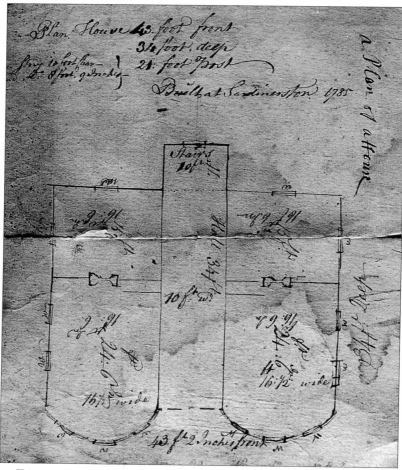

FLOOR PLAN of proposed residence for William Gardiner, son of Dr. Gardiner, on Brunswick Avenue, Gardiner, in 1785. Because William died soon after his father, this house was never built. PRIVATE COLLECTION.

be properly presented in court by a good lawyer, he felt certain that his cause must prevail. William, who appreciated much more justly that a strictly legal innocence was of no use in the present occasion, felt unwilling to get into trouble over a case which he did not believe in. He therefore confined himself to

ELEVATION OF proposed residence for William Gardiner.
The intended site near Skehan's Dairy on Brunswick,
Avenue, Gardiner, would have included gardens
westward to the river. PRIVATE COLLECTION.

complaining, though his father's letters grew steadily more
insistent and were filled with demands for information which
William was too lazy to supply.

The Confiscation Act had directed that all creditors who
could establish a claim must be paid out of the sale of a prop-

erty before any money was turned over to the state. This amounted to offering a present to enterprising people at nobody's expense, and many found it exceedingly tempting. In consequence, Silvester was horrified to find that all sorts of claims were being brought against his estate for debts which he did not owe. Welch, the poor tenant with the family of children whom he had supplied on credit for so long, had trumped up a bill for over three thousand pounds as the expenses of draining his meadow, though Silvester had supplied the tools, provisions, and men. At the other end of the social scale, Goodwin's son, who had rented the Pownalborough sawmill for a number of years, had produced a thousand-pound bill for some repairs that probably have cost him eighteen. Gideon Gardiner, who had made away with large quantities of valuable timber, now added insult to injury by demanding four hundred pounds. Silvester was almost incredulous. He did not understand how so many wicked wretches could have so little fear of God as to swear to the truth of such accounts. "They are all perjured," he exclaimed, "for which if they dont answer for it in this world, they must in another."

Once again Silvester had not allowed for the state of affairs, since the fact was that conscience did not bother such claimants in the least. After his return, Robert Hallowell met Welch and asked him how he could have presented a claim on the estate to which he knew he had no right.

"I would not, Mr. Hallowell, wrong you for the world," was his answer. "The account I presented to the commissioners was correct. I only omitted to say you had paid it. I knew the presentation could do you no harm. Everybody was doing the same, and I was much in want of money."

William was aware of this attitude and too timid to resist it. An act had been passed for the deportation of those who had discouraged men from entering the army or navy during the war. Bowman had threatened William with proceedings, and the mere suggestion was a sufficient hint that he would be wise to make no trouble. His letters became increasingly wild and unsatisfactory.

Silvester now turned in despair from both his sons and applied to Oliver Whipple, who had opened correspondence with his father-in-law and promised to give him early information of all that went on. The position of Oliver Whipple in these family disputes was not an indifferent one. He had visited the Kennebec for the first time shortly before John Gardiner got there, and he had been much impressed with the size of the estate and the manner in which William was living. "He possesses a Lordship," he exclaimed, and began to rhapsodize over the value of the timber, the fertility of the soil, the immense variety of fish, and the agreeableness of the country in general. There was more than a tinge of envy in his attitude to William, whom he represented as doing very well out of the rent of his mills, and by no means sunk in the abject poverty that he complained of to his father. Whipple was thus disposed to make common cause with John against William, on the general grounds that William was living comfortably on property that should have belonged to them all. However, in his approach to Silvester he showed himself far smoother than either of his brothers-in-law. His great desire was to be of service. He shook his head over William's extraordinary neglect and was inclined to blame him for the unfortunate misunderstanding that existed between Silvester and John. He himself had no business more pressing than Silvester's, since his chief hope, and that of Nabby and little Silvester, was to see his dear Father again.

Silvester delightedly replied "with great love to your dear little family," and proceeded to pour out a flood of commissions and advice. Whipple must have learned to dread the arrival of a fresh sheet starting: "I forgot to advertise you in my last...," and too closely crowded with instructions to leave room for paragraphs or stops. He found himself ordered to put forward arguments which he knew would have no weight, to hire lawyers who would not accept the case, to demand postponements which would not be granted, or oaths which would not be applied. Being anxious to please, he dared not explain to Silvester that these matters could not be handled in the fashion of ten years before. Even more annoying was the fact that Silvester would not delegate his affairs to one agent, but wrote to another before he had an answer from the first. Thus a single commission was entrusted to William, to John, to Silvester's old friend Sullivan in Boston, to his cousin and one-time apprentice, Dr. Joseph Gardiner, and to Whipple himself. A final awkwardness was the frequent occurrence of such phrases as "desire my son William," or "Let me know from Billey," which involved Whipple in part of the blame when William did not cooperate. Whipple did his best, but Silvester was too busy for gratitude, and his only sign of approval was another long, involved, and repetitious sheet full of arguments and commands.

O NE OF THE GREATEST difficulties in these negotiations was that most of the papers needed on the Kennebec were with Silvester in England, whereas the documents he wanted himself were largely in Boston. The British government, having failed to persuade the Americans to restore exiled Tories to their rights, had appointed a committee to investigate the losses of Loyalists, and to award compensation. This immediately made it necessary for Silvester to provide some evidence of how much he had lost. He began to write for an authenticated copy from the Boston town records of the sale of his personal estate and two sloops, and of the seizure of his drugs. When he got a statement saying that claims had been allowed against his estate to the value of thirteen hundred pounds, and that only a little over two thousand had consequently been paid into the treasury, he went into a rage and said it was all "vilany." All they had sent him was a certificate reducing his Boston estate to about one quarter of its value. It would be necessary for Whipple to produce an authenticated copy of the sale of every article he had possessed, and to get from billy a detailed account of the losses on the Kennebec property. This entailed a good deal of work, with no help from William, but it brought Silvester to realize the services his son-in-law was rendering. At last he found time to express his appreciation, and did so in terms that must have made Whipple hopeful that his position with the old man was assured. "A duty that every tie of nature called on others to have done, but alas, instead of that, they have taken every means in their power, to add new afflictions to my distress, but blessed be God, who has raised me up other friends in their room, who shall ever be gratefully remember'd by me." A man might well suppose that such expressions were good for some property in Silvester's will.

In the end it was not the arguments of Silvester, the influence of John, or the efforts of Whipple that saved the Gardiner estate. There was a general feeling that the time for reprisals was over, and the nation was ready to turn to more constructive affairs. For a long while the position was delicate, since no one knew whether some interested person might not introduce special legislation against it. Nevertheless, the estate was Silvester's, and it seemed wise after ten years of chaos to make a general effort to assert his authority. For this purpose Whipple was delighted to receive a power of attorney and to go up to the Kennebec and force William to go with him round the estate. No better choice could have been made, since Whipple's smoothness was certain to avoid offense, while his interest in Silvester's affairs made him unlikely to give way as weakly as William. When threatened by an old soldier, he was ready to reply that he himself was a soldier of the American army, though not quite so old, and that he would not endure any insolence. On the other hand, he prudently refrained from pressing damages against Gideon Gardiner and offered him a lease on favorable terms in order to get his acknowledgement that Silvester was actually the owner. As he said, it was not in Silvester's interest to get into a suit, since feeling against the Tories still ran high, and very probably he would not win it. For the first time, Silvester received a clear account of how things actually were and of the position of William, who was boarding at the Great House, which he had let, and living off the rent of the mills.

WHILE ALL THESE matters were being settled in America, Silvester's life in Poole was a lonely and uneventful one. Two or three times he went up to London to present his case to the commissioners, staying modestly at the sign of the Mangle, which was cheaper than his previous lodgings. Robert Hallowell, who had come up from Bristol on the same errand, found him wonderful considering his age and his simple manner of living, so different from what he had once been accustomed to. His memory was failing a little, but he concealed it admirably, and his mind was as acute as it had ever been. He could still converse with fire and spirit, raising his voice as decidedly in an argument as he had done of old. He had no reason to stay at Poole, save that he was used to it and did not like Bristol, where Anne and Hannah were living. Anne Browne was now a widow, straitened in means and with four youngish children. Hannah Hallowell after a succession of delicate daughters had at last had a son in 1782. Neither of these households appealed to Silvester, and yet he wanted companionship. None of his children were particularly pleased when he found it by marrying again.

Silvester's motives for marrying at this time are obvious enough, but it is not so clear what made him acceptable to a girl about fifty years younger. Catharine Goldthwaite was the daughter of a man who had been Secretary of War for the

Province of Massachusetts Bay and had served with fair distinction in several capacities. She had first come to England with her uncle, who had settled in Bristol. Later when her parents had followed, they went to her married sister's near London and lived in what seems considerable style, since there were two liveried servants, a gardener, housekeeper, lady's maid, and cook. Afterwards they established themselves in a small cottage about three miles away, which seems to have been more suited to their restricted means. Catharine's chief quality amid all these changes was perpetual good humor. She never forgot her Boston friends or ceased to regret them, yet she was delighted with England and called it "the garden of the world." Her step-aunt and uncle in Bristol had made a second home for her. When she moved to live with her parents, country life suited her. Reading, writing, or playing the guitar could be diversified by the most delightful walks, or by calls on which she would take her netting, since it was vulgar to have nothing

RESIDENCE OF Colonel Thomas Goldthwaite, third father-in-law of Dr. Gardiner, in Walthamstow, county Essex, England, a few miles north of London. Dr. Gardiner was a frequent visitor to this house.

COLONEL THOMAS GOLDTHWAITE (1717–1799), third
father-in-law of Dr. Gardiner. Prior to his exile to
England, Colonel Goldthwaite was commander of Fort
Pownal on the Maine coast. MUSEUM OF FINE ARTS, BOSTON.
BEQUEST OF JOHN T. BOWEN IN MEMORY OF ELIZA M. BOWEN.

with which to occupy one's hands. She assured her friends that she missed them, but in tones which declared that she had never known a care in the world.

Perhaps it is significant that though other such young ladies liked to exchange hints about suitors, Catharine's letters hardly mentioned a young man. As a refugee in England with no particular fortune, she was doubtless not much sought after and may have feared that she would become an old maid. Doctor Gardiner, though he was living very simply, had an American estate out of which he could certainly provide for Catharine. As he was at least seventy-five, she had but to devote a few years to making him happy. Her match was not romantic, but Catharine was the sort of girl to be content in any circumstances, and doubtless she played her part well.

ONE OF THE REASONS for Silvester's remaining in Poole was that he had become interested in trade with Newfoundland which was controlled by the merchants there. Newfoundland at this time was only a fishing center, though it boasted thirty-five thousand inhabitants during the season. Its supplies were imported by the merchants of Dartmouth and Poole, who had been collecting them mainly from the American continent in exchange for cargoes of fish. When the Revolution interfered with this trade, the island fell on hard times, and after the peace its condition was taken up by the Privy Council and by Parliament. Silvester talked to the merchants who gave evidence, and as he did not agree with their policy, he set to work on a treatise presenting his own point of view.

Silvester's solution for Newfoundland's problems was colonization, which he supported with a typical mixture of factual knowledge and sweeping claims. His recommendations for establishing settlers were based on sound experience. He knew what it actually cost to put up a saw mill and how many feet of board it produced in a day. Yet among many excellent arguments in support of his project, his imagination led him to declare that Newfoundland could easily become Britain's chief source of timber, and that its settlements would "intirely stop all future emigrations from this kingdom or Ireland to America." Its prosperous development, added he, would give England security against the ambitious rival nation which "the late infamous peace" had established so near it. Not content with offending the government by his quite unnecessary aspersion, he launched himself on a spirited criticism of the present administration of the island. The governor was nominated by the Admiralty, the courts were scandalously oppressive, and the present head of the law department was a man of extremely bad character whose last occupation had been keeping a gin shop.

NOTHING IS MORE characteristic of Silvester than the mixture of practical sense in this pamphlet with a universal lack of tact. His recommendations, though fundamentally sound, were not of a nature to make him popular in Poole, where fortunes depended on the existing state of affairs. Nor can his style of argument have pleased the government, however much it may bear out Robert Hallowell's statement that his mind had lost none of its vigor. It would be interesting to know who read this treatise and if anyone pointed out to Silvester that a British pensioner would be foolish to print such a blunt criticism of the very government that was allowing him his income. At all events, the pamphlet never was published, though Silvester may have been intending to arrange for it when he was distracted by a fortunate turn in his American affairs.

Almost from the first it had been John Gardiner's opinion that Silvester should return to his native state of Rhode Island, whence he might petition Massachusetts for repeal of his banishment. So great was the feeling against him in Boston, however, that it had seemed wiser to wait, lest any activity merely result in a penal law confiscating the rest of his estate. Silvester himself longed to return, but as his old friends all told him very bluntly, he had made himself too conspicuous to be easily forgiven. When a petition was drawn up on his behalf, John refused to present it, and Whipple agreed that the time had not yet come. However, in 1785 it was decided that he should come to Newport and try out the temper of the Assembly in Boston himself. Perhaps it was felt necessary to remind Massachusetts that Silvester had performed certain services. At any rate, he petitioned not to return, but to have compensation for some of his losses. Silvester seems to have felt that the strict truth was not necessary on this urgent occasion, since in spite of his private opinion of "that theif Washington," his petition maintains that he had left his stock of drugs behind him in Boston for the good of his country, though his own sloop in the harbor had been ready to sail and could easily have them away. Silvester felt his cause just, and a slight distortion of the truth he evidently thought was as nothing compared to the charges that had been brought up against him without foundation.

Ten years of revolution and war had changed the face of America and had aged Silvester, but it had not altered his character in the least. Catharine Gardiner's picture of him in Newport shows him, just as one might expect, being indiscreet. "Dr. Gardiner," she writes, "has been talking politics with a gentleman very loud ever since I took my pen." Fortunately Newport was tolerant, but a bitter blow from Boston was in store. The King's Chapel had been in a very real sense the center of Silvester's personal life for more than forty years. His services to it had been extremely great. Nevertheless, when the state had confiscated the rest of his property, the church had followed suit and sold his pews. Worse was to follow. Silvester now found that the congregation had followed its pastor in establishing a Unitarian form of worship, and that his own son John was strong in the new faith and had been active in promoting the change.

It is difficult to know which side of this affair hurt Silvester most. After all his other property losses, the sale of his pews was like a blow on an old wound, and from a most unexpected source. "I did not believe," he protested with some justice to the officers of the King's Chapel, "that there could be found so much ingratitude in any society of men professing Christianity." Even more painful was the change in religion to a doctrine which Silvester particularly abhorred. He did not hesitate to denounce the author of it as one who had destroyed the peace and unity of a once happy church, and one who could never expect to find admittance among the faithful in the church above.

No exile could have been more bitter to Silvester than his breach with the King's Chapel, where his children had been christened and their mother buried, and with which all his happiest years and his sincerest desires for good had been connected. The severance was final. Even if he recovered his pews by process of law, to sit in them would be to listen to spiritual damnation. This wicked state was the work, or partly the work of his own son John, whose impious political views were now seen to be combined with a denial of the sacred truths which he had been brought up to revere. John's conduct to his Father in Heaven and his father on earth were all of a piece; and since he had renounced the one, the other would reject him. The Kennebec estate must be left to William, and provision must be made lest the Gardiner name become extinct.

SILVESTER NOW seriously considered the claims of his daughters' children. Anne Browne's were thoroughly English and might be passed by. Dumaresq, Rebecca's husband, Silvester despised. When they had both been in New York, Dumaresq had preferred to borrow and live like a gentleman rather than betake himself seriously to work. Eventually his debts had caught up with him, as it had been obvious they

EXTERIOR VIEW of Trinity Church, Newport, Rhode Island, where Dr. Gardiner is buried. SOCIETY FOR THE PRESERVATION OF NEW ENGLAND ANTIQUITIES.

INTERIOR VIEW of Trinity Church, Newport, Rhode Island, where Dr. Gardiner is buried. SOCIETY FOR THE PRESERVATION OF NEW ENGLAND ANTIQUITIES.

would, and he was now living in considerable poverty in Nassau, where influence had obtained him some sort of a position. There remained Hannah Hallowell's Robert, and Abigail Whipple's Silvester. Hannah was the elder, and with her Silvester had always been on affectionate terms. Neither the name of little Silvester, nor the recent services of Whipple seemed an adequate reason for pushing aside Hannah's claim. Silvester left the chief part of his estate in trust for the benefit of William, providing that in default of his heirs it should go to the children of Hannah, and failing these to the children of Abigail.

The end came shortly. In the fall of 1786, the Doctor contracted a chill. In a few days he was dead and his long-hoped-for petition to return to Massachusetts would now never be presented. Few things are more heartening about the American Revolution than the swiftness with which ill-feeling died down after it was over. Even the hated "Mahogany" Jones lived for years on the Kennebec after the war, while now in Newport the citizens paid Silvester honor with never a word of blame. "He was a native of this state," says his obituary notice, "but for many years prior to the revolution, an inhabitant of Boston, in the state of Massachusetts, where in the line of his chirurgical and medical profession, he long stood foremost. He was possessed of an uncommon vigor and activity of mind, and by unremitted diligence and attention, acquired a large property, which though much injured by the late civil war is not wholly annihilated. His Christian piety and fortitude were

HALLOWELL HOUSE, designed by Charles Vaughan of Hallowell in 1796 for Robert Hallowell, executor of the will of his father-in-law, Dr. Gardiner. MAINE HISTORIC PRESERVATION COMMISSION.

MINIATURE PORTRAIT of Robert Hallowell
Gardiner I (1782–1864). This likeness was painted
by Edward Greene Malbone in 1805, two years
after he claimed his inheritance by changing his
surname to Gardiner. PRIVATE COLLECTION.

exemplary as his honesty was inflexible and his friendship sincere." That this effusion was not the work of some particular friend is attested by the fact that the flags in the harbor flew at half mast when Silvester died. For her own most honored son, Newport could have done no more.

It is difficult to decide who was the most indignant when Silvester's testament was published, the hopeful Whipples or the disinherited John. The latter had been cut off with a shilling, but in a week Silvester had been unable to keep up his anger to the point of disowning him completely. He left him a thousand pounds and half of his Pownalborough property, the remainder being divided among his children. William, to whom the chief part of the inheritance came, did not live long to enjoy the fruits of his brother's indiscretion. A year later he muddled himself out of life by taking an overdose of laudanum to allay the pain of a colic. Robert Hallowell thus found himself the father of the heir, a little boy of five, who was to take, when he reached his majority, the name of ROBERT HALLOWELL GARDINER.

Genealogy of the Family of
DR. SILVESTER GARDINER
Danny D. Smith

1. GEORGE[1] GARDINER, a native of England, born in the 1620s, made his first recorded appearance in the New World in May 1638. Absolutely nothing concerning his ancestry is known, and the claims made by his descendants have been demolished by G. Andrews Moriarty, one of America's ablest genealogists in "Parentage of George Gardiner of Newport, R.I.," *The American Genealogist* 21(1945):191–200 and by the same author in "Herodias (Long) Hicks-Gardiner-Porter: A Tale of Old Newport," *Rhode Island History,* 11(1952):84–92. He married (1) in Common-Law form in 1644 HERODIAS (LONG) HICKS, born *circa* 1624 in England (date deduced by Moriarty in *The American Genealogist* 21:198), and by hypothesis of Moriarty a descendant of a Long family in Somersetshire allied to the Aylesfords. She married first by a marriage license granted by the Bishop of London 14 March 1636–7 at St. Faith's Chapel in the undercroft of St. Paul's Cathedral John Hicks. George Gardiner married (2) soon after 1668 LYDIA BALLOU, daughter of Robert and Susannah Ballou, formerly of Portsmouth, Rhode Island, but then of Boston where Ballou died testate in 1668. Lydia married secondly 14 June 1678 William Hawkins of Providence by whom she had further issue of four children and died prior to 17 March 1721–2, the date on which Hawkins drafted his will (Austin, *Genealogical Dictionary of Rhode Island*, 318).

2. BENONI[2] GARDINER (*George¹*) born probably in Newport, Rhode Island about 1644 or 1645 and died at Kingstown, Rhode Island in 1731, doubtlessly much closer to the age of eighty-seven

rather than the fantastic age of one hundred four, a fiction which has arisen from an uncritical acceptance of data. He married before 1671 MARY ELDRED. whose identity was first stated in Henry Sewall Webster, *Silvester Gardiner* (Historical Series No. 2, Gardiner, Maine, 1913) as a daughter of Samuel and Elizabeth Eldred of Kingstown, Rhode Island. Daniel Goodwin in *The Gardiners of Narragansett* (1919), 202 note 4a, accepts this attribution despite the lack of record evidence and proceeds to outline an argument in its support. Benoni took the oath of allegiance to the government of Rhode Island 19 May 1671. On 29 July 1679 he and forty-one others, of Narragansett, signed a petition to the King, praying that the would "put an end to these differences about the government thereof, which had been so fatal to the prosperity of the place; animosities still arising in people's minds, as they stand affected to this or that government." On 6 September 1687 he was taxed at 5s, 3 1/2d. On 18 September 1705 he and wife Mary deeded to son Nathaniel one hundred acres being the west half of the farm where Benoni then dwelled and on the same day deeded to son Stephen the dwelling house and orchard (John Osborne Austin, *The Genealogical Dictionary of Rhode Island* [Albany, N.Y.: Joel Mussell's Sons, 1897] 81).

3. WILLIAM[3] GARDINER (*Benoni[2], George[1]*) born at Boston Neck, Narragansett, Rhode Island in 1671 and died there 14 December 1732. He was known as William Junior to distinguish him from his uncle William, also of the same place, a naming custom well known to genealogists of colonial families of New England. It was customary in his time to label any free-thinker "wicked," and therefore William Gardiner became known as "Wicked Will," irrespective of the "correctness of his outward life." Although a wealthy shoemaker and large-scale farmer in South Kingstown, Rhode Island, his support of St. Paul's church earned him the reputation as being uncommonly liberal in religious opinion. He married Abigail Remington (1691–1763), daughter of John and Abigail (Richmond) Remington of Newport and Kingstown, Rhode Island. They resided on Boston Neck in that section of Narragansett which became South Kingston. Seven children were born to them, including Dr. Silvester Gardiner, the subject of this biography.

4. SILVESTER[4] GARDINER (*William[3], Benoni[2], George[1]*) was born at South Kingstown, Rhode Island 29 June 1708 and died at Newport, Rhode Island 8 August 1786. He married (1) at King's Chapel, Boston, Massachusetts 11 December 1732 ANNE[3] GIBBINS, baptized at Brattle Street Church in Boston 28 December 1712 and died at Boston in 1771, daughter of Dr. John[2] (*William[1]*) and Rebecca (Gray) Gibbins. He married (2) at Salem, Massachusetts 30 April 1772 ABIGAIL[5] (PICKMAN) EPES, born Salem 22 October 1732 and died at Poole, Dorset, England 3 November 1780, daughter of Benjamin[4] (*Benjamin[3-2], Nathaniel[1]*) and Love (Rawlings) Pickman. She had married previously at Salem, Massachusetts 5 April 1750 William[3] Epes, late of Chesterfield, Virginia, son of Colonel Daniel[2] (*Daniel[1]*) and Hannah (Hicks) Epes of Salem, Massachusetts. He married (3) at St. James Church, Poole, Dorsetshire, England 26 October 1784 CATHARINE[5] GOLDTHWAITE, born Boston, Massachusetts 5 January 1747 and died at Boston on Ash Wednesday 1830, daughter of Colonel Thomas[4] (*John[3], Samuel[2], Thomas[1]*) and Esther (Sargent) Goldthwaite. She married secondly at Boston 2 April 1789 William Powell, born 1726 and died at Boston 1805, son of John and Anna (Dummer) Powell.

Children, surname *Gardiner*, born at Boston and baptized at King's Chapel:

5   i   WILLIAM[5], born 13 June 1736 and baptized 27 January 1737

6   ii   JOHN, born 4 December and baptized 11 December 1737.

    iii   JAMES, born 9 September 1739, baptized 9 September 1739; died in Boston 24 December 1759.

7   iv   ANNE, born 21 April 1741 and baptized 3 May 1741.

8   v   HANNAH, born 18 June 1743 and baptized 27 June 1743.

9   vi   REBECCA, baptized 17 April 1745.

    vii   THOMAS, baptized 18 April 1747; died 1750.

10 viii   ABIGAIL, baptized 1 August 1750.

5. WILLIAM[5] GARDINER (*Silvester[4], William[3], Benoni[2], George[1]*) born 13 June 1736 and baptized 27 January 1737; died at

Pittston, Maine before 16 April 1787 when administration on his estate was granted to his brother John Gardiner. Although he never married or left issue, his position in the dynastic history of the Gardiner family is important because he survived his father and was therefore briefly proprietor of the Cobbosseeconte estate on the Kennebec River in Maine. The land titles in the central Maine area reflect his agency in the area for his father, and this is a critical episode of the region's history. He is buried near the site of the first parish house at Christ Church, Gardiner, Maine.

6. JOHN[5] GARDINER (*Silvester[4], William[3], Benoni[2], George[1]*) was born at Boston, Massachusetts 4 December 1737 and was drowned when the packet *Londoner* capsized near Cape Ann, Massachusetts 15 October 1793. He married in 1763 MARGARET HARRIES born in 1732 and died in 1786, youngest and posthumous daughter of George Harries of Priskilly, Pembrokeshire (who died 13 September 1722), son of John Harries, by Letitia (whom he had married 12 December 1670) daughter of John Owen of Priskilly and sister and in her issue eventual heiress of Thomas Owen, of Priskilly, a descendant through the Wynnes of Wales and through David ap Griffith, Prince of North Wales, of Hedd Molwynog, founder of the ninth noble tribe of North Wales and Powys. She was a near relative of Sir Watkin Williams-Wynn, Baronet, according to Robert Hallowell Gardiner I in his *Early Recollections*—a social and genealogical connection which doubtless brought Councillor John Gardiner into the defense of John Wilkes in that *habeas corpus* suit sponsored by the Grenville party in England which family also had married into the Williams-Wynn family. Dr. Silvester Gardiner cut him off with a pittance in his will but later in a codicil restored a farm in Pownalborough, now Dresden, Maine.

Children, surname *Gardiner*:

  i JOHN SILVESTER JOHN[6], born at Haverfordwest, Wales June 1765 and died at Harrowgate, Yorkshire, England 29 July 1830. He was rector of Trinity Church in Boston, founder of the Boston Athenæum, editor of the *North American Review*. He married and left issue in the male line, collectively known as the "Pennington Gardiners."

  ii ANNE, born 4 January 1771; died May 1799. She married

JAMES NOBLE LITHGOW, son of Dr. Gardiner's nemesis, Colonel Lithgow. She was mother of Llewellyn Lithgow who endowed the public library in Augusta, Maine.

iii WILLIAM. He married but in two generations his line became extinct.

7. ANNE[5] GARDINER (*Silvester⁴, William³, Benoni², George¹*) painted in the pose of the goddess Diana by John Singleton Copley was born at Boston 21 April 1741 and baptized at King's Chapel 3 May 1741; died July 1807. She married at Boston 30 November 1759 Colonel the Honourable Arthur Browne, born 1731 and died 21 July 1799, second son of John Browne, first Earl of Altamont by his wife Anne, eldest daughter of Sir Arthur Gore, second Baronet of the family of the Earl of Arran. Anne was so sure that her husband's invalid elder brother would die in early life and thereby open the succession to the peerage in favor of her husband that she had a countess' coronet painted on her coach door. Her actions were premature because the elder brother did survive, became robust, married, and sired a line of Brownes who elevated the peerage dignities of the family to that of the Marquessate of Sligo which continues to the present.

Children, surname *Browne* :

i JOHN[6], born 1766; married and left descendants in England.

ii GEORGE, born 1760; married and left descendants in England.

iii ANNE, married Major Thomas Bucknall Lindsey, of Turin Castle, co. Mayo, Ireland and died without issue.

iv AUGUSTA LOUISA, married and left descendants in England.

8. HANNAH[5] GARDINER (*Silvester⁴, William³, Benoni², George¹*) born at Boston 18 July 1743 and baptized at King's Chapel 27 July 1743; died 9 February 1796. She married at Boston 7 January 1772 ROBERT[4] HALLOWELL, born at Boston July 1739 and died there 23 April 1818, son of Benjamin³ (*Benjamin², William¹*) and Rebecca (Briggs) Hallowell. He is buried in the southwest tomb on the south wall of Christ Church in Gardiner, Maine. His portrait was painted by Gilbert Stuart.

Children, surname *Hallowell*, except child v who changed his surname to *Gardiner*:

   i   HANNAH[6], born at Boston 27 September 1773; died 1 May 1796.

   ii NANCY, born at Boston 22 November 1774; died 17 September 1775.

  iii ANN, born at Halifax, Nova Scotia 15 July 1776; died at Boston 15 August 1800.

  iv REBECCA, born London, England 29 September 1777; died 14 May 1779; buried at St. Mary-le-Bow, London.

   v ROBERT, born Bristol, Gloucestershire, England 10 February 1782. He is known as Robert Hallowell Gardiner I.

9. REBECCA[5] GARDINER (*Silvester[4], William[3], Benoni[2], George[1]*) baptized at King's Chapel, Boston, Massachusetts 17 April 1745 and died long before 1820 when her nephew, Robert Hallowell Gardiner I, was winding up the probate proceedings arising under the residual bequests mandated by the will of Dr. Silvester Gardiner. She married at King's Chapel, Boston 13 December 1763 PHILIP DUMARESQ (pronounced "Doo-*mer*-rick"), born at Boston 1737 and died at Nassau, New Providence, West Indies, a Loyalist exile 28 September 1800 where he was Collector of the Customs, son of Philip and Susan (Ferry) Dumaresq, and grandson of Elias, Seigneur des Augrés and of Frances de Carteret, through whom Philip Dumaresq inherited twenty-six heraldic quarterings of the noble families of the Channel Islands. Note that the pronunciation is found in the table "Some Pronunciations of Proper Names," in *Titles and Forms of Address: A Guide to Their Correct Use* (fourth edition; London: A. & C. Black Ltd., 1936) at page 21 and is the same pronunciation which the present compiler heard Laura Elizabeth (Richards) Wiggins use on the occasion of several sessions over the tea table at Yellow House in Gardiner, Maine. His death date is stated in David E. Maas, *Divided Hearts: Massachusetts Loyalists 1765–1790: A Biographical Directory* (Boston, New England Historic Genealogical Society, 1980) 50.

Children, surname *Dumaresq* and baptized at King's Chapel, Boston:

i ANNE[6], baptized 27 March 1765; married JOHN
FERGUSON, and left descendants in the West Indies.

ii SILVESTER, baptized February and buried 21 April 1766.

iii REBECCA, baptized 22 April 1768, married CHARLES
GOW and left one son.

iv SUSANNA, buried 26 June 1771, aged twenty months.

v JAMES, baptized 1 January 1772, married SARAH
FARWELL and left numerous descendants.

vi PHILIP, baptized 18 December 1772; drowned at sea,
1806.

vii FRANCIS, baptized 2 February and buried 5 September
1774.

viii HANNAH, baptized 21 December 1775.

ix ABIGAIL, buried 21 December 1776, aged five months.

x DR. FRANCIS, married, had two children who left no
issue.

10. ABIGAIL[5] GARDINER (*Silvester⁴, William³, Benoni², George¹*)
baptized at King's Chapel, Boston, Massachusetts 1 August 1750
and died in 1827 presumably in Gardiner, Maine although no
record is found there. She married at Boston 15 November 1774
(Boston VRs 365) OLIVER WHIPPLE, born at Cumberland,
Rhode Island *c*1743 and died from apoplexy in his law office at
Georgetown (then in the District of Columbia but now in
Virginia) April 1813. His wife obtained a divorce from him in
1796, but when they remarried the following epigram was soon in
circulation:

> Divorc'd, like scissors rent in twain
> Both mourned the river out;
> Now whet and riveted again,
> You'll make the old shears cut.

Whipple, an attorney, graduated from Harvard College in
1766 and obtained an honorary A.M. from Dartmouth in 1773.
He settled in 1771 in Portsmouth, New Hampshire where he
practiced law for twenty years until removing to Hampton where
he practiced law another twelve years. On 4 October 1791 he
bought of the heirs of General Jonathan Moulton eighty and a
half acres of land and on 28 August 1794 obtained a quitclaim
from the estate. Between those two dates he settled on the Gen-

eral Moulton homestead. While in Hampton he was moderator of sixteen town meetings from 1794 and 1800, and of the annual meetings from 1801 to 1803. In 1801 he was also chosen a member of the Hampton School committee. He took part with the town against the Congregational society during the Presbyterian schism and was the town's attorney in the suit against Mrs. Thayer, widow of the former pastor. He was chosen representative in 1796 in which office he continued five years. In December 1802 he sold his farm then consisting of one hundred thirty-eight acres to James Leavitt for $2700. During Whipple's residence in Hampton he published two poems in pamphlet form, "The Confessional Tears of a Louis d'Or" (1794) and "The Historic Progress of Liberty" (1802)

Children, surname *Whipple*:

i SILVESTER GARDINER[6], born *c*1775 and died at Middleborough, Massachusetts 28 May 1822. No issue.

ii ANNE GIBBINS, born *c*1790; died at Gardiner, Maine 29 November 1859, aged sixty-nine. No issue.

iii HANNAH BOWEN, born Hampton, New Hampshire 28 November 1789 and died at Gardiner, Maine 14 April 1848, married FREDERIC ALLEN, well-known attorney of Kennebec County, Maine. Of her six children, only one left issue, but the entire line eventually became extinct.

11. ROBERT HALLOWELL[6] GARDINER I (*Hannah[5], Silvester[4], William[3], Benoni[2], George[1]*) born as Robert Hallowell the younger at Bristol, Gloucestershire, England 10 February 1782 during the occasion of his exiled Tory parents' residence there and died at the second Oaklands, Gardiner, Maine 22 March 1864. He married at Trinity Church, Boston, Massachusetts (with his first cousin the Reverend John Silvester John Gardiner officiating) 25 June 1805 at 8. A.M. EMMA JANE[4] TUDOR, born at Boston 10 March 1785 and died at Oaklands, Gardiner, Maine 24 June 1865, daughter of Judge Advocate General William[3] (*John[2], William[1]*) and Delia (Jarvis) Tudor. The Tudor genealogy is established in William Tudor, *Deacon Tudor's Diary, or "Memorandoms From 1709 , &c. by John Tudor, to 1775 & 1778, and to '93." A Record of More or Less Important Events in Boston from 1732 to 1793, by an eye witness* (Boston: Press of Wallace Spooner, 1896). Accounts of her broth-

ers Frederic Tudor (1783–1864) the Ice King and William Tudor (1779–1830) are in *The Dictionary of American Biography*, Volume 19. The ultimate depositories of Tudor family manuscripts are traced in *Proceedings of the Massachusetts Historical Society*, 97 (1985):103–134. Her mother was the first of four women in an umbilical line—mother, daughter, granddaughter, and great-granddaughter—all named Delia, the last of whom was Delia Parnell (1837–188?) elder sister of Charles Stewart Parnell (1846–1891) the Irish statesman, and whose descent is set out in "Part of Tudor Family Tree," in Jane McL. Côté, *Fanny and Anna Parnell: Ireland's Patriot Sisters* (New York: St. Martin's Press, 1991) page 10. He and his wife are interred at Christ Church beneath a Gothic spire designed by Richard Upjohn. He graduated A.B. in 1801 and proceeded A.M. in 1804 from Harvard College, being the first of six consecutive generations—identically named—to graduate from Harvard. In 1801 Robert Hallowell the Younger was required by the obligatory change-of-name clause in the will with four codicils, all executed 25 April 1786 by his maternal grandfather Dr. Silvester Gardiner (1708–1786) and probated at Newport, Rhode Island 21 August 1786 and administration *de bonis non* established at the Kennebec County Registry at Augusta, Maine 8 August 1820 to change his surname to Gardiner which was accomplished by the Great and General Court of Massachusetts, Acts of 1801, Chapter 75 for the January session.

Children, born under surname of *Gardiner*:

i EMMA JANE[7], born Boston 29 May 1806 and died unmarried at Gardiner, Maine, 8 January 1845.

ii ANNE HALLOWELL, born Boston 5 December 1807 and died at Paris, France 25 April 1878. She married at Gardiner, Maine 18 September 1832 FRANCIS RICHARDS (1805–1858) of North House, Hambledon, Hampshire, England. They had seven children, the youngest was Henry Richards (1848–1949), architect and civic leader, married Laura Elizabeth Howe (1850–1943), author of ninety children's books, daughter of Dr. Samuel Gridley Howe, founder of the Perkins School for the Blind; and of Julia (Ward) Howe, author of the Battle Hymn of the Republic. They left numerous descendants and resided at

Yellow House in Gardiner, Maine, now owned by their great-grandson, John Dyer Shaw, Jr.

iii ROBERT HALLOWELL II, born Pittston, Maine 3 November 1809 and died at Gardiner, Maine 12 September 1886. He married 5 June 1842 SARAH FENWICK JONES (1813–1869) of the historic Jones family of Wormsloe Plantation, near Savannah, Georgia. No issue.

iv DELIA TUDOR, born Oaklands, Gardiner, Maine 16 June 1812 and died at Gardiner, Maine 10 January 1836. She married GEORGE NOBLE JONES, brother of Sarah Fenwick Jones, above. He built the Kingscote mansion in Newport, Rhode Island, now a museum. No issue.

v LUCY VAUGHAN, born Oaklands, Gardiner, Maine 10 December 1814 and died unmarried at Gardiner, Maine 10 November 1847.

vi Colonel JOHN WILLIAM TUDOR, born Oaklands, Gardiner, Maine 5 June 1817 and died at Gardiner, Maine 27 September 1879. He married in Maryland 5 July 1854 ANNE ELIZABETH (HAYS) WEST (1821–1901). A graduate of West Point, he served in the Mexican War, built forts in California, commanded Fort Tejon, and served as Provost Marshall of Maine. President Grant visited him in Gardiner, Maine. He had six children, the eldest of whom was Robert Hallowell Gardiner III (1855–1924), ancestor of the successive owners of Oaklands: Robert Hallowell Gardiner IV (1882–1944); Robert Hallowell Gardiner V (1914–1984); and Robert Hallowell Gardiner VI (born 1944). He was grandfather of Governor William Tudor Gardiner (1892–1953). A younger son of Colonel Gardiner, John Hays Gardiner (1863–1913), author and Harvard professor, was a patron of the poet Edwin Arlington Robinson (1869–1935).

vii HENRIETTA, born Oaklands, Gardiner, Maine 8 March 1820 and died in Austria in 1880. She married in 1846 RICHARD SULLIVAN (1820–1908), a grandson of Governor James Sullivan of Massachusetts, the historian; and first cousin of Richard S. Bowdoin who endowed the construction of the world's largest cathedral, St. John the Divine in New York City. He amassed the largest private library in America. No issue.

viii **The Rev. FREDERIC**, born Oaklands, Gardiner, Maine 11 September 1822 and died at Middletown, Connecticut 17 July 1889. He married in 1846 **CAROLINE VAUGHAN** (1825–1906) of Hallowell, Maine. He was a founder of the Berkeley Divinity School, now part of Yale University, and was a prolific author of theological works. Of his five children, the eldest married the Reverend Henry Ferguson, headmaster of St. Paul's School. The third was the Reverend Frederic Gardiner, ancestor of the Gardiners of Philadelphia. The fourth, Henrietta, was a missionary to China and professor at Wellesley College.

ix **ELEANOR HARRIET**, born Oaklands, Gardiner, Maine 16 July 1825 and died at Peekskill, New York 13 August 1920 where she was Superior of the Sisters of St. Mary. For many years she was an effective administrator of Trinity Hospital in New York City.

Bibliographical Essay

Danny D. Smith

THIS ESSAY TRACES THE intellectual foundation of Olivia Coolidge's biography of Dr. Silvester Gardiner and suggests further sources to the interested reader. Dr. Peter R. Virgadamo of Monterey Park, California, who has taught at the University of California at Northridge, is working on an academic biography of Dr. Gardiner, but it may not appear for several years. As curator of Special Collections at the Gardiner Library, I am frequently queried about Gardiner genealogy and have therefore completed a draft of a genealogy of Dr. Gardiner's ancestors and all his descendants to the present, a work to be published in the future.

1. RHODE ISLAND ORIGINS

Dr. Silvester Gardiner's ancestors are traced in Caroline E. Robinson, *The Gardiners of Narragansett*, ed. by Daniel Goodwin (Province, R.I., 1919) and G. Andrews Moriarty, "A Tale of Old Newport," *Rhode Island History*, 11(1952):84–92. The standard history of Rhode Island, Samuel Green Arnold, *History of the State of Rhode Island* (2 vols.; London, 1878), should be read in conjunction with a modern interpretation pertinent to the period just before Dr. Gardiner's birth, Carl Bridenbaugh, *Fat Mutton and Liberty of Conscience: Society in Rhode Island, 1636–1690* (Providence, R.I., 1974). For detailed accounts of early Rhode Island citizens, see John R. Bartlett, *Records of the Colony of Rhode Island and Providence Plantations in New England* (10 vols.; Providence, R.I., 1856–63) and John Osborne Austin, *The Genealogical Dictionary of Rhode Island* (Albany, N.Y., 1887), wherein appears accounts of the Remington and Richmond families in the maternal ancestry of Dr. Gardiner. For the social context of the

Narragansett planter aristocracy of which the Gardiner family were members, see Christian McBurney, "The South Kingstown Planters: County Gentry in Colonial Rhode Island," *Rhode Island History* 45(1986):81–93, and Daniel Berkeley Updike in "The Restoration of A Colonial Altar-Piece," *Old-Time New England* 22(1932):188–192 provides an account of the Gardiner family church presided over by Dr. Gardiner's brother-in-law, the Reverend James MacSparran. See also *Old Houses in the South County of Rhode Island* (Providence, R.I., 1932). Wilkins Updike anticipated the broad lateral pedigrees linking the study of a social class in his *A History of the Episcopal Church in Narragansett, Rhode Island, Second edition edited, enlarged, and corrected by Daniel Goodwin* (3 vols.; Boston, 1907), noting a modern reprint of James MacSparran's *America Dissected* (Dublin, 1783) in volume 3. Another important source of Narragansett history is James MacSparran, *A Letter Book and Abstract of Out Services, Written during the Years 1743–1751*, ed. by Daniel Goodwin (Boston, 1899). Articles by Peter R. Virgadamo on Dr. Gardiner and by John F. Woolverton on James MacSparran in the forthcoming *American National Biography* (New York: Oxford University Press for the Council of Learned Societies, 1999) will provide the best summary accounts of these two individuals. Portraits of MacSparran and his wife Hannah, sister of Dr. Gardiner, are reproduced and discussed in Richard H. Saunders, *John Smibert: Colonial America's First Portrait Painter* (New Haven, 1995).

2. EDUCATION AND MEDICAL CAREER

The state of medical practice and education in the time of Dr. Gardiner's youth is traced in Leslie G. Matthews, "Licensed Mountebanks in Britain," *Journal of the History of Medicine and Allied Sciences* 19(1964):30–45; Joseph F. Kett, "Provincial Medical Practice in England, 1730–1815," *Ibid.*, 19(1964):17–30; and Sir Humphrey Rolleston, "History of Medicine in the City of London," *Annals of Medical History* 3(1941):1–17. For an account of one of Dr. Gardiner's teachers with particular reference to the pupil, see Francis R. Packard, "Cheselden's American Pupils," *Annals of Medical History*, 9(1937):536–37. An older history, Samuel A. Green, *A History of Medicine in Massachusetts* (Boston, 1881) is brought up to date in Eric H. Christianson, "Individuals in the Healing Arts and the Emergence of A Medical Community in Massachusetts, 1700–1792: A Collective Biography," Ph.D. dissertation presented at the University of Southern California, 1976. Maurice Bear Gordon, in his *Æsculapius Comes to the Colonies* (Ventnor, N.J., 1949) has an account of Dr. Gardiner's medical education in England. For an account of surgery in colonial Massachusetts, see Owen H. and Sara D. Wagensteen, *The Rise of Surgery: From Empiric Craft to Scientific Discipline* (Minneapolis, 1978). The first scholarly account of Dr. Gardiner's medical career was R. F. Seybolt, "Lithotomies Performed by Dr. Gardiner, 1737 and 1741," *New England Journal of Medicine*, 202(1930):109. The most recent examination of Dr. Gardiner's medical career is Eric H. Christianson's "The Colonial Surgeon's Rise to Prominence: Dr. Silvester Gardiner (1707–1786) and the Practice of Lithotomy in New England," *New England Historical and Genealogical Register*, 136(1982):104–114.

3. EIGHTEENTH-CENTURY BOSTON

The location of Dr. Gardiner's residence and medical office is detailed in Robert Means Lawrence, *The Site of St. Paul's Cathedral, Boston and Its Neighborhood* (Boston, 1916). Henry Wilder Foote in *Annals of King's Chapel* (2 vols.; Boston, 1896) gives an extended account of Dr. Gardiner and his family as well as many of Dr. Gardiner's social and professional associates. Foote traces the career of Gardiner's disinherited son and his rôle in transferring the parish from the Anglicanism to Unitarianism. Carl Bridenbaugh in *Cities in the Wilderness* (New York, 1964) and *Cities in Revolt: Urban Life in America, 1743–1776* (New York, 1955) give good account of everyday life in pre-revolutionary and revolutionary Boston. Bruce E. Steiner in "New England Anglicanism—A Genteel Faith?" *William and Mary Quarterly*, 3rd series, 27(1923) examines the social background of colonists who adhered to the Church of England. John Singleton Copley painted portraits of the social elite of Boston. Jules David Prown, in his definitive catalogue raisonné, *John Singleton Copley* (2 vols.; Cambridge, Mass., 1966) reproduces all the paintings, details their provenance, and discusses the social backgrounds of the sitters, including Dr. Gardiner, his daughter Anne, and the reattributed portrait to Joseph Blackburn of Anne (Gibbins) Gardiner. A color plate of the Copley portrait of Dr. Gardiner appears in Carrie Rebota, et al., *John Singleton Copley in America* (New York,

1995). Important monographs on Copley, his work, and subjects also appear in the 1995 catalogue. The starting point for all research in Boston history is Justin Winsor, *The Memorial History of Boston, 1630–1880* (4 vols.; Boston, 1880). The most accessible history of Boston is the elegantly written text by Walter Muir Whitehill, *Boston: A Topographical History* (2nd edition enlarged; Cambridge, Mass. and London, 1968), an indispensible work.

4. FAMILY CONNECTIONS

The major group of Dr. Gardiner's papers are in the Gardiner-Whipple-Allen Collection at the Massachusetts Historical Society in Boston. There are a few documents by Dr. Gardiner in the Maine Historical Society aside from the papers of the Kennebec Purchase Company. A few other original documents are in the Edward Cary Gardiner Collection, 227A, (1632–1939), archives bearing mostly upon allied families of the Gardiners at the Historical Society of Pennsylvania in Philadelphia. There is a fifty-eight page manuscript, "Observations on Newfoundland," detailing commercial opportunities for investment in the fisheries on the Grand Banks, Additional Manuscript 15493, no date, in the National Library (formerly British Museum) in London, attributed to Dr. Silvester Gardiner.

The ancestry of Dr. Gardiner's first wife, Anne (Gibbins) Gardiner, is constructed from *Sibley's Harvard Graduates* 5:313–317 under her father Dr. John Gibbins (1687–1760) and *Ibid.* 10:497 under his namesake son (1722–1743), her only brother whose early death cast her as heiress of one of the largest estates in colonial Boston. Her mother's ancestry is sketched from "Samuel Gray," in James Savage, *A Genealogical Dictionary of the First Settlers of New England* (4 vols.; Boston, 1860–62) 2:299 and amplified by Arthur M. Alger, "Descendants of Philip and John Langdon of Boston," *New England Historical and Genealogical Register* 30(1876):33–37 and Henry Sewall Webster, "Langdon Family Bible Records," *Ibid.* 67(1913):379–80. See also her posthumous cookbook, *Mrs. Gardiner's Receipts from 1763* (Hallowell, Maine, 1938).

The family connections of Dr. Gardiner's second wife are found in John R. Rollins, *Records of Families of the Name Rawlings or Rollings In the United States* (Lawrence, Mass., 1874) 277–278, wherein Abigail's mother, Love (Rawlings) Pickman's identity is established and linked to Benjamin Pickman in the context of his paternal lineage. The remainder of the Pickman ancestry can be assembled from Sidney Perley, *The History of Salem, Mass.* (3 vols.; Salem, Mass., 1926) 2:15 and note 2 as well as the published vital records of that town, births 1:174–176, marriages 2:195–196, and deaths 3:143–145. A close connection who may have influenced Dr. Silvester Gardiner's choice to remain loyalist and never commented upon by any historian was the niece of his second wife, Love Pickman, who married first the loyalist Peter Oliver and secondly Admiral Sir John Knight of the Royal Navy. Abigail's paternal grandmother Abigail Lindall's ancestry is traced in John A. Vinton, "Memoir of the Lindall Family," *New England Historical and Genealogical Register* 7(1853):15–24, noting on page 17 her links to the colonial dynasties of New England, the Wadsworth, Pitts, Curwin, Weld, Higginson, Borland, Winthrop, Temple, and Bowdoin families. Although not mentioned in the Lindall article, the Borlands had genealogical tendrils reaching to the Woolsey, Hillhouse, and Lloyd families of Long Island and Connecticut, a network of commercial and political magnates embracing all of New England. Note also "Burial Inscriptions in Salem, Mass.," *Ibid.* 3(1849):130 for Lindall and page 131 for Pickman and *The Heraldic Journal* 2(1866):26–28. The family connections of Abigail's first husband William Epes are found in Sidney Perley, *The History of Salem, Mass.* (3 vols.; Salem, 1926) 2:92 and note 1 carried over to page 93; the published vital records of Salem, marriages 2:338; and Walter Kimball Walkins, "Epps-Linford-Yale-Endicott," *New England Historical and Genealogical Register* 71(1917):91–93.

The ancestry of Dr. Gardiner's third wife has received treatment in an excellent work, Charlotte Goldthwaite, *Descendants of Thomas Goldthwaite, An Early Settler of Salem, Mass.* (Hartford, Connecticut: Hartford Press, 1899) 37–53, 58–62, 88–98, and 142–149 which starts with her great-great-grandfather of Salem whose immediate descendants established themselves in the clerical and political elite of colonial New England. Because this genealogy gives accounts of the ancestries of the wives of the successive generations of Goldthwaite men, lateral pedigrees of the in-laws which define the social connections of an upwardly mobile family can easily be sketched. Another great-great-grandfather of Catherine Goldthwaite was Ezekiel Cheever (1614–1708), for seventy years a schoolmaster, the last thirty-eight of which as headmaster of the Boston Latin School, terminated only by death at age ninety-four. This pedagogue has found admirers as diverse as Cotton Mather who studied under him and the Episcopal divine Phillips Brooks. Cheever's Latin grammar was the standard textbook in New England until it reached its twentieth and final edition in Boston in 1838. Her father Thomas Goldthwaite (1717–1799) even as a young man was influential in the public life of Chelsea, Massachusetts which he represented several times in the General Court. He as a friend and business partner with Governor Francis Bernard soon rose through the commissioned ranks of the military during the colonial wars until he became a colonel in command of Fort Pownal at the mouth of the Penobscot River in Maine where he stayed until surrendering that post to the American patriots in the spring of 1775. His final settlement on 15 February 1780 at Walthamstow, county Essex, England where he died 31 August 1799 was a comfortable and dignified retreat, owing to the influence of his second wife's nephews General John Coffin and Admiral Sir Isaac Coffin, who presumably were on intimate terms with Dr. Gardiner as well. Catherine as an adoptive daughter was assumed into the household of her stepmother's wealthy and childless brother Henry Barnes at Bristol, England, where she met Dr. Gardiner and married him soon after his second wife's death. Another good genealogy is Elinor Worcester Sargent and Charles Sprague Sargent, *Epes Sargent of Gloucester and His Descendants* (Boston: Houghton Mifflin Company at the Riverside Press, 1923) 44–45, noting the lavish footnotes at both pages showing the connections of Catherine's second husband William Powell. By his first wife Mary Bromfield, daughter of Edward Bromfield of Boston, who died in 1786 Powell had two daughters, Susannah Powell, the elder, who married Jonathan Mason; and Anna Dummer Powell, the younger, who married Thomas Perkins. They were ancestral to the Mason, Warren, Sears, and Perkins, families of Boston, many of whose descendants were to marry descendants of Dr. Gardiner.

A photograph of the Gardiner-Cate house in Dresden, Maine, built by Dr. Silvester Gardiner and inherited by his son John, appears in Charles E. Allen, *History of Dresden, Maine*

(1931) on page 414. John's portrait painted by Copley was in 1931 in the possession of his great-great-granddaughter Caroline (Gardiner) Cabot of Boston who later presented it to Tudor Gardiner. The portrait is now at Westmoreland Museum of Art, Greensburg, Pennsylvania. A summary of John Gardiner is found in Bertram E. Packard, *John Gardiner, Barrister, An Address Made Before the Kennebec Historical Society* (Augusta, Maine: Kennebec Historical Society's Brochures, Series 1, Number 1, 1923) and Henry Wilder Foote, *Annals of King's Chapel* (1896) 2:147 and 189. Laura E. Richards is at her best when she evokes Counsellor John Gardiner, in the ancestral vignettes in her autobiography *Stepping Westward* (New York, D. Appleton, 1932) pages 190–195. Herbert W. Silsby's article, "John Gardiner: Law Prophet," in *Supreme Judicial Court Historical Society Journal*, 2(1996):75–94 is now the standard reference on John Gardiner.

Burke's *Peerage and Baronetage* under the family of the Marquess of Sligo gives the ancestry of Colonel the Honourable Arthur Browne, second son of the Earl of Altamont, who married Anne, daughter of Dr. Silvester Gardiner. The present Marquess of Sligo owns a copy of the Copley portrait of Dr. Gardiner at his seat, Westport House, co. Mayo, Ireland. Should the senior line of Marquesses expire, the title of the earldom of Altamont would revert to descendants of Anne (Gardiner) Browne. The earlier Browne lineage is traced in articles on the Barons of Kilmaine in peerage directories, including Burke's. Dr. Gardiner's daughter Rebecca married into an ancient family from the Isle of Jersey with ties to royalty and nobility in Europe. It is traced by Augustus Thorndike Perkins in his article "Dumaresq Family," *New England Historical and Genealogical Register* 17(1863): 317–324.

5. KENNEBEC PROPRIETORS AND COLONIAL POLITICAL FIGURES

The definitive study, and likely to remain so, of "The Proprietors of the Kennebeck Purchase from the late Colony of New Plymouth," to cite its properly incorporated designation under Massachusetts law in 1752, is Gordon E. Kershaw, *The Kennebec Proprietors: "Gentlemen of Large Property & Judicious Men"* (Somersworth, New Hampshire and Portland, Maine: New Hampshire Publishing Company and Maine Historical Society, 1975).

As Kershaw states, the Kennebec Purchase Company Papers are the best source for an understanding of the corporate body. They are at the Maine Historical Society in Portland, Maine, and consist of nineteen bound volumes and fourteen boxes of loose papers, described by Kershaw at some length on pages 303–305. The only comprehensive account of the Kennebec Purchase Company prior to Kershaw was Robert Hallowell Gardiner, "History of the Kennebec Purchase," *Collections of the Maine Historical Society*, First Series, 2(1847):269–294. Setting the institutional history of joint stock companies for land investments is the classic study Roy H. Akagi, *The Town Proprietors of the New England Colonies* (Philadelphia, 1924) with a modern interpretation by Michael Zuckerman, *Peaceable Kingdoms: New England Towns in the Eighteenth Century* (New York, 1970). An important monograph bearing upon Dr. Gardiner's rivals in the company is William T. Baxter, *The House of Hancock: Business in Boston, 1724–1775* (Cambridge, 1945). Many of the Bostonians associated with the proprietors may be traced in John Langdon Sibley, *Biographical Sketches of Graduates of Harvard University* and Clifford K. Shipton, *Biographical Sketches of Those Who attended Harvard College* (Cambridge, Mass., 1873–). William Shirley and Thomas Powell helped the proprietors steer through political rapids. See John A. Schutz, *William Shirley, King's Governor of Massachusetts* (Chapel Hill, 1961); *The Correspondence of William Shirley: Governor of Massachusetts and Military Commander in America 1731–1760* (2 vols.; New York, 1912); and John A. Schutz, *Thomas Pownall, British Defender of American Liberty: A Study of Anglo-American Relations in the Eighteenth Century* (Glendale, California, 1951). James Sullivan, Boston attorney who represented the proprietors, later became governor of Massachusetts and a noted antiquarian. His *History of the District of Maine* (Boston, 1795; reprinted Augusta, Maine 1970) was the first published history of Maine. Maine was then part of Massachusetts and therefore subject of Massachusetts law. Accordingly James Sullivan, *The History of Land Titles in Massachusetts* (Boston, 1801) is pertinent to an understanding of the establishment of the proprietors' claims to extend their boundaries. The only other proprietors to own shares in the Kennebec Purchase Company comparable to the Gardiner and Hancock interests were the

Bowdoins. Important works on this notable farmily are Marvin S. Sadik, *Colonial and Federal Portraits at Bowdoin College* (Brunswick, Maine: Bowdoin College Museum of Art, 1966); Robert L. Volz, *Governor Bowdoin & His Family* (Brunswick, Maine: Bowdoin College, 1969); Gordon E. Kershaw, *James Bowdoin: Patriot and Man of the Enlightenment* (Brunswick, Maine: Bowdoin College Museum of Art, 1976); and Katherine J. Watson et al., *The Legacy of James Bowdoin III* (Brunswick, Maine: Bowdoin College Museum of Art, 1994). A brother of Dr. Gardiner's second wife is the subject of George F. Dow, *The Diary and Letters of Benjamin Pickman (1740–1819) of Salem, Massachusetts* (Newport, R.I., 1928).

6. SETTLEMENT OF THE KENNEBEC VALLEY

To understand the wilderness conditions which Dr. Gardiner and his fellow proprietors had to combat, the excellent account by Charles E. Clark, *The Eastern Frontier: The Settlement of Northern New England 1610–1763* (New York, 1970) is the best starting point. Two other works by Charles E. Clark are helpful for this period, *Maine During the Colonial Period: A Bibliographical Guide* (Portland, Maine: Maine Historical Society, 1974) and *Maine: A Bicentennial History* (New York, 1977). Louis C. Hatch, *Maine: A History* (New York, 1919) is weak for the colonial period, and therefore the *faute de mieux* remains William D. Williamson, *History of the State of Maine* (2 vols.; Hallowell, 1832; reprinted 1966). Another classic in Maine history is Henry S. Burrage, *The Beginnings of Colonial Maine* (Portland, Maine, 1914). See also Robert E. Moody, "The Maine Frontier 1607–1763," a doctoral dissertation presented at Yale, 1933.

The most important eyewitness account of events on the Kennebec for this period is found in William S. Bartlett, *The Frontier Missionary: A Memoir of the Life of the Rev. Jacob Bailey* (Boston, 1855). In addition many transcripts of Bailey documents which were undertaken by Charles E. Allen, but which his untimely death prevented him from using in his history of Dresden, are at the Wiscasset Public Library. George F. Dow, *Fort Western on the Kennebec* (Augusta, Maine, 1922) and Leon E. Cranmer, *Cushnoc: The History and Archaeology of Plymouth Colony Traders on the Kennebec* (Occasional Publications in Maine Archaeology, Number Seven, Augusta, Maine, 1990) detail an important fort which doubled as a trading center for the proprietors. Charles E. Allen, *History of Dresden, Maine* (Augusta, 1931) is an important source for understanding the first concentrated attempt by the proprietors to settle an entire town by holding out prospects of homestead rights. James North in his *History of Augusta* (Augusta, Maine, 1870) is the only publication to detail the exact shares of individual proprietors and their inheritance by later generations of families of the proprietors. North also gives genealogies, even of those who never settled in Augusta, in his work. An excellent town history of an area in contention between the Kennebec Proprietors and their rival, the Pejepcot Proprietors, is George A. Wheeler, *History of Brunswick, Topsham, and Harpswell, Maine* (Boston, 1878). Robert L. Bradley and James Hewat for the Maine Historic Preservation Commission in "Nomination of the Swan Island Historic District, Perkins Township, Sagadahoc County, Maine, to the National Register of Historic Places," September 1995, give important information about the Gardiner-Dumaresq house built by Dr. Gardiner near Dresden, Maine, which served as his headquarters several summers during the development of his lands on the Kennebec. The suit *Gardiner* v. *Hallowell*, Kennebec County, Court of Common Pleas, September, 1799 (file at the Maine State Archives) contains important data on Dr. Gardiner's holdings in Kennebec County and the devolution of the land title.

Period pieces are *A True State of the Copartnership of Gardiner and Jepson, taken from their Books and Settlements from Time to Time under Jepson's Own Hand* (Boston, 1771); James Flagg, *A Short Vindication of the Conduct of the Referees in the Case of Gardiner Versus Flagg, Against the Unjust Aspersions, Contained in Two Anonymous Pamphlets Lately Published and Handed About* (Boston, 1767); *Plaintiff's State of the Case: the Proprietors holding under Lake and Clark, Plaintiffs, against Proprietors from Plymouth-Colony, Defendants* (Boston, probably Dec. 1756); *The Award and Final Determination of the Referees respecting the Claims of the Proprietors of the Kennebeck Purchase from the late Colony of New-Plymouth, and the Company holding under Clark and Lake, relative to the Lands on each Side Kennebeck River* (Boston, Aug. 1757); and *Remarks on the Plan and Extracts of Deeds lately published by the Proprietors of the township of Brunswick (as they term themselves) agreeable to their Vote of January 27th 1753* (Boston, Jan. 31, 1753). An inflamatory piece, sometimes attributed to James Flagg, *A Strange Account of the Rising and Breaking of a Great Bubble* (1767) and reprinted in *The Magazine of History*, Extra edition (1928), pages 249–268 is a virulent attack on Dr. Gardiner.

Although these two works by Pulitzer-Prize winning authors cover the historical period immediately after Dr. Gardiner's death, they describe conditions on the Maine frontier which had changed little from the time Dr. Gardiner was bringing settlers in. They are Alan Taylor, *Liberty Men and Great Proprietors: The Revolutionary Settlement on the Maine Frontier, 1760–1820* (Chapel Hill, 1990) and Laurel Thatcher Ulrich, *A Midwife's Tale: The Life of Martha Ballard, Based on Her Diary, 1785–1812* (New York, 1990).

7. Sources of Gardiner, Maine, Community History

The only attempt to write a comprehensive history of Gardiner, Maine, is its earliest one, John W. Hanson's *History of Gardiner* (Gardiner, Maine, 1852), now out-of-date. The next history appears as a chapter in Henry D. Kingsbury and Simeon L. Deyo's *Illustrated History of Kennebec County* (New York, 1892) which curiously has hardly any references to the Gardiner family. The 1892 account is strong in tracing the industrial history of the city in the later half of the nineteenth century, but it is sadly out-of-balance with the inclusion of many paid biographies. *Leading Business Men of Lewiston, Augusta and Vicinity* (1889, pp. 141–170) contains accounts of the merchants of the city at the end of the nineteenth century, *Picturesque Gardiner* (Gardiner Board of Trade, 1896) preserves many views of the city at the time. *The Centennial of Gardiner* (1903), edited by Josiah S. Maxcy, agent of the Gardiner estate, preserves the ceremonial addresses at the time of the centennial celebration of the incorporation of the town. Two other secondary accounts give sweeping accounts of Gardiner. First, Evelyn L. Gilmore, *Christ Church, Gardiner, Maine: Antecedents and History* (Gardiner, Maine: Reporter-Journal Press, 1893; reprinted 1962) is filiopietisstic whilst Gordon E. Kershaw, *The Kennebec Proprietors: "Gentlemen of Large Property & Judicious Men"* (Somersworth, New Hampshire and Portland, Maine: New Hampshire Publishing Company and Maine Historical Society, 1975) seems at times hellbent for iconoclasm in reference to Dr. Gardiner. One should read the evocative vignettes in Laura E. Richards, *Stepping Westward* (New York: D. Appleton, 1932). Two painstakingly compiled references, both by Judge Henry Sewall Webster, *Land Titles in Old Pittston* (Gardiner, Maine: Reporter-Journal Press, 1912) and *Silvester Gardiner* (Gardiner, Maine: Reporter-Journal Press, 1913) survey the landed inheritance which Robert Hallowell Gardiner I (1782–1864) found when attaining his majority in 1803. Judge Webster also compiled the volumes of published vital records for the communities of Gardiner, Pittston, Randolph, Farmingdale, and West Gardiner. *One Hundredth Anniversary of the Diocese of Maine 1820–1920: Christ Church, Gardiner, Maine May Thirtieth to June Third* (Gardiner, Maine at the Merrymount Press of D. B. Updike, Boston, 1920), gives information not available elsewhere. The best brief account of Robert Hallowell Gardiner I (1782–1864) is an article by Ralph H. Gabriel, *Dictionary of American Biography*, Volume 7. An intimate account of Gardiner's early life and family connections is his autobiography, posthumously and topically rearranged by his great-grandsons, *Early Recollections of Robert Hallowell Gardiner 1782–1864* (Privately printed for R. H. Gardiner and W. T. Gardiner by White & Horne, Hallowell, Maine, 1936). The squire gives an eyewitness account of the transformation of the community from a sleepy outpost on the frontier to a vibrant center of commerce. Unfortunately the accounts halt abruptly in 1839, leaving his grandson Henry Richards' autobiography, *Ninety Years On* (Augusta, Maine, 1940) to provide the best account of the subsequent twenty-five years. Henry Richards was intimately informed about his descent from Dr. Gardiner and gives a perspicacious account of his ancestor whom he viewed with a curious mix of dread, awe, and veneration. *The Gardiner Story* (1949) is a summary of local history for the centennial celebration of the city charter. *Gardiner and Bostonians* (1951) relates mid-twentieth-century industrial history. Notable houses appears in *An Architectural and Historical Survey* (Friends of Gardiner, 1984), edited by Leroy Congdon and Joanne D. Clark. Danny D. Smith, in both his *Gardiner's Yellow House* (Friends of Gardiner, 1988) and *Yellow House Papers Inventory* (Gardiner Library Association, 1991) gives account of the Gardiner and Richards families. The most recent history of the city is Danny D. Smith and

Earle G. Shettleworth, Jr., *Gardiner on the Kennebec* (Dover, N.H.: Arcadia Publishers, 1996).

8. THE LOYALIST MOVEMENT AND EXILE

One of the most important works on the mounting political tensions between the American colonies and the mother country is Bernhard Knollenberg, *Origin of the American Revolution* (New York, 1965). See also Philip Davidson, *Propaganda and the American Revolution, 1762–1783* (Chapel Hill, 1941). Because Dr. Gardiner's loyalty to the crown was strengthened by his devotion to the Church of England, Carl Bridenbaugh, *Mitre and Sceptre: Transatlantic Faits, Ideas, Personalities, and Politics, 1609–1775* (New York, 1962) is essential to an understanding of the crisis which eventually crushed Dr. Gardiner. Bartlett's *Frontier Missionary*, cited in section six above, gives account of the flight of the loyalists. The brutal conditions they encountered during their brief stay in Halifax is detailed in Duncan Campbell, *Nova Scotia in its Historical, Mercantile and Industrial Relations* (Montreal, 1873). The extent of Dr. Gardiner's losses is itemized in H. E. Egerton, editor, *The Royal Commission on the Losses and Services of American Loyalists 1783 to 1785, Being the Notes of Mr. Daniel Parker Coke, MD* (Oxford: Roxburghe Club, 1915). E. Alfred Jones, *The Loyalists of Massachusetts* (London, 1930) gives citations to Dr. Gardiner's petitions to the English Crown for assistance during his exile in England. These documents are housed in the Public Records Office in London. The classic account of all exiles is Lorenzo Sabine, *Biographical Sketches of Loyalists of the American Revolution* (2 vols, Boston, 1864) which gives biographical and family information. Another source on the Gardiner and Hallowell families is James H. Stark, *The Loyalists of Massachusetts* (Boston, 1910). Dr. Gardiner's obituary was published in the *Newport* [R.I] *Mercury*, 14 August 1786.